EAT FIRST—
YOU DON'T
KNOW WHAT
THEY'LL GIVE YOU

EAT FIRST— YOU DON'T KNOW WHAT THEY'LL GIVE YOU

The Adventures of an Immigrant Family and Their Feminist Daughter

Sonia Pressman Fuentes

Library of Congress Number: 99-091125
ISBN Numbers   Hardcover: 0-7388-0634-X
                Softcover: 0-7388-0635-8

This book was printed in the United States of America.

To order additional copies of this book, contact:
Xlibris Corporation
1-888-7-XLIBRIS
www.Xlibris.com
Orders@Xlibris.com

CONTENTS

To my daughter, Zia, and the memory of my parents,
Hinda Leah Dombek Pressman and Zysia Pressman,
and my brother, Hermann

This book could not have been written if my parents and
brother had not shared with me the stories of their lives until
those stories became an integral part of my own life.

I wish to thank the following publications that published various versions under diverse titles of the following stories that appear in these memoirs:

Hard Copy

D.C. Bar Journal: "Passing the Bar"
Jewish Frontier: "How I Got My Mink Stole"
Café Solo: "Coming to America"
IRIS: "Sex Maniac"
Frontiers: "Sex Maniac"
Moxie: "Sex Maniac"
Jewish Currents: "Harry Golden and 'the Coat'"
Catskill/Hudson Jewish Star: "Graduating with My Class"
Humanistic Judaism: "Jewish Blood" "If You Speak His Language"
Outlook (Canada): "Weinberg's Glasses"
The Sweet Annie & Sweet Pea Review: "If You Live Long Enough"
Evolving Woman: "And Baby Makes Three"
Spindrift: "Our Winter Vacation"
Der Bay: "Jewish Geography"
Passager: "Moving to 'the Mountains'"

Internet

JoyZine (www.joyzine.zip.com.au):
    "Weinberg's Glasses"
    "Sex Maniac"
    "A Seder in Shanghai"
Harry Leichter's Home Page (http://home.earthlink.net/~leichter/):
    "Graduating with My Class"
    "A Seder in Shanghai"
Jewish Internet Magazine (http://www.jewishinternet.com/):
    "How I Got My Mink Stole"
Jewish Magazine (http://www.jewishmag.co.il/):
    "Jewish Blood"
    "Harry Golden and 'the Coat'"
Writing Now (http://www.writingnow.com):
    "Weinberg's Glasses"
i*Agora* (http://www.iAgora.com):
    "Accidental Birth"
    "Thai Silk"
    "Return to Germany"
Whispers (http://www.whispersmagazine.com):
    "Sex Maniac"
    "Weinberg's Glasses"
    "Thai Silk"
    "Return to Germany"

For me, writing is a way of living in an imperfect world without having to suffer in silence.

Barbara Kingsolver

Memory is a passion no less powerful or pervasive than love. What does it mean to remember? It is to live in more than one world, to prevent the past from fading and to call upon the future to illuminate it. It is to revive fragments of existence, to rescue lost beings, to cast harsh light on faces and events, to drive back the sands that cover the surface of things, to combat oblivion and to reject death.

Elie Wiesel[1]

INTRODUCTION

I did not intend to write *this* book. I intended to write one that was altogether different—a serious, historical study. And I didn't intend to write it alone. I knew that my roles as the first woman lawyer in the General Counsel's office at the Equal Employment Opportunity Commission (the EEOC) in 1965 and as one of the founders of the National Organization for Women (NOW) a year later were historic. I'd known that for years. For that reason, I had kept a diary during my first six months at the EEOC. I saved many documents involving my EEOC and NOW activities, speeches I had given on women's rights, and articles I had published.

Shortly after I retired from the US Department of Housing and Urban Development (HUD) in May of 1993, I began to think about commemorating my role in the women's movement. But I didn't want to devote the time needed to pour through all my papers and write a lengthy tome. I wanted the book written, but I didn't want to write it, at least not alone.

So I embarked on a search for a writer to work with me. I spent a year in libraries, talking to friends, writing to publishers and writers' organizations, and meeting with writers. What I learned was that a writer would work with a non-celebrity only upon the payment of thousands of dollars. I was loath to invest that kind of money in a project that might never result in publication.

A friend suggested I go to the library of the Foundation Center, a nonprofit organization that focuses on foundations, in Washington, DC, to research information on grants. There I could learn how to apply for a grant, which I could then use to pay a writer.

When I contemplated going to the Foundation Center, I knew I had come to the end of the road. I had tried to get this book written for a year, with no success. I decided that if my trip to the Foundation Center didn't produce results, I would give up and devote myself to other activities. So before I left for the Center, I spoke to God, something I rarely do. "God," I said, "if you want this book written, you'll have to make it happen. I've done all *I* can do."

At the Center, I found that grant seeking was a world unto itself. It required an expertise I did not have and could not easily acquire. Mixed in among the brochures on grant seeking, however, were a résumé and business card from a woman named Sara Fisher. She described herself as a "Writer, Editor, Proofreader." Although her résumé indicated that her specialty was fiction, I decided to call her. This was, after all, going to be the end of my efforts. We agreed to meet for coffee at Zorba's Café in Dupont Circle.

At coffee, Sara and I exchanged biographical information. She had been raised as a Catholic and was, on a part-time basis, serving as the managing editor of the publication of the Paulist National Catholic Evangelization Association. Her other part-time activities included writing fiction and book reviews, editing, teaching freshman composition at the Northern Virginia Community College, and serving as a tour guide in Washington, DC. "It's obvious, we have nothing in common," I said, after hearing this. She ignored my statement and continued the conversation. After we chatted some more, she made a comment that changed my life. "That's not the book you want to write," she said, speaking about my efforts to write a history of my involvement in women's rights. "You want to write a book of humorous stories about your parents, the kind of stories you've been telling me. And you want to write it yourself. I'll help you with the editing."

With Sara's guidance, I started this book.

But there were other reasons why I continued it. The raconteur and author, Alexander King, once wrote, "Whenever anyone dies, a world dies with them." A world died when my parents died. I did not want that world to disappear without a trace. I did not want my own life to disappear either.

And so, I wrote this book about their world and mine.

ACKNOWLEDGMENTS AND AUTHOR'S NOTES

While this is *my* book, many people helped along the way. I would, therefore, like to thank those people, in addition to Sara Fisher, who helped turn this, my first book, into a reality. First, those who encouraged me when I doubted my ability to write a book: my friends, Ed Fein, Gloria Riordan, Joan Davies, Ed Bomsey, and Rita Kleinerman.

Special thanks are due Dan Greenburg, the best-selling author of *How To Be a Jewish Mother* and many other books, who took the time to write me an extensive letter detailing his experiences with publication; the International Women's Writing Guild (IWWG) and its newsletter *Network*, which was an invaluable networking resource and guide to potential publishers; the Elderhostel program of the Iowa Writers Workshop, which I attended in the summer of 1996, where I learned a great many things, including the enjoyment of writing in a community of writers; the Writer's Center in Bethesda, Maryland, whose course, Beginning a Book, provided helpful insights; and Doris Booth of Authorlink! (a service for writers, agents, and publishers on the Internet), who selected me as mainstream nonfiction author for March 1997.

I never thought when I entered upon the writing of these memoirs that it would entail much research. But it did. I needed to check my recollections against the facts and to fill in the details. Much of this research was tedious, but it also brought me some unique thrills of discovery. At the National Archives, through the help of technician Dan Law, I held in my hand a copy of the manifest of the ship that brought my family to the US, the *S.S.*

Westernland, containing the names of my parents, my brother, and myself. In the US Holocaust Memorial Museum Library, I found a book about Bendin, Poland, where my paternal grandmother and other family members had lived, containing pictures of the residents taken from the identity cards the Nazis required Jews to carry. Six of those pictures were of members of my family. In researching the history of birth control in Germany, I found the name of Dr. Ludwig Levy-Lenz, one of my mother's abortionists, who turned out to be the inventor of a contraceptive sponge and the author of a book called *Memoirs of a Sexologist*.

My brother, Hermann, was an invaluable resource to me for the story of how my family left Germany. One day many years ago, he opened a rarely-used drawer of his night table and discovered a diary he had begun on his eighteenth birthday, July 21, 1932, at the beginning of the Nazis' rise to power. He kept it until November 29, 1935, in the German shorthand he had learned in school, and it is rich in its depictions of my family's day-to-day life and of political developments in Berlin. His granddaughter, Debbie, transcribed it into English and, at my insistence, Hermann, who had planned to leave it only to his children and me, donated it to the US Holocaust Memorial Museum. In what was to be the last year of his life, I had innumerable telephone conversations with him, during which he supplied me with further details of our escape from Berlin, for which he was wholly responsible.

Others to whom I am indebted are Ruth Dym Shapiro and Barbara Quanbeck, my editors; Virginia Harrington and Myrna Mikkelson, my Iowa Writers Workshop colleagues, and Elizabeth Stevens, for their editing and advice; the late Dorothy Bilik, my invaluable resource on Yiddish; Aviva Kempner, a writer, director, and producer of films with Jewish themes; Edith Mayo, a feminist historian; Dr. Margherita Rendel, for sharing her experiences on sex discrimination legislation in the United Kingdom; James Woycke, author of *Birth Control in Germany 1871-1933*, who graciously shared his expertise on birth control and abortion practices in Germany in the 1920s and '30s; Michael Spitzberg, who definitively located Piltz, the small town where my parents were born and married, for me; Michlean Amir, the then-librarian at the Isaac Franck Jewish Public Library in Rockville, Maryland; Beila S. Organic, the then-Upper School Librarian at the Charles E. Smith Jewish Day School in Rockville; Marion M. Dumond, the then-town historian for Ellenville, New York; Patricia Christian, a staff member at the Ellenville Public Library and Museum; the staffs at YIVO (the Institute for Jewish Research), the US Holocaust Memorial Library, the library of Congress (with special gratitude to Katy Kapetan, the then-research analyst at its Federal Research Division), and the Jewish Information & Referral Service in Rockville; the various other librarians who patiently answered my countless questions; John and Anna Jamerson, for their invaluable help with my computer problems; and the many others who gave so freely of their time and effort.

A word about the transliteration of Yiddish used in this book. Yiddish, like all languages, had different regional pronunciations; my parents spoke the Yiddish of Poland and the Ukraine, using the inflections, pronunciation, and intonations of that region. However, with regard to the Yiddish words in this book, I have by and large followed the standardization recently established by YIVO.

This is intended to be a book with a light touch. I feel the need to say something about that. From childhood on, when I was the bespectacled, asthmatic child of older, immigrant parents in a new country, I learned to cope with life by using humor, and I do so still. Apparently, I came by it naturally. In my teens, I learned from my mother that my maternal grandfather earned his meager living by entertaining at social functions.

Jews have long been known for their sense of humor and wit as a way of dealing with the anomaly of being the "chosen people" who have been subjected to thousands of years of discrimination. As one wag put it in addressing God, "Do me a favor. Next time, choose someone else."

The number of Jewish comedians and writers of humor in our

society attests to the continued vitality of humor in Jewish life. I am proud to carry on the tradition.

The stories in this book are by and large true. I was either involved in them myself or learned of them from my parents and brother. My childhood was filled with my parents' stories about their lives in Poland and Germany. But here and there, I have used my author's license and taken slight liberties with the facts to improve the story.

One of the effects of the women's rights movement has been in the titles used before the names of girls and women. Before the movement, although boys and men were referred to as "Mr.," regardless of their marital status, marital status determined the titles of girls and women. "Miss" was used for those who were single and "Mrs." for those who were or had been married. To eliminate this distinction, the women's movement espoused the term "Ms." for all girls and women.

As a feminist, I favor the use of "Ms." for all girls and women. As the writer of these memoirs, however, I felt it would be historically inaccurate to use "Ms." before it was in general use. I have, therefore, arbitrarily chosen July 2, 1965, the effective date of Title VII of the Civil Rights Act of 1964, which prohibited employment discrimination based on sex, as a line of demarcation. I have used "Miss" and "Mrs.," as the case may be, to refer to girls and women involved in incidents occurring before that date and "Ms." to refer to girls and women involved in incidents on and after that date.

In some cases I have used fictitious names to protect the privacy of persons, places, or organizations, or because I did not know the real names. In each such case, I have asterisked (*) the fictitious name on first use.

PART I

1.

THE NIGHT MY FATHER RAN AWAY FROM HIS OWN WEDDING

My parents had seen each other for fifteen minutes before their marriage.

They were both born in Piltz, a *shtetl* near Cracow in Poland in the Pale of Jewish Settlement. *Shtetl* is the Yiddish word for a small town in Eastern Europe with a sizeable Jewish population. Piltz was the town's name in Yiddish; it was known as Pilica in Polish. It was under Russian domination at the time, and about two-thirds of its 4,500 inhabitants were Jewish.

My mother, Hinda Leah Dombek, knew the month and day of her birth, March 15, but not the year. Her father didn't bother going to the registry office with just one child but waited until he had several children and then registered them all at once. It appears that my mother may have been born in 1891; my father, Zysia Pressman, was born on December 24, 1893.

Although they came from the same town, my parents never met until about a year before their wedding. Both of them had left Piltz when they were quite young. Hinda Leah's mother, Schandla, whose maiden name was Zjeschkowska, died when Hinda Leah was ten, and her father, Jzek-Moschek, remarried shortly thereafter "so Hinda Leah would have a mother." He married a spirited woman with a daughter of her own who had no use for her husband's daughter from his first marriage.

Jzek-Moschek was a *marshalik*, a *badkhn*, a jester, someone who told jokes and stories at weddings and bar mitzvahs. This did not bring in much money.

Because two of her maternal uncles in Piltz were teachers, Hinda Leah had an opportunity to get some schooling. In the classes she attended, she developed a lifelong love of learning. She became a studious child who recited the *khumish*, the first five books of the Bible, out loud daily when she came home from *kheyder*, Jewish elementary school. This incessant intoning increasingly disturbed her stepmother. When Jzek-Moschek came home one day, his wife shouted at him and complained that Hinda Leah's recitations were giving her a headache. Jzek-Moschek seized Hinda Leah by the hair and threw her across the room. She ran outside and sat on the stoop, crying. At just that moment, her "rich Uncle Hirschberg," her late mother's half-brother from *Varshe*—Warsaw—came by on one of his visits. When he saw her weeping, he said, "Lonishu, why are you crying?" When she told him, he was outraged and stormed into the house. After berating her father, he arranged with him and her more-than-willing stepmother to take Hinda Leah back with him to Warsaw.

And so it was that Hinda Leah grew up in the capital of Poland in the wealthy household of her uncle and aunt and their two children, their handsome son, Dalik, and their sickly daughter, Helche. Hinda Leah's role in this household was somewhere between member of the family and household retainer. As the years went by, she and Dalik became close and fell in love, but Hinda Leah knew she had no future with him because of the difference in their backgrounds. When Dalik pleaded for sexual favors, she reluctantly turned him down. She reminded him that if they had sex and she became pregnant, there would be no alternative for her but to throw herself out the window.

Zysia's father, Ephroim Pressman, died when Zysia was a young boy. Ephroim was the last of the three husbands of Zysia's mother, Udel Olmer. Udel was one tough lady. She not only survived three husbands but also owned and operated a bakery. Unlike Hinda Leah, Zysia never had the opportunity to attend school. From early childhood, he worked at his mother's bakery. At the age of nine, since he was not interested in spending the day under his mother's watchful eye, he took a job with a local tailor delivering clothes. After several years of this, he was ready to move on. But there were few opportunities in Piltz for a boy, especially one who was illiterate. So Zysia decided to go to Germany to seek his fortune. He did this by racing across the Polish-German *grenets*, the border, one dark night when he was fourteen. The border guards, who chased him, did not stop him but managed to put a bullet through his cap. Someone later returned that cap with the bullet hole in it to his mother and told her that the border guards had killed her son. Udel had no reason to doubt this report. Thereafter, since Zysia was not able to write to her, she continued to believe he was dead.

Zysia found work in Germany in a shop that manufactured cloth for military uniforms in Neu Isenburg, a town just outside Frankfurt am Main. He moved up a notch some years later when he became a tailor's apprentice. He did so well that by the age of eighteen, he had become shop foreman. He was then financially able to return to Piltz for his first visit.

Upon arriving in his hometown, he headed straight for his mother's house. When Udel opened the door to his knock and saw him, she flung her arms about and cried, "Spirit, return to your *keyver*—grave." It took Zysia a while to convince Udel that he was not a ghost but her son who was still very much alive.

At the same time, Hinda Leah also returned to Piltz. In spite of the treatment she had received in her father's house after his remarriage, she nonetheless periodically returned to visit him. By this time, she had already had a romance with a blind violinist. He had escorted her all over Warsaw and knew every nook and cranny of that beautiful city. Hinda Leah had wanted very much to accept his offer of marriage, but her uncle had convinced her not to marry him. "When you have children," he had pointed out, "he won't be able to see them and that will make you sad." Hinda Leah had had another offer of marriage from a chicken farmer, which she had turned down. No other marriage prospect was in sight. She was twenty-one years old and already an "old maid" by the standards of Piltz.

One of Hinda Leah's cousins, anxious to earn a *shadkhn's*—matchmaker's—fee, arranged for her to meet Zysia. When they met, Hinda Leah lowered her eyes. Zysia was so handsome she hardly dared to permit herself to look at him. He asked her to join him in one of the few activities open to courting couples in Piltz, a walk to the River Piltz. They walked in silence, and, during the walk, Hinda Leah sneaked glances at Zysia. When they reached the river, Zysia showed her his photograph. She admired the likeness, but when she offered to return it to him, he told her it was hers to keep. She knew then that this young man was interested in her. So she asked him how much money he earned. Not wanting to be loved for his money, he gave her a figure much lower than the actual amount. Hinda Leah nonetheless seemed satisfied and agreed to keep the photograph. Zysia told her that he had to return to Germany but promised to write.

Hinda Leah wondered if she would ever hear from this handsome young stranger from Germany, but he was true to his word. Short in stature himself, he admired this tall, slim, young woman with the long braids down her back. He knew she had managed her uncle's household and would make him a good wife. Besides, he had long been looking for a young woman who could read and write. He planned to go into business for himself one day and such a wife would be useful. And, like frosting on the cake, there would be the *nadn*, the dowry she would receive from her rich uncle. Yes, it was definitely a good match for him.

And so, Hinda Leah began to receive beautiful postcards with photographs of lovers and romantic poems on one side and notes from Zysia on the other. Of course, she did not know that these notes were written for him by one of his friends. After she had received a number of these postcards, one arrived in which Zysia addressed her as "Darling."

Hinda Leah immediately wrote back, "Dear Mr. Pressman: Please do not address me in that manner, or I shall have to stop writing to you." It was then that Zysia told her it was all right for him to call her "darling" because he intended to marry her.

Word of the intended marriage spread from Hinda Leah in Warsaw to her family in Piltz, and the residents of the town began to make preparations for the wedding. It would be a momentous affair! An "old maid," and a *yesoyme*—female orphan—at that, was getting married to a handsome *bokher*—a young man—from Germany. The *shtetl* had never had such an affair. Chickens and geese were slaughtered, jellies and wines brought up from cellars, and cookies and cakes baked.

But Hinda Leah remained downcast throughout these festivities, for only she knew that she had no *nadn*. True, she had had one, supplied by her uncle in gratitude for her many years of service in his home. But over the objections of her uncle, she had yielded to the entreaties for funds from her cousin, "the gambler." And he had lost her *nadn* at cards. She had gone pleading to him for the return of her money, but what could he do? "When money is gone, it is gone, eh, Lonya," he said. She spoke to her uncle, but he reminded her that he had advised against the loan in the first place. He had not offered a second *nadn*, and she was indeed worried.

Zysia, ignorant of this history, made plans to leave Neu Isenberg for Piltz. When his employer learned of this contemplated second trip to Piltz, he refused to release the young man from work since it was the height of the season. Zysia, never one to brook refusals, announced haughtily that he could always get another job, but he couldn't always find another wife—and he left.

When Zysia arrived back in Piltz, he was no longer so self-assured. Udel was less than pleased with her handsome son's choice of a wife. What did he see in this young woman anyway? She was tall and thin, with hardly any bosom, she was left-handed, she was almost three years his senior, and, what's more, she had freckles. Who knew what she might have done in that big city of Warsaw? Hadn't they just read that a young unmarried woman with the same last name—Dombek—had just given birth to twins there?

How did Zysia know that that woman and Hinda Leah weren't one and the same? If he insisted on marrying into *that* family, why didn't he marry Jzek-Moschek's red-haired stepdaughter? Now, there was a beauty for him. And, better still, why didn't he marry the young woman to whom his mother had betrothed him before his birth when she was in the *mikve*—the ritual bath? That young woman had grown up to be a schoolteacher.

Zysia was assailed by doubts. How much did he really know about this woman that he was about to marry? He had after all merely taken a short walk with her a year earlier and received some letters from her thereafter. Was that enough on which to base a lifetime together?

That night when Zysia was asleep, Schandla Dombek, Hinda Leah's long-deceased mother, appeared in his dream, and said, "Zysia, marry my daughter. She will make you a good wife." Zysia awoke, convinced that he had received a sign from on high. Thereafter, all his mother's entreaties went for naught.

And so, July 14, 1913, the day of the wedding, arrived. Zysia, decked out in a tuxedo and collapsible top hat, found himself talking to Uncle Hirschberg at last. The uncle kept putting his hand in his pocket, and Zysia was sure that each time it would come out with the long-awaited *nadn*. But, instead, each time Uncle Hirschberg's hand came out empty or holding his pocket watch. Finally, Zysia broached the question and learned that there was to be no *nadn* after all. Uncle Hirschberg told him some ridiculous story about a gambler, but Zysia knew better: he had been tricked. They had trapped him with these elaborate preparations, thinking he would have no choice but to go through with the wedding. If that was the case, they didn't know Zysia Pressman! He was no fool they could trick into marriage by deception. He hadn't gotten this far in life without learning a thing or two. So he did what he had always done when faced with a problem. He acted. He ran away.

Then followed one of the most bizarre events in Piltz's history. Everyone who had been making ready for the wedding—the town elders, Yeshiva *bokherim*—young male Talmudic scholars, house-wives, children, dogs, even some stray chickens—ran through the streets of Piltz chasing Zysia. Up and down the narrow alleys they went, the women brandishing broomsticks, the men, canes, shout-ing at Zysia as they ran. Finally, the leader of this motley group, a bearded patriarch, caught up with Zysia, raised his cane, and struck him on his high hat, which instantly collapsed. Immediately, the rest of the community was upon Zysia, berating him for his con-duct and threatening him with all forms of earthly and heavenly retribution. How could he run away from his own wedding after everything had been prepared? How could he shame Hinda Leah, a *yesoyme*, in front of the whole community? Why, her dead mother would rise up out of the grave if this were permitted! Even Uncle Hirschberg was there, and now he did indeed offer a second *nadn*. The wedding had to go on.

By this time, Zysia was no longer interested in Hinda Leah or her dowry, but the combined forces of the *shtetl's* wrath were too much for him. Reluctantly, he agreed to return to the synagogue.

And so they were married. As they stood under the *khupe*—the wedding canopy, Zysia, instead of whispering his eternal devo-tion, told Hinda Leah he was marrying her under duress and would be leaving for Germany the next day—alone. Hinda Leah nodded and determined to kill herself as soon as she could decently do so after the wedding. The ceremony ended with Zysia's refusal to kiss the bride. Instead, he told her he would continue to save his kisses for his mother, who had been right all along.

When the festivities ended, the whole *shtetl* escorted the couple to their bridal cottage. Some maintained their vigil throughout the night, peering into the windows to see what was happening, as was the town custom.

Inside the cottage, Hinda Leah went into an anteroom and undressed surreptitiously, away from the prying eyes at the win-dows. Then, Zysia went through the same process. Hinda Leah was already under the covers when Zysia came in with two big cotton wads in his hands. "What on earth are these?" he asked.

Haltingly, Hinda Leah explained that these were what passed as her breasts. Now that he knew, she thought, Zysia would surely keep his promise to leave her. Instead, he burst into uproarious laughter, and Hinda Leah wondered whether he might not be ready to forgive her after all. Perhaps things could still work out for them. And that night, in spite of the occasional faces appearing at the windows, they did.

Next morning, Hinda Leah and Zysia bade everyone goodbye and boarded the train for Germany with their suitcases. They were just getting settled in their seats when Zysia exclaimed, "Oy, Lina, I forgot one of my bags." Before she realized what was happening, he jumped off the train, promising to catch up with it at the next stop. Hinda Leah was stunned. A fellow passenger, seeing her distress, came over and asked what was wrong, and she told him. "You don't mean to tell me that that young man who just jumped off the train is your husband?" he asked. "And he's going to join you later? You don't really believe that yourself, do you?" She had to admit that she didn't. "Why, that's the oldest trick in the book," he continued. "He's taken your *nadn* and run away. You'll never see him again."

With that, the stranger returned to his seat, and Hinda Leah was left alone to face the complete desperation of her situation. She was twenty-two years old, no longer a virgin, married but without a husband, on her way to Germany, where she knew neither the language nor any person and had hardly any money. She started to cry softly.

And this is how Zysia found her when he came aboard the train at the next stop, true to his word, missing suitcase in hand. [I never learned how he managed this feat.] Zysia comforted his distraught bride, calmed her fears, and held her hand all the way to Neu Isenburg.

Once they were settled in their small apartment, Hinda Leah became her old resourceful self again. While Zysia was out one day looking for work, she went to see his former employer. Didn't he know skilled tailors and foremen were hard to find? Didn't he believe in marriage? Didn't he realize she would be able to help with the light sewing at home? He did indeed, and Zysia was reinstated in his job.

The couple settled down to married life, but Hinda Leah still did not completely trust her young husband. He had already run away twice, once from Poland and once from her. One never knew when he might take it into his head to leave again, this time never to return. She was not a young woman any more, but a matron, and she had to take care of herself. Just before she and Zysia had left Piltz, her uncle had thrust a small packet of bills into her hand, and she was determined to keep it for herself. She wrapped it in cloth and hid it in one of the kitchen cupboards. Every day, when she came home from her shopping, she checked to make sure her money was still safe. And each time she found her packet of bills, she relaxed, secure in the knowledge that all was well.

But then came the day when Hinda Leah went to the cupboard to find it bare. Frantically, she searched throughout the closets, the entire kitchen, and the rest of their small apartment. Her savings were nowhere to be found. There was no sign of a break-in, nor was there the type of disarray that accompanies a robbery. There was only one answer. Obviously, Zysia had found the money and taken it. That was all he had really been after from the beginning. Now her life was truly over.

That evening, when Zysia came home, she told him about the missing money. "Of course I took it," he said. "Did you think I married you for love? I married you for your money, and now I have it. Now I have what I wanted."

Hearing her worst fears confirmed, Hinda Leah ran to the window determined to end her life. But before she reached the window, Zysia caught her. He cradled her in his arms and smothered her face with kisses. "Lonya, darling," he said. "Did you really think I stayed with you all these months because I wanted your money? Why, I make more than that in a month now. Don't you know I love you? I only took that money to teach you a lesson. We don't need to keep such secrets from each other. Here, take it back."

He reached into his pocket, pulled out the packet of bills, and handed it to her. Hinda Leah looked at the money briefly, returned it, and mumbled something about putting on the tea.

Zysia never again told Hinda Leah he had married her for love. Throughout the fifty-four years of their marriage, he always said he married her for her *nadn*.

2.

ACCIDENTAL BIRTH

I've often read romantic novels of how the hero or heroine of the story was conceived. Usually, it was under perilous circumstances. There the lovers were, seeking shelter from a storm, stranded on a desert isle, snowbound on an icy peak. What else could they do? But while there are many stories explaining how a person was conceived, few explain why that person was in fact born. That's my story.

My parents had been married for fourteen years and were living in Berlin in 1927 when Mother discovered she was pregnant again. This was cause for considerable concern in the household. Mother was thirty-six and a year earlier she had had an ectopic pregnancy. It had taken her many months to recover, and her gynecologist had warned her against ever becoming pregnant again. Hermann was thirteen years old and had no interest in sharing the household with an infant. Finally, enlarging the family wasn't fashionable for well-to-do couples in pre-World War II Berlin society.

Fortunately, Berlin society, while setting the standard for small families, also provided the means for achieving that standard. Mother had already undergone seven abortions when she became pregnant with me. The services of abortionists, while illegal (except for prescribed therapeutic reasons), were available. Between 1900 and the 1920s, there was in fact a veritable abortion epidemic in Germany. Thereafter, more women were using alternative methods of contraception, but abortion remained the final recourse. While such a choice was not celebrated, neither was it cause for social opprobrium.

Not only did Mother have the option of an abortion, she even had a choice of abortionists. First, there was *Doktor* Ludwig Levy-Lenz, Mother's Jewish abortionist. And then, when the stars were right, *Doktor* Karl Wilhelm* might be available. *Doktor* Wilhelm was a tall, handsome swashbuckler who had an unusual relationship with some of his clients: he was often responsible both for the commencement and conclusion of their predicaments. That, of course, was not the case with my mother.

Mother preferred *Doktor* Wilhelm, whose technique, even on women who were comparative strangers to him, was infinitely superior. And so, when she learned that I was on the way, after the usual discomfiture that one encounters at the discovery of an unpleasantness, she decided to deal with the situation. One brisk Friday morning in September of 1927, Mother bid *auf Wiedersehen* to my father after breakfast and set off for the office of *Doktor* Wilhelm. As fate would have it, *Doktor* Wilhelm had made other plans. He was just then en route to the Swiss Alps for a vacation with one of Berlin's prima ballerinas.

Disconsolate at this turn of events, Mother came home and went to bed, where Father found her that evening, obviously the worse for her experience. "Well, Lina," he greeted her heartily, "It's all over? Everything's all right?"

"No, Zysia," moaned Mother. "It's not all right. *Doktor* Wilhelm went to Switzerland. I'll have to see *Doktor* Levy-Lenz next week.

"No," said father. "Let it be already."

And so I was born. But that was not the end of the story, as Mother told it. Whenever she described her visit to *Doktor* Wilhelm, she always ended it by lowering her voice and saying, "We didn't know it was going to be *you*."

So that's why I was born—not because my parents had a romantic interlude under perilous circumstances, but because *Doktor* Wilhelm was out of town. On second thought, maybe my story's not that different after all. I, too, am here because of two lovers on an icy peak—*Doktor* Wilhelm and the ballerina.

3.

COMING TO AMERICA

In January of 1933, my family was living well in Berlin, the capital of Germany. My mother was forty-one years old, my father thirty-nine, Hermann was eighteen, and I was four.

Jews constituted four percent of the city's 4.2 million people and less than one percent of the 66 million in the country. My parents had lived and worked in Berlin since 1919. Father rented and managed under his German first name the Siegmund Pressman Herren Kleider Fabrik, a men's clothing store and factory. It was located at 135 Skalitzer Strasse, the former location of the Dresdner Bank. My father manufactured men's clothing in back rooms for sale in the store. My mother and Hermann helped out in the store. In addition, my parents had recently bought a building consisting of forty apartments and four stores at 26 Koepenicker Strasse as an investment. We lived in a rented apartment at another address, 88-99 Kottbusser Damm, where full-time maids did the housework.

On January 30, 1933, President von Hindenburg appointed Hitler Reichs Chancellor of Germany. A year earlier, Hermann had become concerned about the growing power of Hitler and the Nazis (the National Socialist Party). After Hitler's accession to the Reichs Chancellorship, Hermann became increasingly aware of atrocities perpetrated by the Nazis. Hitler and Joseph Goebbels, initially chief of Nazi Party propaganda and later given the euphemistic title of Minister for Propaganda and Public Enlightenment, encouraged the terrorization of Jews. On March 9, there were several attacks on Jewish-owned department stores. Throughout Germany, the song one heard was "*Wenn das Judenblut vom Messer spritzt, Dann geht's noch mal so gut.*" ["If Jewish blood spurts from our knives, then things will be twice as good."]

On March 30, while listening to the radio, Hermann heard the announcement of a planned boycott of Jewish businesses and professional persons. It was scheduled to begin that Saturday, April 1. Germans were urged not to employ Jews or do business with them. Special parades and demonstrations were organized and signs and placards prepared.

The newspapers and airwaves were flooded with news of the anticipated boycott. All over the country, Jewish business and professional people and employees were told not to report to work; Jewish employees, moreover, were to be demoted or even stripped of their jobs.

During the night preceding the boycott, Jewish-owned stores, businesses, and the homes of Jewish professionals were painted with the words "Jude" and "Juden" and emblazoned with swastikas. On the morning of April 1, my father found "Jude" painted on the windows of his store. He was either courageous or foolish enough to immediately have one of his apprentices wash the paint off. Then he locked the store and went home.

That day, Nazis with cameras in hand were stationed at the doors of Jewish-owned stores. Customers entering these establishments were photographed and beaten either on the spot or later.

On April 5, the boycott against Jewish businesses was temporarily discontinued because neighboring countries had threatened repercussions.

Before that happened, however, Hermann was already thinking of leaving Germany. An incident on April 15 as well as subsequent events convinced him that it was time to leave. A taxi accidentally hit him as he was cycling around a traffic circle near our apartment that day. Fortunately, the taxi was a Hanomag, a battery-operated car then in vogue, which did not travel as fast as gas-driven cars. Nonetheless, Hermann's bicycle was bent out of shape, his clothes were torn, and his right knee was injured. As he lay on the ground, bruised and bleeding, he heard bystanders who recognized him yelling, "Kill that Jew. Who wants him to live?"

Five days later, police came to our house with a search warrant and searched the house. The family was given no reason for this search, and nothing came of it.

Our Jewish neighbor, Mr. Nachman, did not fare as well. The members of a non-Jewish German family, the Voltsehlegers, were set on appropriating a ring Nachman wore. They forced him onto their truck, and, when they were unable to remove the ring, they broke his finger. Thereafter, he was detained in a barracks for Jews for several days before being allowed to return home. After he had been home for a few days, the police picked him up one evening for "interrogation." A few nights later, Mrs. Nachman was called and told to pick up her husband's body. In order to retrieve it for burial, she was compelled to sign a form stating that her husband had died of natural causes.

On April 29, when Hermann went to see Mr. Rosenberg, the tailor with whom Father did business, he learned that the police had detained Rosenberg in "protective custody." Hermann never saw Rosenberg again.

The last straw for Hermann occurred the day a group of six men came into my father's store, intent on stealing the merchandise. Hermann recognized a number of them: they had worked for the business in the past as part-time salesmen and *shleppers*, men whose job it was to entice customers into the store. The thieves announced to the sales staff that the staff had nothing to fear; they were only after "the principals," Father and Hermann, whom they planned to place in the vault. The Dresdner Bank had left this vault on the premises; my father used it for storing piece goods.

Hermann ran to his private office and locked the door. He grabbed a pistol that he had bought recently for security when collecting rents at the apartment building. This pistol shot gas pellets to incapacitate its targets. With the pistol in one hand, he used the other to dial the *Überfall* Commandos, the police unit that specialized in holdups. As he looked up from the phone, he saw one of the thieves outside the window of his office, trying to enter. When the thief realized the door was locked, he attempted breaking in through the window. Then he saw the gun, abandoned his efforts, and returned to the store.

Shortly thereafter, a van with about half a dozen *Überfall* Commandos came and chased the thieves out of the store. But as the Commandos were leaving, their leader said to Father, "We came this time, *Herr* Pressman, but don't call us again because we won't come. You are *Juden*."

Hermann told my parents that it was time to leave Germany. My father snorted with contempt. He had lived in Germany for over twenty years, was the prosperous owner of a men's clothing store and factory, and had just bought an apartment building. Leave Berlin? Because of this madman? Hitler and his Nazi thugs would soon blow over.

Hermann decided to leave alone. Since he had studied English in school, he initially planned to go to London. But when he had difficulty getting a visa for England, he opted for Antwerp, Belgium, instead. We had a cousin, David Mendelson, there. Hermann was able to secure a temporary visa for a four-week visit to Belgium, and on May 9 he boarded the train for Antwerp.

After his arrival, he explored the possibility of remaining in Belgium as a permanent resident. The Committee for German Refugees and Immigrants told him that he might have a chance to remain if his parents applied for visas, too. Hermann shared this information with our parents, and they agreed to apply for short-term visas. Their plan was to remain in Belgium temporarily until Hitler blew over and then return to Berlin.

Even though our parents applied for visas, Hermann continued to have difficulty in securing permission to remain in Belgium. Although he had been born in Germany, the Germans had never granted him citizenship because they had never granted our parents citizenship. Hermann, like my parents, was considered Polish. As a Pole, he did not qualify as a German refugee or immigrant.

On June 16, our parents wrote to Hermann asking him to return to Berlin temporarily as the situation had quieted, and they needed his help with some financial matters. They told him that the entire family would move to Belgium four weeks later. Hermann refused to return. He had heard that the Nazis were arresting returnees and holding them in "protective custody," from which few returned.

Two days later, our parents called Hermann and again asked him to return to Berlin. He said if they *ordered* him to return, he would; otherwise, he would remain in Belgium. Two days later, Mother called Hermann and demanded his return. She followed this up with a letter to the same effect.

Hermann made plans to return to Berlin. As he was packing, the phone rang. It was Mother. She and Father had decided to leave Germany. Hermann unpacked his bags.

Then Father met with a small group of Nazis and agreed to turn his store and factory as well as the apartment building over to them for a fraction of their value, and they agreed to let us go.

On July 16, Father and I arrived by train in Belgium. Mother stayed behind to supervise the shipping of our furniture; she arrived three days later. My parents rented an apartment in Antwerp, and I was enrolled in kindergarten.

My parents missed Germany. When my mother needed a new pair of shoes, she returned to Berlin. After all, we were going to return there soon when the Nazi regime ended.

Father had doubts about remaining in Antwerp, even for the short term. In August, he returned to Berlin to look into establishing a business there. He learned, however, that Jews were now barred from participating in commercial enterprises, and he returned to Belgium the following month. He then began to look into the possibility of getting into business in Czechoslovakia. Nothing came of that either.

Months passed, and Father remained unemployed and unoccupied. My parents believed that they had been better off in Germany, where they had been in business and knew the language. In

Belgium, neither was the case. Hermann was to blame for this state of affairs.

In early October, Father began to think of moving the family to Palestine, but Hermann and my mother were opposed to this; they feared anti-Semitism there. Then, on a visit to Paris, my father learned from French Jews who had gone to Palestine that the weather there was oppressive and business opportunities were limited. So he decided against moving the family to Palestine. Instead, he considered opening a beauty salon in Paris with a friend of his in the business. He suggested that Hermann register at a beauty school, and we made plans to move to Paris.

The beauty salon venture never materialized and, in early November, Father decided to invest in a cooperative to be established by a group of wholesale grocers in Antwerp. In return for my father's investment, Hermann would be given a job in the cooperative. This venture, too, did not come to pass.

In mid-November, Father bought the stock of a men's suit store in Antwerp and stored the merchandise. Then he looked for a store where he and Hermann might sell these suits but was unable to locate one. It took him and Hermann months to sell the stock to department stores, individual buyers, and at auctions.

Father then decided to return to the trade he had embarked upon when he first came to Germany. He had business cards printed saying, "Zysia Pressman, Men's Tailor." But by early December, he abandoned that idea. He had met a wholesaler in the textile business and decided to go into partnership with him. The business would also provide a job for Hermann. My father and the wholesaler could not, however, agree on terms, and that deal fell through as well.

On December 19, two policemen arrived at our home, took Hermann's temporary visa, and gave him a notice directing him to leave Belgium within eight days, or he would be deported. No reason was given. Mother and Hermann went to the mayor of Antwerp and pleaded for his assistance. On December 22, the deportation order was halted, and Hermann was given a temporary visa pending review of his status. No explanation was given then either.

Meanwhile, a new year, 1934, rolled around. The family had been in Antwerp six months, and none of my father's intended business ventures had materialized. He then explored the feasibility of opening a raincoat factory in Antwerp, a business he had been in years before in Germany.

To while away the time, Father began to study Yiddish. He had never learned to read or write in any language. In Poland he hadn't had the opportunity, and in Germany he hadn't found it necessary: Mother and Hermann always handled the paper work. But in Antwerp Mr. Krimilovsky, one of our friends, came to our house and gave Father Yiddish lessons. So Father learned to read Yiddish, but, for some reason, he was never able to read silently. He would sit in his easy chair reading the newspaper out loud in Yiddish. He was reading that way one day at the end of January, when he turned to Mother and said, "Lina, did you hear that? It says here that ships are leaving for the United States. [A certain number of displaced Europeans were permitted to enter the United States.] Why don't we go to America?" Since there did not appear to be any sign of conditions changing in Germany and nothing was working out in Belgium or any other country, Mother agreed. She had an uncle and aunt, David and Hattie Gold, in Brooklyn. Many years earlier, they had urged our family to move to the United States and had sent us the necessary papers. But my family was doing well in Germany at the time and did not consider it. Now, Father thought perhaps he could go into business with David. He intensified his Yiddish lessons because he had heard that in order to enter the United States an immigrant had to be literate in at least one language.

The raincoat factory idea was dropped. Hermann was dispatched to visit the American Consulate to look into the possibility of our moving to the United States. We had Polish passports and would fall within the Polish quota.

Weeks passed. My father was dubious about our being admitted to the United States and began to think about Czechoslovakia again. On March 2, however, the American Consulate notified us that our papers were in order. We could leave for the United States.

From the time Hitler had come to power, Father had been sending his money to banks in Poland and Czechoslovakia. After we moved to Antwerp, he had arranged for it to be transferred to a bank there. Now he arranged for our funds to be transferred to a bank in New York City.

On April 20, we boarded the Belgian Red Star Line's *S.S. Westernland* at Antwerp and sailed for New York City. The ship left harbor early that morning on a ten-day voyage, during most of which the entire family was seasick. After stops at Le Havre, Southampton, and Halifax, we disembarked in New York City on May 1, 1934.

Neither of my parents had any education to speak of, and, except for Hermann, none of us knew a word of English. My mother was forty-three years old, my father forty, Hermann was nineteen, and I was five. Now, it was up to us to create a new life for ourselves in this foreign land.

PART II

4.

MOVING TO "THE MOUNTAINS"

I never saw any pictures of my parents when they were children. The earliest picture I have of either of them is their wedding picture. Dad was a handsome young man of nineteen and Mother a serious, attractive young woman of twenty-two.

My father as *I* knew him, however, was a short, slight, bald, unprepossessing man, whose long nose was his only distinguishing physical feature. My youth was shadowed by the fear that I would inherit that nose, but Mother always assured me: "Don't worry, if you get Daddy's nose, you'll have an operation."

Father had a number of outstanding character traits: he disdained education; his principal motivation was to provide for his family; and he was a terrific businessman who could make a living wherever he found himself and with whatever was at hand. In making a decision, he consulted no one, and, once his mind was made up, the proverbial wild horses couldn't get him to change it.

My mother, when I knew her, was about 5'5" and solidly built; she wore a size forty-two or forty-four in dresses. Because of her size, she had difficulty finding clothes with style and bright colors. They didn't make them for large women in the 1930s and '40s. She always told me how lucky I was to be short because I had my pick of clothes.

Mother's hair was a grayish-white and she wore it in tight curls around her head, which she kept in place with long bobby pins. She was fair-skinned, with a mass of freckles on her face and arms.

I had a stronger resemblance to my father—I was built like him and had his coloring. I also looked to him much more as a role model than to my mother. He was the decision-maker in the family, the one with the power. My mother busied herself largely with housekeeping and cooking, activities that did not interest me.

Though much larger than my father, my mother was a much softer person—but she wielded a power of her own. Father's decision to move to the Catskills illustrated that.

After our arrival in the United States in 1934, we first settled in the Bronx at Five Hundred Southern Boulevard. That's where I learned to speak English. Our apartment was in a building that was built in a semi-circle around a small garden. I would stand in the garden listening to the other children at play, and whenever I caught an unfamiliar word, I'd run upstairs, repeat it to Hermann, and he'd give me the German equivalent. A month after we arrived in the United States, I turned six and started kindergarten.

My father returned to the business he knew. He opened a men's clothing store in Manhattan with a partner, but the business did poorly. And my father found that he could not take the pace of life in New York City. In Berlin, he had closed his store at midday, gone home for lunch and a rest, and then reopened until 7:00 PM. That was the schedule to which he was accustomed. The hurly-burly of life in New York was too much for him.

In the summer of 1935, the family took a few weeks' vacation in the Catskill Mountains of New York, *the* summer resort area for New York City's Jews. Shortly after our return, Father announced to the family that we would be moving to a village in the Catskills. He would buy out his partner and run the business as long as necessary to pay off his creditors. Then we would move to the Catskills, where he planned to go into the resort business. My father had never been in the resort business or in anything even approaching such a business, but that issue was never raised. Instead, my mother exploded for another reason. "Are you *meshuge*, crazy?" she asked. "Do you think I'm going to leave this city for a *dorf*, a village, in the mountains?" All their lives, wherever my parents lived, my father wanted to move, and my mother wanted to stay. When they visited neighbors, my father wanted to sell our house and buy theirs. This time was no different. But my mother adamantly refused to consider the idea of moving.

Father said no more. He was a man of few words, but those few words one needed to listen to. Since no one was listening, he turned around and left the apartment. Hermann said, "I don't like the look in his eyes. I'm going to follow him." So saying, he went out the door after Father.

Father went down to the East River and sat on a piece of lumber, staring out at the water. Hermann went over to him and suggested they go home together. He pushed Hermann aside and told him to go home to Mother, but Hermann was worried by the vacant look in Father's eyes. He ran to the nearest bystander and asked him to call the police. When Hermann returned, Father was walking into the East River. The police came and pulled him out of the water. His eyes had rolled up into his head, and he no longer knew what he was doing. The police wanted to call an ambulance and send him to the hospital, but Hermann persuaded them to release Father into his custody.

Hermann brought Father home, soaking wet and incoherent.

Mother took one look at him and said, "All right, we'll move to the Mountains."

That's how we came to the village of Woodridge, New York, in 1936, a village one square mile in area with a population of about seven hundred people.

5.

IN THE SWIM

I had always been different from my American-born classmates, with my foreign-born and older parents, and being foreign-born myself. Whatever village, town, or city we lived in, I hadn't grown up there. In addition, I'd worn thick glasses for nearsightedness and astigmatism from the age of eight. I was unattractive, a book-worm, and had no social graces.

One of the skills I lacked was the ability to swim. "Don't worry," Mother told me when we moved to Woodridge. "Someday, Daddy will build a pool for you, and you'll learn how to swim." This was preposterous, and I told Mother so. We were not in the economic and social class of people who had their own pools.

For our first five years in Woodridge, Mother and Dad rented a house from an elderly woman with a witch-like appearance named Mrs. Maloff, whom Mother and Dad called derogatorily *di Malofke*—the Maloff. They turned the house into a *kokhaleyn*, a "cook-alone" place. Stefan Kanfer, in his book *A Summer World*, had this to say about *kokhaleyns*:

> These "cook-alones" were improperly named. The patrons slept in separate rooms of a large house but shared the over-populated communal kitchen. There, the heat, combined with the squalling children underfoot, the closeness of bod-ies, and the absence of men during the week led to desperate cooperation and violent argument.[2]

The *kokhaleyn,* which was near the bottom of the ladder in the resort business, was common to the Catskills. A family would rent a single room for the season, from Memorial Day through Labor Day. The women would cook in the communal kitchen, the men would work at their jobs in "the City" [New York] during the week and join their families for the weekend.

After five years in Woodridge, Dad came home one day and announced that he had just bought a parcel of land in Monticello. It was time to move up the ladder in the resort business, from a *kokhaleyn* in the village of Woodridge to a bungalow colony in the town of Monticello, about ten miles northwest of Woodridge. Monticello was the county seat of Sullivan County, with a population of about 3,500 in the winter, which swelled to 75-100,000 during the summer season. My father bought fifty acres of land from the Gusars, a family that owned a drugstore in Monticello. This property, on route 42, the Port Jervis Road, had a frontage of 500 feet and acres and acres of pine trees. Father said he would build twenty-five bungalows on the property and name it The Pine Tree Bungalow Colony. He was true to his word.

By 1941, when we moved from Woodridge to Monticello, there were just the three of us. Hermann had met Helen Wurman, a summer vacationer, while we were living in Woodridge. He subsequently married her and opened a candy store in Long Beach, Long Island.

After the bungalows were built, my father added a handball court and a swimming pool. My mother's prediction had come true. My father did indeed build a swimming pool. And that's where I learned to swim.

6.

FATHER GETS A B+

When I was in high school in Monticello, girls were required to take Home Economics and boys, Shop. I had never shown any aptitude for domestic duties, but, nonetheless, as a girl, I was required to take Home Economics.

I learned to operate a sewing machine in that class. The class project for the semester was to make a dress using the sewing machine. We were allowed to choose the type of dress we wanted to make, and I chose a jumper. (After all, that was only half a dress.) I bought some attractive blue rayon fabric and selected a design for a v-necked jumper. The design had pretty embroidered flowers in many colors along the neck.

Fortunately, we had a Singer sewing machine at home, and I worked on my jumper all semester. I particularly enjoyed doing the flowered embroidery. On the day before I was to turn it in, I finally finished it and put it on. As I looked at myself in the mirror, I was appalled! Everything about the jumper had turned out fine—except that it did not fit. It was too tight. Tears rolled down my cheeks when I saw the work of a semester wasted. My mother heard my sobs and came running from the other room. When she saw me in the jumper, she realized what was wrong.

I was totally distraught. "Don't worry," Mother said. "Did you forget that your father was a tailor?" I was too upset to see what my father, excellent tailor that he was, could do in the part of the day that was left to rectify the situation. But he and my mother both saw the solution immediately.

The jumper was constructed of two pieces of fabric, front and back, joined at the sides. All my father had to do was buy another piece of fabric for the back, larger than the one I had, and substitute that for the back piece of the jumper I had made. He dashed off to the yard goods store, matched the fabric, came home, and redid the jumper. This time, it fit beautifully.

I wore my new jumper to class the following day—and passed Home Economics. My grade, however, was only a B+. I thought my father deserved an A.

7.

GRADUATING WITH MY CLASS

The year was 1945, and we were living in our home at the Pine Tree Bungalow Colony in Monticello. I was seventeen and in my senior year at Monticello High School. Late one afternoon, the front door opened and my father walked in, beaming, followed by Sheiner and a well-dressed, middle-aged couple. My father introduced the couple as Mr. and Mrs. Greenbaum* and said to my mother, "Bring out the *shnaps*—whisky, Lina. We just finished a little business." Mother left to get the bottle of whisky and the liqueur glasses we kept for special occasions.

Sheiner, who was never referred to in my home by anything more than his surname, was the most aggressive realtor in Monticello. As soon as I saw him that day, I was gripped by fear. He was the type of salesman who could sell ice to the Eskimos. Five years earlier, he had negotiated our purchase of the property from the Gusars. At that time, the fifty-acre property was filled with pine trees and huckleberry bushes. Out of this wilderness, with my father's imagination and my mother's endless uprooting of bushes, had sprung our bungalow colony consisting of twenty-six separate buildings (twenty-five bungalows and our house), a parking lot, a swimming pool, a handball court, and a general store. Now Sheiner was here again. Why?

It turned out that the "little business" Father had just concluded was the sale of our colony to the Greenbaums for $120,000. When I heard this news, only one thought came to my mind. I would not graduate with my high school class. Instead, I would have to transfer to yet another school in the middle of my senior year, as I had already transferred from Antwerp to the Bronx; to Woodridge; to Miami Beach; to Monticello; to Long Beach; back to Monticello; back to Miami Beach; and, finally, back to Monticello. Again I would have to become familiar with a new school building, a new school system, new teachers, and a new class, most of whose students, unlike me, had grown up together. I could not bear it.

I let loose a stream of acrimonious language against Sheiner that shocked the assembled small group. I told him no one had put the property on the market (which was true), that his presence was unwanted, that he had no right to come in here with these customers, that we were not going to sell the property, and so on.

He took all this without saying a word. There was utter silence after my torrent of abuse until Mrs. Greenbaum turned to her husband and said, "When we are paying so much money for a property, I certainly don't want to feel like I'm taking it away from someone." With that, she turned around and calmly walked out of the house, followed by Mr. Greenbaum. Sheiner was stunned. He could not believe he was losing a $7,000 commission due to the ravings of a 17-year-old high school student. But he said nothing and followed the Greenbaums out the door.

I thought my father would kill me. Customers for $120,000-properties did not come along every day. Furthermore, this was the time to sell the property. My father always knew when to get into a business and when to get out. This was the time to get out. The piers were starting to shift and needed to be redone, and the tenants were beginning to demand new services, like a casino, entertainment, and childcare.

But, instead of killing me, Father slowly took Mother's arm, walked to the window with her, watched the departing Greenbaums and Sheiner, and calmly said, "Lina, we'll never get a customer like that again." After that, the matter was never raised in my presence.

That spring, I graduated with my high school class, and in the fall I began my freshman year at Cornell. That winter, I received a call from Mother one evening. "I have some news for you," she said, with hesitation. "I hope you won't be angry." I couldn't imagine what Father had done now.

"We sold the place again," she said,"but not for $120,000. We got $125,000 this time. Is that all right?" I told Mother it was quite all right, and she heaved a sigh of relief. "Thank God." she said, "Daddy was worried."

PART III

8.

MOTHER AND THE
NIGHT SCHOOL

With the increasing number of women working outside the home, one of the issues of our day is how women with families can balance the competing interests of work and family. This was never an issue for my mother. She didn't distinguish between work and family; she simply did whatever had to be done. When my father was in the men's clothing business, she helped him in the store and with the bookkeeping. When they ran the bungalow colony in Monticello, she joined the cleaning women at the end of the season in cleaning the bungalows.

But the core of her life was her husband and children. And from the time I was ten, children meant me, because Hermann married then and moved to Long Beach.

Mother cleaned the house, cooked the meals, did the laundry and ironing, took care of Father and me when we were ill, and supplied liberal doses of love. She had only one abiding interest that ever took her out of the home or the family business: education.

When we moved to Long Beach, Mother was able to feed her hunger for learning by attending the local night school, where she quickly became the star of the class. At first, she made some attempt to get my father to go along with her, but this was doomed to failure. Father had always kept a healthy distance between himself and formal education and was not about to change.

Every Thursday evening, Mother would prepare the evening meal, leave it on the stove ("Just turn on the burners and put it on the plate.") and leave for her night school class. She would come home later with wonderful tales of what she had learned, interspersed with exclamations at the erudition of her teacher, Mr. Quinn ("A regulah Einstein.") When Christmas time rolled around, Mother naturally was placed in charge of collecting for Mr. Quinn's gift and managed to add a little *Yiddishkayt* to the holiday festivities.

After several years of this, I was surprised to come home at dinnertime one Thursday to find Mother busy at the stove. "What are you doing home, Mom?" I asked. "Isn't it time for your class?"

"I'm not going to class anymore," she said. It turned out that Mother had been feeling increasingly guilty about the fact that on Thursday nights Father and I had to heat our meal ourselves, bring it to the dinner table, and eat without her presence. She was failing in her duty to her family. She could not continue to indulge herself in night school attendance at her family's expense.

Nothing we could say could change Mother's mind. She never attended night school again. I don't know who bought Mr. Quinn's present at Christmastime after that, but I do know who was with us every Thursday evening at dinner—my mother.

9.

IF YOU SPEAK HIS LANGUAGE

Every once in a while one of those magazines for learned Jews will publish a symposium with the slightly mysterious title of "What Makes a Jew?" It may contain a dissertation by a leading Jewish sociologist proving that Jews are nothing more than an ethnic group with a common cultural heritage. Another may argue that Jews are indeed a race apart as evidenced by their outstanding intelligence and achievements. A renowned theologian will enunciate his thesis that the belief in one God lies at the root of all Judaism and that a Jew is one who adheres to the Jewish religion. Yet another may argue that religion is irrelevant to Jewishness and that even an atheist can be a Jew if he or she identifies as a Jew.

My father was never one to quibble over such subtle distinctions. He had one invariable standard for determining if someone was a Jew: if you spoke his language, you were a Jew. That was it. No complications.

This was obviously a gross oversimplification, which I knew wouldn't stand the test when confronted with reality. And so I waited for Father's theory to meet a challenge. It looked as if my chance had come one night in the mid-'50s when Harry Belafonte appeared on our TV screen singing "Hava Nagila."

"Howja like dot?" asked my father.

"Not dot," corrected Mother, unperturbed by Father's twenty-year resistance to the niceties of English pronunciation. "Not dot. Dat. T—h—a—t. Dat." For some inexplicable reason, Mother's tutorial method with a man who had never mastered the alphabet was premised on spelling. I suspected this technique owed its application not so much to Mother's belief in its validity as a teaching tool but to her desire to demonstrate her own superior grasp of the language. "All right," said Father, in his I-stand-corrected tone. "Dat. Howja like dat?" And, then he said, in astonishment and delight, "'Herry' Belafonte turns out to be a Jew!"

No amount of refutation from Mother and me had the slightest effect on him. "Herry" Belafonte sang in Hebrew. Who else but a Jew would do that? He was obviously one of those Black Jews, like the Falashas of Ethiopia.

Strictly speaking, Hebrew wasn't my father's language. Yiddish was. But Hebrew was the language of the Bible, the other sacred texts and, in recent times, the language of Israel. That was good enough for Dad.

From then on, "Herry" was a favorite in our house. On those notable occasions when he made a TV appearance, the family would gather before the set and sit in hushed and grateful silence. One of our own was on.

Accordingly, it came as no surprise to Father when "Herry" divorced Marguerite, his African American wife, and married Julie Robinson, a young Jewish dancer with the Katherine Dunham dance troupe. "Nu," said Father, with that know-it-all sparkle in his eyes. "What did I tell you? A Jewish fellah. First, he's got to marry a *shikse*—a gentile girl or woman. And then he finds a nice Jewish girl."

The acid test of reality never had a chance with my father. He had the exasperating ability to conform reality to his own vision of it.

10.

WEINBERG'S GLASSES

My father always liked to bring things home. He believed that it was the responsibility of the head of the household to bring provisions into the house, and he performed this duty assiduously, whether the goods were needed or not. If no one else had use for them, he would find a use. Nor was he particular about the means of acquiring these things. Legitimacy of acquisition was not one of his standards. He might receive items through purchase, gift, barter, or a more unsavory means. The important thing was to bring something home to cast before my mother's often-horrified eyes. He brought home an endless supply of dirty towels cast up on the beach; an expensive German camera that someone had sold him; and huge containers of fruits and vegetables that produce merchants gave him in exchange for the fish he caught. Mother dutifully baked pies with the peaches and blueberries and made casseroles of the vegetables. When Father wasn't looking, she would retrieve all the dirty towels around the house and throw them out. She would sooner have walked on burning coals than permit a stranger's towels to mix with her own, even in the most thorough of washing machines.

When we were living in Long Beach in the early '50s, Father brought home an unusual item—at least, for a man with 20/20 vision—a pair of dark, horn-rimmed spectacles he found one morning in front of Hermann's candy store. He then proceeded to put these glasses on as he read the *Forverts*—the *Jewish Daily Forward*. Mother and I were alarmed that Father might be harming his eyes by wearing these glasses. Our distress was heightened when we learned the identity of the owner of the glasses perched so jauntily on Father's ample nose. One day, Mr. Weinberg came into Hermann's store, wondering if he might have left his glasses there. Weinberg, an elderly Jew who lived with his wife and adult daughter, was a friend of our family. After Weinberg left the store, despite all our entreaties, Father stated that he had no intention of returning the glasses. He defended his position with two arguments. First, he went into an involved legal analysis of the law of personal property and its application to lost articles. He concluded that as Weinberg's glasses had been found in front of *his* son's store, the Pressmans had acquired legitimate ownership of them. His second theory, pronounced in his most sonorous judicial tone, was that he had no proof that these were in fact Weinberg's glasses. Weinberg, who was then wandering about the streets of Long Beach groping his way, might have made the whole story up.

There was nothing to be done. Like his hero, Winston Churchill, who hadn't become Prime Minister of the British Empire to oversee its destruction, Father hadn't fought his way up from the streets of Piltz to relinquish his booty now. The glasses would not be returned. Hermann surreptitiously gave Weinberg money on some pretext to cover the purchase of new glasses, which, when Father saw them, only confirmed his theory that Weinberg had not lost his glasses in the first place.

Years went by. We moved from Long Beach to Miami Beach, and Mother and I no longer had to live in dread of Weinberg's walking into our house unexpectedly and discovering Father wearing *his* glasses. But Mother and I continued to be worried about possible damage to Father's eyes. He was using "Weinberg's glasses," as they came to be known around our house, more and more: for reading, driving, TV, the movies. Something had to be done.

Finally, Father succumbed to years of prodding. He and Mother had recently purchased a new home in North Miami Beach, and—as befitted a new homeowner in "Florida's Finest Residential Community"—he finally agreed to go forth, flanked by Mother and me, to be fitted for his own spectacles.

We could not, of course, divulge the origin of "Weinberg's glasses" to the optometrist. Instead, we told him that Father had been having difficulty with his reading and, therefore, thought he might need a new pair of glasses. He wanted a thorough eye checkup. The optometrist proceeded to put Father through the standard eye examination. This was difficult because Father couldn't read English--but somehow he managed to let the optometrist know what he saw and when he saw it. Mother and I were already congratulating ourselves on finally getting rid of "Weinberg's glasses" when the optometrist, with a bewildered look on his face, said, "I don't understand why you've been having trouble, Mr. Pressman. The glasses you're wearing are exactly the right prescription for you." Father beamed, and Mother and I knew we were beaten. We collected "Weinberg's glasses" and went home.

Some years later, when I came home from Washington for a visit, I was astonished to find Father reading the paper with a spanking new pair of glasses perched crookedly on the bridge of his nose. "Mom," I shouted in amazement, "Is that what I think it is? Has Daddy gotten himself a new pair of glasses?"

"Yes," came back my Mother's voice. It sounded strangely resigned. "He found them last week. On the beach."

I shuddered a moment, thinking of the latest Weinberg stumbling about somewhere on Miami Beach. But it was only for a moment. Then I realized that I was home again, and Father hadn't changed at all. Impulsively, I reached out to embrace him in a great big hug, knocking the glasses right off his face. He didn't seem to mind.

11.

OUR WINTER VACATION

In the late '30s and early '40s, when my parents and I would drive to Miami Beach for the winter, it was usually just the three of us. These trips always required lots of preparation because we had to pack kosher food and a small ice chest as well as clothes. But, eventually, we would be ready to go.

Traveling with my parents was never dull. I was usually in the back seat laughing at their antics, but on one such trip in 1940, when I was twelve, Hermann and Helen joined us for the first few weeks. I had their additional eccentricities for amusement.

At every southern store where we stopped—for food, gas, or to use the bathroom—regardless of the condition of the place, which was often little more than a lean-to, Hermann would say to the proprietor, "Nice little place you got here." That phrase became a byword in the family, sure to convulse us all.

Helen, always cold, although the heater was on and we were driving south, was wrapped in at least three blankets.

All went comparatively well until we started looking for a place to spend the night in Summerton, South Carolina. On this trip, we needed three rooms. It wasn't always easy to find three vacant rooms, but in Summerton we found them in a lovely tourist house, a rambler that looked like a private home. We rented the rooms and began to prepare for the night. I was in a room adjoining that of my parents, and Hermann and Helen were around the corner. We noticed that the heat for the entire house came from a grate in the hallway, so Father suggested to Mother that she leave their door open throughout the night so that the heat would waft in.

At 2 AM a loud thud awoke me and then I heard noises coming from my parents' room. Father had fallen off the bed again. This happened regularly when he slept in a strange bed. Immediately the remonstrances began. Whenever Father fell off the bed and awoke to see my mother kneeling beside him on the floor, he would ask her what on earth she thought she was doing. She would explain that he had fallen off the bed and that she was trying to help him get back into bed. He always flatly denied her explanation. He had not fallen off the bed! A grown man didn't fall off a bed.

This time, as usual, it was Mother's fault. She must have disregarded his instructions to leave their door open, and the shock to his body from the biting cold in the room must have propelled him out of bed and onto the floor. Mother's defense that she had opened the door, and that it must have closed on its own was to no avail.

By this time, Hermann and Helen were awakened by the to-do and were standing about discussing the situation. Then Father announced that he was going to take a hot bath because his side hurt from the fall. Mother pointed out that it was ridiculous to take a bath at 2 AM; she suggested that the sensible thing for him to do was get back into bed, go to sleep, and bathe in the morning. That did it! Now he was definitely going to take a bath.

Off he went to the adjoining bathroom. Shortly thereafter, we were startled by my father's cry for help. "Lina," he called to my mother, "come quick." Mother dashed to the bathroom to discover Father sitting upright in the tub, covered from head to toe in soapsuds, but with no water in the tub. As was his custom, Father had gotten into the tub, turned on the water, and proceeded to cover himself with lather. After some trickles of water, which he had used to make the lather, no more water came out of the spigot. It seemed that the owners of our tourist house, unaccustomed to 2 AM bathers, had shut the water off for the night. Now there was no water with which to rinse off. So, as he sat there sheepishly, Mother wiped her soaped-up husband off with towels.

When he was finally cleared of all soap and dried, we all prepared to return to bed, but Father would have none of it. He had been soaped and dried, he felt fine, and was ready to proceed and "make some time while it's light yet." As usual, when his mind was made up, nothing would dissuade him. So, at 3 AM, we said good-bye to Summerton, South Carolina, and resumed our trip to Miami Beach.

12.

OUR SUMMER VACATION

While we were living in Long Beach in the early '50s, Father decided that we should take a trip back to the Catskills. Since we no longer owned a resort there, now we could go "like guests." We would stay at one of the local hotels and be tenants instead of landlords. Knowing my father's views on paying rent ["money down the drain"], and eating in restaurants ["I have better food at home."], I did not look forward to this vacation. Something always went wrong on those infrequent occasions when Dad paid rent or ate in a restaurant. But I brushed my fears aside and prepared for the trip.

Father decided we would return to Monticello ("the Garden Spot of the Mountains," the signs proclaimed) in mid-August. So Mother and I spent July shopping in New York for proper outfits for me. One never knew when the son of a New York garment manufacturer might be dropping by at the hotel's casino and "a girl had to be dressed." Mother had the quaint idea that love always bloomed when a young woman was "dressed" and I didn't want to disabuse her of that notion.

Finally, the big day came and we all piled into the car, loaded with suitcases, cartons, my father's fishing equipment, and enough kosher food for several trips ("God forbid, you should get hungry.").

When we reached Monticello, we discovered that "the Garden Spot of the Mountains" was in the throes of a polio epidemic. Residents and guests had been advised to avoid swimming pools and crowds. As a result, hotels, rooming houses, and bungalow colonies were closing for lack of business. In view of this, we decided to abandon our summer vacation and return home as soon as possible. We would stay overnight at the rooming house of Mrs. Perel, who lived across the street from our former colony on the Port Jervis Road, and drive home the following morning.

That night we all went to a local delicatessen to have a kosher meal before tucking in for the night. We gorged on *gedempte*—stewed—chicken, *kasha varnishkes*—buckwheat groats with bow ties, and *kishke*—stuffed derma (intestinal beef membranes). Then, we bedded down for the night. Mother and Dad had a large double room and I a single across the hall.

At about 3 AM, I was awakened by a throbbing in my upper lip. I got out of bed, went to the mirror, and looked at my face. My entire upper lip was swollen to such proportions that it hung over my lower lip. Three pinpoints appeared in the center of my upper lip, out of which a sticky, yellowish liquid was oozing. My knees began to shake.

The thought that kept going through my head was: "No one will ever kiss me again, no one will ever kiss me again, no one will ever kiss me again." With this thought reverberating in my mind, I quickly made my way across the hall to my parents' room and knocked at the door. I expected that it would take a few moments before my parents awakened and opened the door. To my surprise, Mother opened the door immediately, and behind her I saw my father, bent over the basin, throwing up. Father was again suffering from a case of "indigestion." (We found out years later that he had gallstones.) Apparently, something in the dinner the night before hadn't agreed with him. Mother was sure it was the *kishke*—it always was.

When Mother saw my overhanging lip, she shrieked, "*Oy, gevald!*"—"Heavens!" and asked me what had happened. I told her I didn't know, but perhaps it was bedbugs or some vile Catskills disease that lingered in the mountain air. Whatever it was, I asked Mother to have Father drive me to the doctor in town immediately. Mother said, "How can Daddy drive you to the doctor? He's sick himself." I then said I'd go downstairs myself and hitch a ride to town. Mother absolutely refused to permit this, arguing that I'd surely be raped by anyone who picked me up at three o'clock in the morning. "With this lip, no one will rape me, Mother," I counter-argued. But, to no avail. At last, it was decided that Father would continue his heaving by himself and Mother would come to my room to calm me down for the remainder of the night. In the morning, we'd go to the doctor.

That morning, we dressed, paid Mrs. Perel ("Are you sure you wouldn't like to stay a few days more?" she entreated.), packed our things, and left for the doctor's.

Doctor Cohen examined Father and me. He said that both of us had been allergic to something in the food we had eaten the night before. He gave me an injection to take down the swelling of my lip and some ointment, which I was supposed to apply for the next three days. Father was given a prescription for his digestive problem. Mother was given a sedative.

Father paid Dr. Cohen, and we began the trip back to Long Beach. Our summer vacation was over.

PART IV

13.

FAR ABOVE CAYUGA'S WATERS

I never had any intention of going to college. I grew up in the rural communities of Woodridge and Monticello, whose population contained a mix of farmers, small business people, and those engaged in renting *kokhaleyns*, bungalows, and hotel rooms for the summer. These were, by and large, unsophisticated communities and "college" was not a word I heard often.

Upon entering high school, I had the option of enrolling in the College Entrance or Introduction to Business program. I chose the latter and prepared to become a secretary. Then, three persons intervened to change the direction of my life—one of my teachers and two classmates. The first was Miss Gallagher, whose Introduction to Business class I attended during my freshman year of high school. At the end of that year, she told me my abilities were more suited to the College Entrance program and recommended that I switch. I decided to do that, not only because of her recommendation. The Introduction to Business course was largely filled with the less intellectual members of my class, and I missed being with my friends, all of whom were in the College Entrance program. But I still had no intention of going to college.

Then came the second influence on my life, my classmate Elaine Robbins*, whose father was a prosperous businessman in Monticello. When Elaine and I met in the ladies' room one day during our junior year, she said, "What are you going to do when you graduate?"

"Do?" I asked, surprised at the question. What was there to do after high school? Graduation alone was enough of a pinnacle, and then I'd become a secretary.

"Well," said Elaine, "*I'm* going to college. Aren't you?"

"No," I answered. "I'd be too old. If I went to college, I'd be twenty-two when I graduated." Most of my classmates would be seventeen on graduation from high school. Because of my arriving in this country when I was almost six and starting kindergarten then, I'd be eighteen. Too old for further education.

But my conversation with Elaine stayed in my mind. She was so sure of herself.

The third influence on my decision to go to college involved another classmate, Jake Nemerson. Jake, whose father was an optometrist, asked me one day whether I wanted to go with him to Middletown, a city about thirty miles from Monticello, to take a test for the George LeFevre Scholarship. The winner of the scholarship would get $400. I told him I'd have to ask my father.

I didn't know how Father would react to my question about the test for the scholarship since there was a $7 fee for taking the exam, and Father did not favor higher education for young women. But he was unpredictable where money was concerned. At one moment, he might refuse me $15 to buy a new dress ("The cellar is full of *shmates*—rags—already."), and at the next, he might urge me to get a new fur coat for $1,000. It depended on his mood.

When I explained things to Father this time, he had no trouble making a decision. "Seven dollars, and you win four hundred?" he asked. "What's the question? Of course, take the test." I tried to explain to him that not everyone won the $400, but he was uninterested. He even went to Mother and laughingly told her how ridiculous I was to even ask him such a question. Who wouldn't pay $7 to get $400?

So I accompanied Jake to Middletown and took the test. Some time later, I learned that I had indeed won the George LeFevre Scholarship. As soon as I learned this, I excitedly told my father. He couldn't figure out what all the excitement was about—that's how he had understood it in the first place. You paid $7 and you got back $400.

I applied to only two colleges, both in New York State: Hartwick, a small college in Oneonta, and Cornell in Ithaca. I was accepted at Hartwick and accepted their offer to attend. Then I received an acceptance from Cornell and chose that more prestigious school over Hartwick.

When I went to Cornell, I found that most of my classmates had scholarships. I have no doubt that winning the George LeFevre Scholarship and later being awarded a New York State Scholarship were responsible for my acceptance at Cornell.

Even though my father had agreed to my taking the test for the scholarship, both my parents were totally opposed to my going to college. They felt that what a young woman needed to know was how to cook and sew so she could attract and keep a husband. Too much book knowledge would only frighten away eligible males. Nonetheless, since this is what I wanted to do, my parents drove me up to Cornell. We knew how to get to the general area, but when we got there, we didn't know where the university was. None of us had ever seen a college or university. My only familiarity with college came from movie musicals. So I pictured Cornell as a large white mansion with pillars, on whose porch students like Mickey Rooney and Judy Garland would be sitting, dangling their legs, and singing a song.

But when we arrived in Ithaca, we saw no such building. We did see a number of small buildings nestled in the woods, which I later learned were fraternity houses. We stopped at one; I went over to the house and knocked on the door. A young man came to the door, and I asked him where Cornell was. Spreading his arms wide, he said, "This is Cornell." It took me a while to understand what he meant. The entire area was Cornell. How very odd.

After we found Balch Hall, my freshman dormitory, and my father had brought my bags to my room, he made ready to leave. The housemother, Miss Helen Armor, noticing this, came over to me. Father was short and unprepossessing, and Miss Armor took him for a driver. "Aren't you going to tip that man?" she asked.

"No," I answered, "I don't have to tip him. He's my father."

14.

SAM KAPLAN

From the moment my parents left Cornell, I was homesick. I had never been away from home before, and I was thrust into a world that seemed incredibly sophisticated. It was full of attractive, well-dressed young men and women, most of whom seemed to know each other and what to do. They not only went to class and participated in sorority and fraternity life, but they were engaged in fascinating extracurricular activities. They wrote for the *Cornell Sun*, rowed for the Crew Club, and performed with the Octagon and Savage Clubs. I would never be able to attain their level of savoir-faire. I wanted to go home.

But I had no home to go to. My parents, as usual, had gone to Miami Beach for the winter. Furthermore, even if I could have returned to my parents' home in Monticello, the entire community would know I had failed at college. I decided to stick it out.

After I'd been at Cornell for three months, I could stand the homesickness no longer. I realized that I could return to Monticello for a visit and reconnect with it and my friends there. My high school classmate and friend, Doris Smookler, would put me up. I talked my roommate, Patricia Stewart*, into hitchhiking the 150 miles to Monticello with me for the weekend.

So, one Saturday morning in December, Stewie and I, dressed in our college blazers and skirts, said good-bye to our friends and headed for the main highway out of Ithaca.

Almost immediately, we got a ride to Monticello. Two men in their fifties, Harry and Jack, stopped for us; they had just visited their sons at Cornell, and were going through Monticello en route back to New York City.

As the trip progressed, the men became more and more personal and kept proposing alternatives to our stopping at the Smookler residence in Monticello. "How about staying with us at the Concord Hotel, girls?" suggested Harry, the more aggressive of the two. "It's pretty fancy." When we turned that down, he said, "Why do you want to go to Monticello? It's a hick town. Come with us to New York. We'll show you *Radio City*."

I became frightened that they would not drop us off in Monticello. What would we do if they drove straight through town? But when we got to Monticello, to our surprise and relief, Jack gallantly opened the door and let us out.

We spent a fun day and evening with Doris and other friends. Sunday morning, Doris drove us to the outskirts of Liberty, the neighboring town, and we took up our stand on the road again, thumbs raised. The first vehicle to stop for us was a broken-down truck, full of chicken feathers in the back. I was loath to accept the ride because I had been allergic to chicken feathers as a child, and the thought of riding 150 miles with the smell of old hens was more than I could bear. But Stewie was already running to the cab of the truck, so I ran behind her. We jumped up, and found ourselves sitting next to a short man in his sixties, with stubby white hair. His name was Sam Kaplan, and he was in the chicken and egg business. He was going to Cortland, thirty miles from Ithaca, and would drive us that far. We were not too pleased at the prospect of hitching yet another ride from Cortland to Ithaca on a Sunday night, but since we were already riding along in Sam's truck, there didn't seem to be much we could do about it.

As we drove along, Sam had a story about the inhabitants of every house that we passed along the way. At first, it seemed incredible that he could know everyone along the route, and then it dawned on us that he was making these stories up. He was one of the most charming liars we had ever met. We began to test him, by asking if he knew any number of famous people.

"Did you ever meet General Pershing, Sam?" I asked.

"Oh, yes," he replied. I used to deliver eggs to the General up in New England—after the First World War. A wonderful man."

He went along that way for the remainder of the trip, telling us about the foibles and eccentricities of every farmer, merchant, and customer who supposedly lived in the little houses along the way.

"I bin in three-quarters of the world, girls," he said, "and done business with the other quarter."

When we got to Cortland, Sam insisted that we come up to see his house. He had lost his wife the year before and was lonesome. We sensed what our visit would mean to him and went along.

Sam lived in a little white-shingled house in the center of town. Old egg crates and other paraphernalia were scattered about the place. It was plainly a home that lacked a woman's touch, and we could see how happy Sam was to have some feminine company. He fluttered about, cleaning up, scrambling some eggs for us, serving us cookies, and generally keeping busy. After we had eaten and relaxed, he insisted that we all pile back into the truck so he could drive us to Ithaca.

During the remaining thirty miles back to Cornell, Sam entertained us with stories of the professors who lived in the houses we passed and who bought eggs from him. When he bade us good-bye at the door of our dormitory, he had tears in his eyes, and Stewie and I were weepy, too.

During the rest of my college days, every once in a while I would dial Sam's number in Cortland, and, after I identified myself, Stewie and I would hear his, "Hello, girls," coming over the telephone. He would regale us with new stories about his customers, and we would tell him about the courses we were taking.

It's been almost fifty years since I've heard from Sam. I hope he's still selling eggs to the "other quarter."

15.

ALMOST IN THE ARMY

As my senior year at Cornell progressed, I began to get panicky. I had started majoring in languages, then shifted to psychology, and now I was in the Graduate School of Business and Public Administration. But in a matter of months I'd be graduating. What would I do then? What did languages, psychology, and business and public administration add up to?

With this question in mind, I picked up the school newspaper, the *Cornell Sun*, one morning, to see the following headline: "Graduates To Be Commissioned As Second Lieutenants." The article stated that college seniors who applied to the Army, including women who applied to the WAC (the Women's Army Corps), would be commissioned as officers, second lieutenants, upon graduation. What an exciting answer to my problem. There was a ready-made position waiting out there for me, with the glamour of interesting work and travel to foreign places. "Stewie," I shouted to my roommate. "Look at this. We can join the Army—and see the world." Stewie, a Liberal Arts major, as I had been, was equally concerned about her future and equally excited about the prospect of joining the Army. We resolved to go to the recruiting office in downtown Ithaca the next morning.

The following morning at 10, dressed and ready, we boarded the bus that went from campus to downtown Ithaca and back again. We spoke excitedly of the future that awaited us in the service. In our mind's eye, we saw ourselves looking spiffy in our

brand-new uniforms, saluting smartly, giving orders, and traveling to exotic locales. What a heady life it would be.

When the bus stopped at the street where the recruiting office
was located, we saw to our surprise that the office was closed. Of
course—it was Sunday. In our excitement, we had totally forgotten that. We would have to return tomorrow. We did not even get
off the bus but just returned to campus.

The next morning when I awoke, the folly of our action hit
me. We were going to join the Army—an organization that told
you where to live, what to do, and how long you'd be doing it. An
organization you couldn't just leave when you felt like it. Where
you'd be wearing the same outfit as thousands of other women—
all day, every day. *We* were going to join the Army—an organization devoted to stamping out individuality, whose creed was following the chain of command?

"Stewie," I shouted. "Do you realize what we were going to
do?"

"Yes," she said, breathing a sigh of relief.

The matter was never raised again. My Army career never had
a chance.

16.

LAW SCHOOL

I entered the University of Miami School of Law in Coral Gables, Florida, in September 1954 when about three percent of the law students in this country were women. How did that happen?

My earliest career goal as a child, and one that never left me, was to be a writer. But I felt that I didn't have the necessary self-discipline. My next choice of a profession, which came to me in the third grade, was to be a teacher. But I abandoned that when I realized that teachers were not accorded the respect and prestige in this country that they were given in Poland, according to the stories my mother told me; nor did they get much in the way of monetary rewards. Next came languages. That interest came from my background and my romantic nature. My first language had been German. My second was Flemish, learned during the months my family lived in Antwerp. In the United States, I learned English. I also knew Yiddish as that was the language, along with German and English, which my parents spoke at home. In high school, I had had three years of Latin, which I loved, and also studied French. In thinking about my future career, I pictured myself as an interpreter at the UN.

Thus, I began my studies at Cornell majoring in languages and took a fourth year of Latin. Then, I had a change of heart. I was concerned that working as an interpreter would not be sufficiently challenging intellectually. Due to my long-standing interest in interpersonal relations, psychology became my next major. I stayed with that until I realized that in order to have a meaningful career in that field one needed to get a Master's and probably a PhD. Since a college education was already more schooling than I'd originally planned, I had no inclination to go on beyond that.

Thus, I found myself in my junior year of college needing to find yet another major. I considered many things, but law was not one of them. By this point, I was so confused I gave serious consideration to switching to Home Economics, a field in which I had never previously had any interest, with a major in meat cutting. I cannot now fathom what could have possessed me to think of that, and what I thought I would do with it. Fortunately, I abandoned that idea in short order and ended up spending my senior year in the Cornell Graduate School of Business and Public Administration. That school awarded graduates a Master's in Business at the end of two years, but one could attend for only one year as one's senior undergraduate year, and that's what I did.

After graduation, I returned to live with my parents in Long Beach and waited for the world to beat a path to my door. After all, I'd graduated as valedictorian of my high school class, Phi Beta Kappa from Cornell, and first in my class for one of my two semesters at the Graduate School. While these were impressive credentials, they seemed even more impressive to me because I was the first member of my family to attend college.

No one beat a path to my door; no one even called. After some time, I realized I'd have to start looking for a job. From the time of my graduation from Cornell, my parents had strongly urged me to study shorthand. I'd already taken typing in high school and with shorthand they thought I'd be able to get a job as a secretary. Whenever they raised this prospect, I pooh-poohed the idea. That might have been my goal when I began high school, but I'd gotten a college education since then. Cornell graduates did not become secretaries; they found positions of significance and influence.

Anyway, at this time, I paid slight attention to any of my parents' comments. For about two years after my graduation from Cornell, I barely spoke to them. I lived in their house, ate their food, and was supported by them—but did not share my thoughts with them. They hadn't gone to Cornell. (They had only paid *for me* to go there.) So what could I possibly have in common with these people?

I began my job hunting by sending out 200 résumés to companies around the country. That produced no tangible results. So I decided to apply for a job with the State of New York and took the qualifying exam. Subsequently, I was told that I qualified for a position with the New York State Liquor Authority, and an interview was set up for me at the Authority's offices in Albany.

My parents drove me up for the interview. After a 150-mile drive, we arrived in Albany and found ourselves in a rundown area with dilapidated houses and stores, unkempt vacant lots, and a general air of seediness. I could see my parents' despair at leaving me in such a place. "Don't be concerned," I said, "This is just the area around the railroad tracks." But then we realized that there were no tracks in sight. This was just the way Albany looked. That being the case, we turned around and drove the three hours back to Long Beach. That was the end of my career with the State of New York.

Next I answered an ad for a managerial trainee at McCreery's Department Store in New York City and was hired. When I began work, I learned that managerial trainee was a fancy title for sales person. I enjoyed the work but, due to my flat feet, was unable to stand all day and did not last beyond three days. McCreery's went out of business shortly thereafter, and I always felt somewhat responsible.

After I left McCreery's, I was so desperate for a job that I answered an ad for a telephone operator at the Lido Beach Hotel (now the Lido Towers, a condominium development) in Point Lookout, just east of Long Beach, the swankiest hotel in the area. After being hired, with no training, I was put at the switchboard and given a set of earphones. So, when the red lights came on signaling a caller, I pulled a telephone line out of its socket, inserted it into another socket, and hoped for the best. For some reason, the management was not satisfied with these efforts, and I was relieved of my duties after only half a day. (Like McCreery's, this hotel subsequently went out of business.)

By this time, seven months had passed since my graduation, during most of which time I had been unemployed. Finally, I decided to take my parents' advice and enrolled in a shorthand course at the Browne Business School in Hempstead, Long Island. I attended classes three hours a morning studying Gregg Simplified Shorthand, after which Mother spent several hours a day dictating to me at home. After two months, I set a school record for achieving a speed of 120 words per minute in that length of time. I finished my course on a Friday, and that Monday I was hired for what turned out to be my first permanent job. In May of 1951, I began work at *Today's Woman* magazine, one of several magazines published by Fawcett Publications. I was the secretary to S.T. "Sunny" Sunshine, the fashion advertising manager, and Ken Dillenbeck, an advertising salesman. Fashion advertising manager was another fancy title, this one for the job of selling advertising space to companies in the fashion business. My salary was $50 a week. For that, I commuted four hours each day round trip—by bus, Long Island railroad, and subway.

Shortly before Christmas, I was called into the management office and told that my superiors were pleased with my work, and therefore, I'd be getting a raise to $52.50 a week!

I liked being a secretary and enjoyed my work and the camaraderie at *Today's Woman*. However, when anyone asked me what I did for a living, I winced inwardly when I answered, "Secretary." While the questioners found nothing déclassé in this—after all, being a secretary was a perfectly legitimate occupation for a young woman in the early '50s, and was in fact one of the few occupations open to women in those days—I felt that it was wholly out of line with my education and my desire to do something meaningful with my life.

So, I began to look for ways to get out. These efforts led me in two directions—studying for an advanced degree and trying other jobs—both of which resulted in failure. First, I enrolled at New

York University to get a Master's in sociology. With my interest in people and social relations, I thought this might be an interesting line of study, although I had no idea what I would do with it. During the time I went to NYU, I worked at *Today's Woman* by day and took sociology courses twice a week at night. Although I enjoyed the courses, at the beginning of my second semester I decided I had to give it up. On those days when I had classes, I had to get up at 6:00 AM to get to my job in Manhattan by 9:00 AM, and I didn't get home to Long Beach after class until midnight. It was too exhausting.

Then, I decided I needed to try other positions. In April of 1952, I left *Today's Woman* to begin a job as personnel assistant at the Lane Bryant Department Store in New York City. I felt an affinity for Lane Bryant, which catered to large-sized and pregnant women because my mother was a size 44. She had always complained that large-sized women were unable to find attractive, brightly colored dresses, and Lane Bryant was making an effort to remedy that situation.

The personnel department consisted of two male managers and the woman I was due to succeed, who had been in the job for sixteen years. I noticed that the two managers were very devoted to this woman and that her knowledge of the job, after sixteen years, was awesome. At the end of my first day, I felt I would never be able to replace her in the hearts of these managers or equal her proficiency, so I never went back.

A few days later, I got a job as assistant to the publisher and editor of two magazines, the *Fishing Gazette* and the *Bicycling Institute*. After two weeks on that job, I concluded that neither fishing nor bicycling was meant to be my life's work. Happily, Sunny Sunshine took me back, and I returned gratefully to *Today's Woman*.

During this time, every December or January, my parents would go to Miami Beach for several months, and they would invite me to join them. On a number of occasions, I did. I would tell Sunny Sunshine that I was leaving to go to Florida, would resign my job, and, when I returned in April, he would rehire me.

But Sunny knew I was anxious to move out of secretarial work. In the fall of 1953, he told me there was an opening at *True Confessions*, another magazine published by Fawcett. While this job was essentially secretarial, I was told it might lead to editorial work. That November, I transferred from *Today's Woman* to *True Confessions*. This magazine, like *Today's Woman*, was targeted to the women's market. It was filled with allegedly true stories, often of romance gone awry. A typical issue, like the one for August 1950, sold for fifteen cents and featured stories like "Alone With My Shame," "The Man You Love Belongs to Me," and "My Husband's Sin Was Mine." The "Glamor Careers" section that month, "If You Want To Be an Air Hostess," concluded:

> One year as an Air Hostess—and then matrimony seems to
> be the rule on all air lines. And most of the girls either marry
> crew members—or men they met on the planes.

Ironically, eighteen years later, as an attorney for the Equal Employment Opportunity Commission (EEOC), I drafted the EEOC's Opinion finding that the airlines discriminated against stewardesses on the basis of sex by grounding or terminating them on marriage or on reaching the age of thirty-two or thirty-five. Apparently "the rule on all airlines" wasn't marriage to crewmembers or passengers; it was grounding or termination on marriage or reaching one's mid-thirties.

In addition to my secretarial duties, I was also responsible for plowing through the magazine's slush pile—the unending flow of unsolicited submissions—to look for promising material.

I enjoyed my duties but didn't seem to be moving very quickly into additional editorial work. When my parents asked me to accompany them yet again to Florida for the winter, I resigned from *True Confessions* and joined them. (Like my previous employers, Fawcett Publications subsequently went out of business.)

On my return from Florida in April, I again had to find another job. Without much difficulty, I found one on Broadway

with Cohn-Hall-Marx, a producer and seller of synthetic and cotton goods and a division of United Merchants and Manufacturers,
one of the largest textile manufacturers in the US. After I was hired,
I was told that there was not a permanent job available for me;
instead, I would be rotated from job to job. I found this very
disconcerting—every few days I had a different boss, a different
location, different colleagues, and different assignments. For someone who liked a structured environment, this was discomfiting.

After several weeks, I was given a permanent assignment, working for L.S. Sollfrey, a highly respected man at the company who
was a vice president in the Ameritex division of United Merchants
and Manufacturers. I found him forbidding and unfriendly; he
never responded when I greeted him with "Good morning, Mr.
Sollfrey." Nor did he speak to me during the rest of the day. Instead, he handed me my assignments without comment.

After several months, I was called into the personnel office and
told that I was being transferred to temporary work again, at Mr.
Solfrey's request—because *I* was unfriendly. The vision of returning to temp work—and the discomfiture it would cause me—was
too much. "Oh no," I said, "you're not transferring me to temp
work again. I'm leaving. I'm going to go to law school." The personnel official was dumbfounded by this announcement. Young
women did not leave secretarial jobs in the early '50s to attend law
school. But he was no more surprised than I was. Until that moment, I had not known I was going to law school either. I had
thought about it but hadn't made any decision.

But I couldn't think about law school right after I left Cohn-
Hall-Marx. There was a more immediate problem. For the first
time in my life, I was eligible for unemployment insurance. Or so
I thought. Cohn-Hall-Marx thought differently. The New York
State Unemployment Office in Hempstead denied my application
for unemployment insurance because Cohn-Hall-Marx took the
position that I had not been fired but had resigned after being
offered temporary work. I appealed and argued that since I had
been hired for a permanent job, offering me temporary work was

tantamount to a dismissal. This was my first legal victory, and I collected unemployment insurance for two weeks. (In 1989, Cohn-Hall-Marx, too, went out of business.)

But I did not feel comfortable living on unemployment insurance. Also, the law required that a recipient of unemployment insurance actively seek employment. With my secretarial skills, I quickly found another job. In June, I became the secretary to the editor-in-chief of Collier's Encyclopedia published by the Crowell-Collier Publishing Company.

But what was I going to do about my announcement at Cohn-Hall-Marx that I was going to enter law school? Actually, there had been influences impelling me to law school since my childhood. They'd never coalesced as a determination to attend, however, until I made that announcement. Probably, every significant event in my life led up to it, but it started with my childhood in the Catskills. Since my parents had an imperfect grasp of English, at a young age I handled their correspondence and drafted the agreements for their summer rentals. In addition, I had a role model—Ethel Kooperman. As a sideline, from the time we moved to Woodridge, my father invested in second mortgages. His attorneys for these investments were a husband-and-wife legal team, Joe and Ethel Kooperman, who lived and practiced in Ellenville, twenty-two miles from Monticello. So, from an early age, I had seen a woman attorney and a husband-and-wife legal team. When I thought about entering law school, I did so with the idea of marrying an attorney with whom I would practice law.

During my junior year at Cornell, I had an encounter in the ladies room with a classmate, Dottie Berner, much like the one I had had with Elaine Robbins in high school. Dottie, who planned to go on to graduate school, asked me what my plans were for continuing my education after Cornell. "After Cornell?" I asked her. I had no intention of going on beyond Cornell. But her question planted a seed in my mind.

In my senior year at Cornell in the Graduate School, one of my courses, Legal Problems of Business, was taught by an assistant professor at the Cornell Law School. It was one of my favorite courses.

In the early '50s, I joined a Great Books group. I was intrigued by one of the selections we read and discussed, Thomas Aquinas's *Treatise on Law*, and its discussion of eternal, divine, natural, and human law.

Then, in the winter of 1953-54, while in the Miami Beach area on our annual winter stay, I happened to be driving by the University of Miami. It had a lovely campus, and I found myself thinking, as I have all my life whenever I come upon a beautiful college campus, that I'd like to matriculate. But I couldn't attend the university because I'd already graduated from college. Then it occurred to me: I could attend if I went to law school. I took the Law Aptitude Test and scored higher than nine out of ten law school freshmen.

Then, it was April of 1954; the family returned from Miami Beach, and I began working at Cohn-Hall-Marx. When my parents learned that I was considering going to law school, they were appalled. They had been opposed to my going to college because they felt that too much education would hinder my chances of getting married. Attending law school would, for them, put the final nail in the coffin of my spinsterhood. All his life, Father had maintained a stout opposition to education in general and women's education in particular. It was his opinion that all a woman needed to reach the apogee of success was the ability to cook and sew. Also, he scoffed at the idea that someone so devoted to "da true business," his contemptuous way of referring to my partiality for the truth, could even think of becoming a lawyer. Mother thought that in addition to domestic skills, a young woman would also need some *mazel*—luck—to succeed in life. But no one could seriously argue that she needed a law degree.

Mother had her own way of dealing with the issue. We'd be at the North Miami Beach shopping mall when she'd suddenly accost a man she noticed nearby. "Look at this little girl," she'd say, pointing to me, her 5'3" daughter. "Do you think such a little girl could be a lawyer?" The man would be totally taken aback. "Uh— I don't really know," he'd say and leave as soon as he could decently do so.

Friends and acquaintances, like my parents, were taken aback to learn that I was thinking of becoming an attorney. Young women in the '50s did not become attorneys. Everyone asked why I had chosen such an inappropriate occupation. I tried explaining that I felt I had the skills required by the practice of law and was impelled to use those skills much like a person with talent in art or music was driven to use that talent. But these explanations generally met with glazed looks.

I was thinking along these lines when the events surrounding my twenty-sixth birthday sped the process along. I realized that my birthday, May 30, was only a week away and I had no plans for celebrating. So I decided to give myself a birthday party and invited a number of friends, including my current beau, Hal Levine. I was greatly disappointed when everyone turned me down because they already had plans for the weekend, which was Memorial Day. I did not, however, understand that. What I saw was that when I needed them, none of my friends—not even Hal—were there for me. I determined never again to rely on friends and beaux. From now on, I would stand on my own two feet. I would go to law school. I applied and was admitted to the University of Miami School of Law.

But even after that, I was still in doubt. Should I attend the law school at the University of Miami or apply to a more prestigious law school, perhaps one in California, a place I'd always wanted to visit? Did I really want to go to law school for three long years? I took so long thinking about these questions that the decision as to which law school to attend was made for me. It was too late to apply to any other law school—it had to be the University of Miami.

Two weeks before I was due to leave for law school, however, I was still in doubt as to whether to go. Returning to Long Beach on the train one evening after work, I noticed the sister of an acquaintance sitting across the aisle. I remembered that she was an attorney and crossed the aisle to sit with her. I told her of my confusion and asked her advice. She strongly encouraged me to go to law school. That did it. In September, I left Crowell-Collier and prepared to attend the University of Miami School of Law.

There remained only my brother's opposition. While my parents opposed my going to law school, they knew better than to argue with me when my mind was made up. My brother hadn't yet learned that lesson. Since he was fourteen years my senior, he always tried to act like a father to me. I, on the other hand, repeatedly told him I had a father, and it wasn't he.

Nonetheless, when Hermann learned of my decision, he came to our house and spent two hours expounding upon all the reasons why I shouldn't attend law school. When he was through, I packed my bags and took the train to Miami. I had $1,500 in savings, enough to get me through the first year. After that, I had no idea what would happen.

PART V

17.

FLORIDA AND BEYOND

The University of Miami Law School put me up in a garden apartment type of building with three other young women. The four of us shared two bedrooms, a living room, dining room, and a kitchen. We were an unmatched lot. None of the others were law students. One was in graduate school; one never attended classes and did not intend to, although her parents thought she did—she was there only to meet college men; the third turned out to have psychological problems: *she* was my roommate.

Our first arrangement was to rotate the responsibility for preparing dinner on a weekly basis. Even though cooking had never been my forte, I managed to prepare the first week's dinners. Thereafter, however, none of the other three did any cooking. Seeing this, I suggested that we each maintain our own food supplies and cook for ourselves. My housemates took umbrage at this proposal but eventually agreed.

This new system necessitated my labeling all the food I had in the refrigerator. It also resulted in a considerable amount of awkwardness since I appeared to be the only one doing any cooking. When I would seat myself at the kitchen table to eat, the others would circle around me and give me dirty looks.

One morning shortly after I moved into this apartment, I realized something was terribly wrong with my roommate. When I awakened, she was holding her hairbrush in her hand and shrieking in a hysterical voice, "You moved my hairbrush!" She believed her hairbrush was not in the exact same spot on the dresser where it had been the night before and that I had moved it, and she was terribly disturbed about this. From then on, I went into our shared room only for my clothes and slept on the floor of the living room.

I wrote my parents, telling them about my experiences on campus but not about my living situation. I did, however, mention casually that it was somewhat difficult for me to grocery shop without a car.

When my mother read this letter to my father, he didn't say a word but left the living room for the bedroom. My mother, surprised by this, followed him a few minutes later, only to find him packing a suitcase.

"What are you doing?" she asked.

"Didn't you hear that letter?" he responded.

"Yes, so?" she asked.

"The girl needs a car," he said. "I'm going down to buy her one."

"But it's *erev* Rosh Hashanah—the eve of the High Holy Days," protested my mother.

My father repeated, "The girl needs a car," and continued packing. Then he took the train from New York City to Miami, checked into a Miami Beach hotel, and called me.

"Who is this?" I asked.

"It's your father," he answered.

"My father's in Long Beach," I said. "Who is this?"

I did not believe it was my father because my father had a strong Yiddish accent and this man did not, and because I had left my father in Long Beach only a short time ago.

"It's your father," he said again.

"Is this Hal?" I asked.

I had just broken up with Hal Levine, a man I'd dated off and on for a couple of years. I'd met Hal one New Year's Eve in Miami Beach on one of my family's winters there. He lived in New Haven, Connecticut, but it would not have been out of character for him to follow me down to the Miami area.

"No," he said, "This is your father.

"If you're my father," I asked, "what's my Yiddish name?"

"*Sheyndl*," he said.

"Hi Dad," I said.

I'd never spoken to my father on the phone before. He never made phone calls, and when I called home, my mother always answered the phone. Apparently, my father's Yiddish accent was not evident on the telephone.

My father arranged to meet me so he could buy me a car. After we accomplished that, he came by to see my living quarters. That's when he learned that I was sleeping on the living room floor. He said nothing to me about it.

When he returned home, the first thing he said to my mother was, "Lina, we have to sell the house and move to Florida."

"Why?" she asked.

He explained that "the girl" was sleeping on the floor and they had to move down there so I would have a decent place to live while I attended law school.

Within two weeks, my parents had sold the house to Hermann, who was then a realtor in Long Beach; had had their furniture and personal belongings shipped; and were ensconced, with me, in a newly-built home in North Miami Beach.

Three years later, when I graduated from law school, I was twenty-nine years old. My mother was still preparing all my meals, washing my laundry, and doing my ironing. She still waited up for me when I went out for the evening. When I attended law school, if I ever came home later than my mother expected, the police were always there to greet me.

The moment Mother heard that I was going to move to Washington, DC, to take a job with the Department of Justice, she began planning a move there with my father. I told her she could not continue following me around the country, and, reluctantly, she and my father agreed to remain in Florida.

18.

FATHER AND THE AIRLINES

Sometimes I think our mass education in this country is a mixed blessing. Our years of schooling seem to take something from us: a drive, a dream, a push toward life—and the willingness to act irrationally and outside the bounds of acceptable behavior. It leaves us eggheads and thinkers, not doers. It leaves us as passive acceptors of life, rather than fighters for a cause. We know too much to take a chance.

Fortunately, my father was not so handicapped; he was not even tainted. He had never gotten as far as kindergarten in Piltz, so he'd never learned to accept what life brought him; instead, he fought for what he wanted.

My father taught me the uses of irrationality and emotionalism one summer in the '50s. My parents and I were scheduled to fly from Miami to Long Beach to visit Hermann and his family. My father had wanted to drive and save some money but remembering difficult times we'd had with him on the road, we persuaded him to go by plane.

We arrived at the airport forty-five minutes before our 8:45 AM scheduled departure only to learn that the flight had been canceled due to mechanical failure. We were told we would be given first-class seats on another carrier at no additional expense. I could almost taste the gourmet food when we were next advised that the first-class flight was completely booked and that the first available flight was a coach flight that was due to depart at 2:00 PM. This caused quite a bit of consternation among the passengers. One elegant woman was particularly distressed. She was due to connect with a cruise ship leaving for Europe and would be unable to make her connection.

Mother and I accepted the change in plans with equanimity. After all, we had no plans that required our presence in Long Beach at any particular time. We wondered, however, what our best course of action would be: should we drive home and come back later or just wait in the terminal for the 5½ hours? We decided to settle down and wait for the flight.

But not Father. "I told you I wanted to drive," he said, "You just can't trust those planes." He could not accept the fact that we wouldn't be leaving at 8:45 AM as scheduled. Finally, he made up his mind: he would get his money back and drive to Long Beach as he had wanted to do in the first place. He began to race around the terminal, cursing the airlines in a loud voice, accosting airline officials, and generally proving of extreme embarrassment to Mother and me. There was no holding him back. Mother and I were mortified to see him heading for the terminal manager's office, still voicing his complaints at the top of his lungs.

Five minutes later, Father was back with the manager, and we found ourselves being escorted to a waiting limousine. We were driven to an adjoining airstrip, where we were placed on a plane leaving for New York momentarily. The manager dispatched a telegram to Hermann, telling him of our arrival at a different airport in the New York area.

We were the only passengers from the 8:45 AM plane on that flight. Neither the elegant woman with the cruise connection nor any of the other passengers were to be seen. Mother and I were happy and grateful to be aboard. But not Father. He didn't know why we had to be behind schedule and arriving at a different airport. As I said, he was uneducated.

19.

HOW I GOT MY MINK STOLE

In the '50s world that I knew and read about, the ultimate in fur was mink. Potentates of exotic foreign countries gave them to their mistresses; Hollywood producers gave them to their favorite starlets; and successful garment manufacturers bought them for their wives. I didn't get my mink stole that way. My mother got it for me—and she didn't get it from a foreign potentate but from the man in our house who was the source of all our possessions—my father. It took her ten years.

Sometime after my parents bought our house in North Miami Beach in 1954, Mother began to talk about a mink stole. This was unusual for her; I couldn't recall her ever before expressing an interest in clothes for herself. Our picture album showed she had been an elegant, fashionable woman in Berlin, but that had been years ago. In the United States, her life was different. It was focused on her husband, her children, and her home. Her mission was nurturing, a goal she warmly embraced. Clothes were something she needed only to take care of her real priorities.

Nonetheless, Mother began to ask Father for a mink stole. Perhaps it was only natural. Miami Beach was the second home of the mink. No respectable garment manufacturer's wife or mistress would think of setting foot in that oasis of affluence without some type of mink draped about her shoulders. It just wasn't done. And my mother, unlike these visitors, wasn't just down for two weeks or even for the whole *sizzen*. She lived there. Furthermore, my father could well afford the $500 or $1,000 that a mink stole cost in those days, so why not?

"Why not?" was that my father didn't embark upon a course of action simply because all rational reasons pointed in that direction. That wasn't his style. That didn't require any gumption. On the contrary, it was going against the tide that showed a man's strength. If everything pointed one way, *dafke*—for spite, Father went the other. So when it came to buying Mother a mink stole, Father refused.

There followed a series of arguments and rationalizations. Mother pointed out that she needed a stole to go to the synagogue; so Father discontinued what was already his very limited synagogue attendance. Mother invited Cousin Sarah from Philadelphia to visit us. Since Sarah was related to us on Father's side of the family, her arguments in favor of Mother's having a mink stole should have carried considerable weight. Father negated that ploy, too, by pointing out that Cousin Sarah herself didn't have a mink stole.

At times, Father took the initiative. "You'll get a mink stole when Sonia gets married," he'd say. "You'll have a mink stole for the wedding." (He was on pretty safe ground here since I was already in my late twenties at this time, with no serious suitor in sight.) "After all," he continued, "what kind of mother would you be careering around Miami Beach covered in furs when your only daughter is still single?" This was a double whammy for Mother: not only was she told she wouldn't be getting a fur stole in the near future; she was also reminded that her only daughter was still unmarried. Nonetheless, Mother stood her ground. She pointed out that with my law school education not even half-completed, with my ambitions for a career in the future, and with my lack of current suitors, my chances of an imminent marriage were dim—and she needed a stole now.

Undaunted, my father then played the "Jewish homeland" card. "Why should I spend money on a mink stole when we could put the money to better use for a trip to Israel, see what's doing over there, and visit my brother, Iser?" This approach was flawed because Mother, the keeper of the family finances, knew that Father could easily afford both the stole and the trip to Israel. Rather than getting into an argument about finances, however, Mother was quick to agree that a trip to Israel made sense and said she'd be delighted to accompany Father on such a voyage. To which Father replied, "Israel? What for do I need Israel? What, am I crazy to go down there with those *Araber* shooting at Jews all the time? A man has to be crazy to go down there. Takes his life in his hands." And then, figuratively draping the American flag around himself, he continued, "Why should I go to Israel when I haven't seen my own country yet. *First*, we'll go to California. After Sonia's married. Then, maybe later, when things have calmed down there, we'll go to Israel." And so it went. He had succeeded in completely changing the subject.

We entered the next phase when Hermann bought Helen a mink stole and, being a loving son, bought my mother one, too. When Dad came home that night and saw Mother cavorting in her slip and mink stole, he was livid. Imagine the nerve of that son of his! Trying to show up his own father. He could afford to buy a stole for his own wife if she needed one. He didn't need his son to buy it for him. But the thing was—his wife didn't need a stole. Had no use for one. He advised Mother once and for all to decide whether she wanted a stole or a husband. With that, Father stormed out of the house, and Mother reluctantly returned the stole to Hermann.

I learned about the next act of this drama when Mother came to visit me several years later in Washington, DC, bearing in her hands a horrible white piece of fake fur. It seemed that Father, on his own volition, had bought it for her. It was made of cheap synthetic material and was the sort of froufrou one associates with streetwalkers. Father had seen it in the window of a storefront on the Lower East Side. He thought he might make it up to Mother with this offering after all their arguments about a mink stole. Mother wanted to know if I had a cleaning woman to whom I could give this fur piece since she wouldn't be caught dead wearing it in Miami Beach. I told her no self-respecting cleaning woman would wear this item and suggested she return it to Father with her compliments.

When Father got this fur piece back ("What's wrong with it? Looks just like a mink stole to me."), he realized that the jig was up. He had tried everything. He then quietly went to one of the finest furriers in Miami Beach and bought Mother her stole—a beautiful gray-white fur. Let the neighbors see that his wife could look good, too.

When Mother saw this beautiful fur—which she'd fought for for so many years—she exclaimed, "A stole? What do I need that for? An old woman like me? Do I need it to do the dishes? To carry out the *garbitch*? To go to the synagogue with those *yentes*—gossipy women? (They had resumed their sporadic synagogue attendance.) What do I need a fur stole for when my child is freezing in Washington?" Father was nonplused at this reaction, but before too much time had passed, he was driving Mother to the post office, where she could ship the stole to me "freezing in Washington." She then accompanied him to the synagogue for Friday night services, in her cloth coat, which was "more than good enough for those *yentes*."

I never figured out whether this result had been in back of Mother's mind all along, or whether she had simply embarked upon a battle with my father that she was determined to win, only to find when she did, that it was the battle and not the prize that was significant. At any rate, that's how I got my mink stole—not from a foreign potentate or a lovesick swain—but from a battle waged by my mother and won over tremendous odds. I was proud to wear it.

20.

PASSING THE BAR

In the summer of 1957, after three days of studying for the Florida Bar exam, I noticed an odd phenomenon. Slowly, imperceptibly, the diploma-covered walls of my den were closing in on me.

My mother had decorated the den as a combination shrine and memorial to me. It was a small room, sparsely furnished with a desk, a sofa, and some bookcases. The walls, however, were another story. They were covered from floor to ceiling with every conceivable type of document and picture illustrating my upward climb on the scholastic ladder. My kindergarten certificate was there, frayed but still inspiring; and the picture of my law school dean handing me my law school diploma, while the swordfish mounted on his wall looked benignly down on the scene.

Into this arena of past glories, I had hurled myself, armed with my schedule, various sets of notes, and a supply of hornbooks and casebooks. The first few days went rather well, and I congratulated myself on my perseverance. But then I noticed the moving of the walls and decided I had better call a classmate.

"Throw away Clark," the book I was then outlining, he said, "He's too superficial."

I called a second. "Just read Clark," she advised. "He really lays down the law for you." Hmm.

The advice from others was just as confusing.

"Stick to your outline."

"Throw away that schedule."

"Concentrate on class notes."

"Don't rely on the cram course."

"Memorize the landmark cases."

"Forget everything you learned in law school."

And so on. I felt the first glimmers of panic.

I had graduated from Law School in May and taken the cram course in Miami. Now it was time to map out a study schedule. I spent quite some time on this project, and the result was a masterpiece of organization and comprehensiveness. Torts, Contracts, Criminal Law, Civil Procedure, Constitutional Law, Real Property, Tax Law—every subject had a time slot of its own.

I allotted myself about a month in which to cover all these subjects and began work in my den.

I had had no trouble preparing for examinations in the past. In grade school, I had developed a method that always stood me in good stead. I would review the material covered during the semester, analyze the teacher, decide what that teacher would concentrate on, and memorize it. Then, armed with that knowledge, I would venture forth, like St. George, to slay the dragon.

But this examination was different. It was prepared by a faceless group of individuals whom I did not know and could not analyze. Its scope would range over the entire body of the law. How did one cope with a prospect like that?

One of my friends had recommended that I concentrate on the leading cases in every field. It was not a technique I had used in law school, but new problems obviously called for new methods. To do this, however, I would need the facilities of a well-stocked law library. Judge Samuels, who had been a part-time professor at my law school and practiced law in Hollywood, Florida, graciously offered me the use of his library. I was delighted at the prospect of studying in such congenial surroundings. Immersion in the atmosphere of a successful law practice could not help but inspire me to greater heights of concentration.

I revised my study schedule to accommodate to this procedure and began my research in the judge's library. It was an inspiring experience—poring through old lawbooks, listening to the judge's reminiscences of past cases, chatting with the secretaries, and watching the clients come and go. The days passed quickly in this manner, until I realized that a week had gone by and I was still in Torts. At this rate, I might get to Criminal Law at about the time my classmates were completing the examination. Obviously, the field of law was too strewn with landmarks for this approach. I revised my schedule, said good-bye to the judge and his staff, and pondered my next move. Time was running out.

Meanwhile, friends were hearing about my dilemma, and offers of help were coming in. Bob Bader, an attorney, invited me to lunch, during which he promised to give me the key to passing bar exams with equanimity. I grasped at this opportunity to learn the secret. During a sumptuous luncheon, Bob reviewed the highlights of his law school days, his legal career, and even his personal life, all of which had led to his present eminence. During the course of his conversation, he did mention that he had, of course, passed the bar examination—"at the first crack, y'know." But after this minor digression, the subject was never touched upon again. Any clues to success—in bar examinations or otherwise—contained in his autobiography completely eluded me.

There were two weeks remaining before the examination. I revised my schedule and determined to really concentrate during this final period. If I bore down now and impressed the material on my mind, I could still make it.

But then I got ill. Every morning when I awoke, a picture of my den would float before my eyes—the walls plastered with certificates and the floor and furniture covered with notes, briefs, and lawbooks. The contrast between my success on those walls and my failure in the rest of the room was overwhelming. The fear of ever bridging that chasm came over me in great, engulfing waves. The nausea was overpowering, and I could barely rise from my bed.

Mother, solicitous as ever, would bring me tea and toast, as I wasn't able to eat much more. With her care, my condition would improve during the day, and I was often able to accompany my parents to the beach for a few hours. By evening I would be well enough to watch some television, and I would vow that next morning, after a slight revision in my schedule, I would begin work promptly on arising. But the next morning, the fear was there again, and the whole horrible process would repeat itself.

My mother insisted that I see her doctor. After hearing a meticulous recitation of my symptoms, he delivered a brief discourse on his trials and tribulations before taking the medical boards, which he had then passed with flying colors. He then gave me some varicolored pills and assured me that he wasn't a bit worried about my passing the exam.

It was clear that this doctor of the body didn't really have a treatment for one about to take the bar exam. Perhaps what I needed was a doctor of the mind. I looked in the yellow pages for a psychiatrist. When I called one and learned his hourly fee was $15, I quickly ended the conversation. I wasn't *that* sick.

Then Max Danton called. Max had started law school with me; and his home boasted one of the finest law libraries I had ever seen. *Corpus Juris* vied with Blackstone's *Commentaries* for space on his shelves and in his closets. Max had flunked out of law school after his first year, but he had heard of my difficulties and wanted to help.

"Don't take that exam," he warned in his most lugubrious tone. "If you go in there, you'll crack up. It's happened to others before. They'll hand you that exam paper and your mind will go blank. You'll probably have to be carried out of the room. Relax. There'll be other bar exams." He went on like that, and I realized he was right. I'd been pushing myself too hard. Three years of law school, and now this. What I needed was a good rest. Then, perhaps six months or a year from now, thoroughly grounded in legal knowledge, I would calmly and coolly walk into that room and take the exam. My only regret was that I hadn't thought of this originally and spared myself weeks of turmoil.

I thanked Max for his advice, replaced the receiver, and donned one of my mother's kimonos. Thus attired, I draped myself on the living room sofa and informed my mother that I had found the perfect solution. I simply wouldn't take the examination. Not now, anyway. Perhaps some other time. The important thing now was to recoup my health. My mother didn't flutter an eyelash. Nothing I did could rattle her any longer.

But it was a different story when my father came home that evening. I was still lying on the divan, dressed like Madame Butterfly, but obviously in the last throes of the illness that had ravished Camille. Brushing aside this incongruity, my father asked how the studying was coming along.

"I'm not taking the exam, Dad," I announced. "Max told me to take it some other time."

My father was infuriated at this turn of events.

"Max?" he bellowed. "Who is he?"

"You remember Max, Dad. The fellow who flunked out after his first year of law school."

"Max. Shmax. Where was he when I was paying your way through college and law school?"

My father then embarked on a lengthy narration of my past history, during all of which Max had been notable by his absence.

"Now that's all behind you," he continued. "You've got your degree, you ordered your ticket to Jacksonville (the site of the exam), and you paid for your hotel room (that really clinched it for Dad). Now you'll take the exam."

"If worst comes to worst," he concluded, "at least you'll see what the questions look like, and it won't be so bad next time."

I had to admit this made some sense. "But Dad," I remonstrated, determined to make one last feeble attempt. "Don't you see how sick I am? How can I take an examination? I won't even be able to get on the plane."

"Sick, shmick," said my father. "You'll get on that plane if I have to carry you on." Since Max had already suggested my being carried out of the examination room, it seemed altogether fitting that I should arrive the same way.

My father then had the temerity to suggest that all my preparations had been a waste of time: "The whole problem is that lousy den your mother fixed up. And all those books and papers in there. The place needs a good cleaning." Father had his own theory for passing bar exams. All one needed was to be a smart man or woman, as the case might be, attend law school for the requisite number of years, and then take the examination. Since I had already satisfied the first two requirements, I could best prepare for the third by spending the remaining time at the beach with him and Mother.

It was ridiculous, of course, but since I had only two days left, what was the harm? I discarded my badly scarred schedule, cleaned up the den, and exchanged the kimono for a bathing suit. Two days later, tanned and glowing, I arrived at the airport to take the plane to Jacksonville. There my mother noticed Fay Becker, a classmate of mine, and went over to her. "Keep an eye on her," she said. "She's been sick. She can't eat any food unless you cut it up into small pieces for her." Fay, with whom I'd had only a slight acquaintance during our law school days, was taken aback by this request but agreed to be responsible for me. We boarded the flight for Jacksonville together.

From then on, I had a wonderful time. As soon as the plane left Miami, my feelings soared with it. It seemed that the worst was over. And it was good to have Fay's company.

Max turned out to be wrong about the exam. I didn't faint when I saw it. In fact, the questions looked quite easy; they were no different from those I had been answering for three years at law school. I left most of the sessions early and spent my free time touring Jacksonville with Fay. We visited historic shrines, saw *Love in the Afternoon*, a romantic comedy with Audrey Hepburn and Gary Cooper, and sipped cocktails at the hotel lounge. In between our roving, we managed to complete the exam.

And then, on the flight home, the full impact of our frivolity assailed us. Neither of us had been adequately prepared beforehand. But we might have applied ourselves during the last few days and snatched victory from the jaws of defeat. Instead, we had gone on a senseless frolic. Now we realized the extent of our folly.

We had failed to discipline ourselves at a crucial time in our lives, and now our entire future careers would be affected. For the rest of our lives, this black mark would be on our records. And what was even worse, in six months we'd have to go through the whole grisly business again.

Our doleful ruminations were interrupted by the sounds of revelers across the aisle. Two of our classmates were confidently celebrating their forthcoming victories. They boasted of their intensive studies and raised toasts to the successful practices they would embark upon shortly. We sat by morosely.

In this mood of gloom, I deplaned and slowly walked over to where my parents were waiting for me in the terminal. Sorrowfully, I greeted them, defeat in every gesture. Across the way, their wives and children met the bons vivants with whoops of joy and congratulatory exclamations. Father took it all in at a glance. "Don't worry," he said, taking my arm. "They didn't pass it. You did."

Three months later I learned he was right. But by then, I was no longer concerned with the Florida Bar exam. I was engrossed in preparations for the District of Columbia Bar. But that's another story.

21.

LABOR LAW

After my second year of law school, I got a summer job with the Miami Beach law firm of Kovner & Mannheimer. I was to serve as a law clerk in an office that consisted of Walter Kovner, a forbidding man; Milton Mannheimer, a cordial man; Jack Brooks*, a young attorney; and Jeanette Posner*, the secretary. My salary was $10 a week.

My father was appalled: for twenty-seven years he had provided me with food, clothing, shelter, and all the necessities of life; he had bought me a car; he had paid my medical and dental bills; he had sent me through college; now he was sending me through law school—all so I could earn $10 a week.

I, on the other hand, was excited about getting this position. Jobs as law clerks were not easy to obtain. Since my dream in going to law school was eventually to open my own law office where I'd practice in partnership with my husband, this would put me on the road to fulfilling that dream.

Furthermore, $10 for a law student didn't seem all that paltry a sum. Jack Brooks, the junior attorney, who had graduated from the US Naval Academy and *cum laude* from a leading Eastern law school and had practiced law for three years in Boston before coming to the firm, earned only $60 a week.

My work consisted of research into a variety of legal issues, drafting memoranda and briefs, appearing at hearings, depositing office funds in the bank, and running other errands.

A frustrating aspect of my work was the fact that I was never able to see my memoranda in print—or even in type. Jeanette was always too busy with the work of the permanent members of the firm to get to mine, and Walter Kovner was not convinced that my work was sufficiently important to warrant hiring additional secretarial help.

I had two disillusioning experiences that summer, one with each of the partners. The first involved Milton Mannheimer. I was due to accompany him to a hearing one day on a motion before a judge in Miami. Just before we were due to leave, Mannheimer pointed to several books that were sprawled on a nearby table and said, "Take them along."

"Are they related to this case?" I asked. "I haven't read them."

"Don't worry," said Mannheimer. "The judge doesn't know that."

That was not how I viewed the practice of law.

The second experience occurred shortly before my summer employment was due to end. During my ten weeks with the firm, Mannheimer or Jack Brooks had given me all my assignments. Kovner was too busy to trifle with me; and, besides, he was a cold and impersonal man. During the entire period of my employment, except for my initial and final interviews, he never called me into his office to discuss my work or anything else; never introduced me to any of his clients or colleagues; and, of course, never invited me to lunch.

I was, therefore, agreeably surprised when, during what I thought was the penultimate week of my employment, Kovner called me into his office. He said nothing about the quality and quantity of my work for him all summer. Instead, he said that he realized that since Rosh Hashanah (the beginning of the Jewish High Holy Days) would begin on the Thursday of my last week, I'd only be working three days that week instead of five. I had not thought this would present any problem, especially as Kovner came from an illustrious Jewish family. He, however, indicated that he did not relish paying a full week's salary for only three days' work and suggested that I end my employment that very week. I did so and, shortly thereafter, returned for my final year of law school.

Jack Brooks did not fare any better. Shortly after I left the firm, when he had completed a year's work with Kovner & Mannheimer, he asked Kovner for a raise. He was told that if his interest in the law was motivated by money, he had best look for work elsewhere.

Towards the end of my final year of law school, I received a phone call one afternoon from Minnette Massey, a professor at the law school who was also the law school librarian. I had never taken a course with her but we knew each other.

"Sonia," she began, "Did you see the announcement at the law school that recruiters with the US Department of Labor are coming to interview seniors for jobs in Washington, DC?"

"Yes," I answered, "But I have no interest in going to Washington." For years, I had driven through Washington with my parents en route to Miami Beach and then back home. It had always impressed me as a gray city, full of massive government buildings. I believed those buildings were filled with faceless government workers who toiled in anonymity. I never intended to become one of them.

"Well, I think you should go to that interview," said Minnette, "and I've set up an appointment for you for 2 PM tomorrow." I suppose I could have declined to go, but since Professor Massey had gone to all that trouble for me, and I was flattered at her interest in someone who wasn't even a student of hers, I decided to keep the appointment.

The interview went all right, and shortly thereafter I received an offer of a job from Bessie Margolin, Associate Solicitor for Fair Labor Standards in the Department of Labor. Since I had no other job offers, and my summer in private practice had been disillusioning, I decided to accept it, remain in Washington about three months, and then see what I wanted to do next.

Shortly thereafter, recruiters for the US Department of Justice came to the law school. Since I'd already gone to one interview with the government, I decided to go to this one, too. Sometime after that interview, I got an offer for a job with the Department of Justice, too. I wasn't sure now what to do, but I was ultimately swayed by the fact that the Justice Department's offer involved a prestigious-sounding program called the Attorney General's Honor Program. That program had been established only several years earlier, in late 1953, to recruit outstanding law graduates into the Department of Justice. I wrote to Miss Margolin explaining that I'd been offered a job with the Attorney General's Honor Program and would, therefore, not be joining the Department of Labor. She responded with a very nice letter accepting my rejection of her offer.

I came to Washington in August 1957 and moved into the Meridian Hill Hotel on 16th Street in Northwest Washington. This was a hotel for women, a wonderful place for a young, single woman new to Washington. It was conveniently located and offered me the opportunity to meet other similarly situated young women. I had a single room for $14 a week and was able to take my meals in the hotel's inexpensive cafeteria.

At the Meridian Hill, men were not allowed above the first floor at any time. I lived there happily for a year until my mother made her first visit. When she entered the ground floor elevator with me, she saw the large sign that announced, "No Men above the First Floor."

"How can you live here without men?" Mother inquired loudly. I was shamed by the fact that my 67-year-old mother was aghast at my living in a building that didn't allow men while it hadn't bothered me at all. Shortly thereafter, I rented my first apartment at the Arlington Towers in Arlington, Virginia, across the bridge from Washington. (Many years later, it was turned into a condominium and is now named the River House.)

I furnished both my apartment in the Arlington Towers and my second apartment in Potomac Towers with rental furniture. My parents had always told me that when one got married, one bought furniture for one's home. Since I was not married, it was not appropriate for me to buy furniture. In time, I became the rental company's longest continuous customer and the butt of many of my friends' jokes. At the age of forty-two, when I married, I finally bought furniture.

The Justice Department consisted of various divisions: Civil, Criminal, Antitrust, Lands, and so forth, and the-then freestanding Office of Alien Property. The Department asked me where I wanted to work, and I chose the Office of Alien Property. I'd never heard of it, but it had a mysterious name, with international connotations. With my foreign background, it seemed a natural for me. I could see myself flying around the world on intriguing foreign missions.

In August 1957, I began work as a law clerk at a salary of $3,500 a year at Alien Property, which was then located at Third Street and Indiana Avenue, Northwest, near Union Station. Shortly thereafter, when I passed the Florida Bar, my position was upgraded to attorney. The Office of Alien Property had been authorized during wartime to seize and administer property and property interests in the United States owned or controlled by our enemies, such as Germany and Japan, and their citizens. In 1953, the Office held almost $400 million worth of property it had seized in World Wars I and II. The applicable law, the Trading with the Enemy Act, provided for the return of seized property if it came within certain statutory categories. My work as a claims attorney did not involve flights to exotic locales. Instead, I was charged with the task of processing claims for the return of property.

I shared a large office with two other claims attorneys, Joe Jaskiewicz and Wendell Colson. Joe was a quiet, unassuming, excellent attorney. Wendell was the more colorful character. He was a blustery Colonel Blimp type, who talked endlessly about the achievements of his son, Chuckie, and the marvelous togetherness of Chuckie and his wife Nancy. Several years later, Chuckie became known not only to Joe and me but also to the nation. He was Chuck Colson of Watergate fame, White House special counsel, who has been described as President Nixon's "top hatchet man."

Chuckie went on to spend some time in prison and divorce Nancy. In prison, he underwent a religious conversion and became a born-again Christian. He founded the Prison Fellowship Ministries, which he now heads, an organization designed to change the lives of convicts through a combination of practical assistance and re-lentless evangelism. He wrote a number of books, remarried, and in 1993 was awarded the most lucrative religious prize on the face of the earth: the Templeton Prize for Progress in Religion, which carried a $1 million-plus award and had previously been granted to Mother Teresa and Billy Graham.

The Office of Alien Property was under the stewardship of the grandfatherly Colonel Dallas S. Townsend, the assistant attorney general and director. His son, with the same name, gained fame as a CBS radio and television correspondent. The highlight of the year was when the Colonel took all the attorneys at the Office who were in the Attorney General's Honor Program out to lunch at the tony Golden Parrot on Connecticut Avenue.

Beyond that luncheon and several others, the Attorney General's Honor Program was a disappointment. I had thought that after bringing outstanding law graduates into the Department of Jus-tice, the program would give them training and job opportunities to enable them to move up the career ladder, but it did no such thing. It was purely a recruitment device.

After I had been at the Office for about 1½ years, a represen-tative of the Department of Justice came to speak to those of us in the Honor Program. He said that since the functions of the Office were diminishing with time, in the near future the Office would become a section within the Civil Division of the Justice Depart-ment rather than a freestanding office. It appeared that the pat-tern of organizations closing after I joined them was as applicable in the federal government as it had been in private industry.

The Justice Department representative said we'd all need to find other jobs, but that that would be no problem because the Justice Department would have us all placed in offices of United States Attorneys around the country. One of my colleagues at this meeting, more sophisticated than I was, sneered at this and said to me, "They can't do that."

"How can you say that?" I asked. "This is a representative of the US government promising to place us all in jobs." In response, he merely snorted.

The Justice Department representative then asked each of us to give him our choices of locations of US Attorneys' Offices where we'd like to be placed. I chose one of the offices in New York City, and shortly thereafter interviews with the management and staff of that office were arranged for me.

I went to New York, excited about the possibility of doing trial work as an Assistant United States Attorney. I had always been known for my verbal skills, and trial work would give me an opportunity to show them off. I spent an entire day meeting with various representatives of that office. At the end of the day, I was asked if I could come back for a second day to see the United States Attorney himself, who was out of town that day. I rearranged my schedule so I could return the following day.

Early the next morning, I walked into the impressive office of the United States Attorney. It was a long walk on the carpeted expanse of his office toward the desk behind which he was sitting. As I walked toward him, the United States Attorney said, "I thought you'd be older than you are."

"How can I be older than I am?" I shot back. I do not remember the rest of our discussion, but it didn't matter. I was not to get that job.

That was the extent of the assistance given to me by the Attorney General's Program in finding another position.

Thus, after only 1½ years in Washington, I was out in the job market again. I called Paul Elkind, an experienced attorney who had left Alien Property some months earlier. I knew he had done a considerable amount of job hunting before he landed his job at the National Labor Relations Board (NLRB), and I thought he might have some leads for me.

"Why don't you come over here?" he asked. "They've got some

openings. I'll set you up with Lou Schwartz."

Shortly thereafter, I was in the office of Louis Schwartz, the supervisory general attorney in the NLRB's Division of Law. My interview went like this:

Schwartz: "You're here because you studied labor law in law
    school?"
Me: "No."
Schwartz: "You studied labor law in high school?"
Me: "No."
Schwartz: "You are planning to take courses in labor law at a
    local university?
Me: "No."
Schwartz: "You have an interest in labor law?"
Me: "It never occurred to me."
Schwartz: "Why are you here?"
Me: "I need a job."
Schwartz: "You're hired."

That's how I came to join the NLRB in May of 1959 as an attorney in its Contempt, Legal Advice and Services Branch. My job was to advise the NLRB's regional directors in regional offices around the country on novel and complex issues of law. Since they were experienced labor law professionals and I was a neophyte in the field, this made perfect sense.

I stayed with the Labor Board for more than six years, during which time I worked in its Pittsburgh and Los Angeles field offices and as a legal assistant to two of the five Board Members, Gerald Brown and Chairman Boyd Leedom. When I left in October of 1965, it was to go on to other jobs in the labor law area, with other government agencies and multinational corporations, remaining in the field for a total of twenty-five years.

22.

PRIVATE PRACTICE

In 1960, although I was working for the NLRB, I had not given up my dream of private practice. I was constantly mailing résumés to firms in Washington, New York City, California, and even a few in the Midwest. In addition, I advertised in the *ABA Journal*; I attended innumerable luncheons and meetings of the Junior Bar, the District of Columbia Bar, the Federal Bar, and the Women's Bar; I lounged about the National Lawyers Club; and advertised my availability to various friends and colleagues.

This produced a variety of responses. Four attorneys with firms in the District of Columbia who had received my résumés asked me to come in for interviews. The first was aghast to learn that I was seeking $10,000 a year. "Why, if we paid you that," he protested, "you'd be making more than some of the men in this office." He was appalled at the effrontery of such a demand. He added that the expense of my salary, the cost of building a women's restroom for my use, and the difficulty of enforcing a rule against profanity that my employment would require were just too much.

The second interviewer asked me to reconsider my request for employment as a *lawyer* and consider instead a position as a legal secretary with his office. His suggestion was not without logic: he was paying his junior attorney $75 a week and his secretary $100.

The third, upon taking a closer look at my résumé, was taken aback by the fact that I had been an honor student throughout my high school, college, and law school years. He himself had barely gotten through college, had been thrown out of two law schools, and had finally graduated from a third non-accredited institution. And yet, he pointed out, here he was in a luxurious office, earning huge fees on the strength of contacts made on the golf course, while *I* was coming to *him* for employment. Obviously, there was a moral to be found in the different paths our lives had taken so far. He could not hire me because he was convinced there was an inverse relationship between scholastic achievement and success in the law.

The fourth, in the midst of our interview, pointed to his pregnant secretary, and blurted out: "How do I know that won't happen to you?" I was dumbstruck and couldn't think of an answer. At the time I was neither married nor dating anyone. The thought of an imminent pregnancy had never previously occurred to me.

After I went home, however, I thought of a number of responses. I could have said:

"Well, sir, I have here a medical certificate attesting to my infertility;" or,

"I carry my diaphragm with me at all times;" or,

"I've been lucky so far;" or

"You don't. Isn't that exciting?"

But by the time I thought of these responses, it was too late. I'd already been turned down for the job.

I mentioned my interest in private practice to Miriam Rosenblatt*, one of the secretaries at my former office, the Office of Alien Property. Miriam suggested I apply for a job with her nephew, Hyman*, who was engaged in the practice of gas and oil law. I had no particular interest in gas and oil other than as fuels, but one had to start somewhere. I went through an extensive interview with Hyman, an hour of which was devoted to his articulation of the importance of utilities to the American economy. I never heard from him again. But several weeks later, Miriam told me that Hyman hadn't hired me because I was "too Jewish."

Then, I got two responses to my advertisement in the *ABA Journal*. The first came from a 54-year-old lawyer in Colorado, who was looking for a woman attorney to serve as both law partner and wife. He pointed out that when he died, I would inherit the firm. Since I had no intention of moving to Colorado to marry a man more than twenty years my senior so I could inherit his firm, I did not respond.

The second response was from a lawyer who had just been hired to revitalize the trial section of a distinguished Chicago law firm. He was looking for lawyers with good law school records. He stated in his letter that he was due to come to the East on other business and could stop in Washington to interview me. I was most interested in this opportunity, and we made an appointment for an interview.

This lawyer was an intelligent, urbane man. While somewhat concerned about the rigors of Chicago's winters, I was intrigued by the opportunity to do trial work. Two months later, he wrote me that regretfully one of the firm's senior partners would not countenance the firm's hiring a woman.

At about this time, I was beginning to wonder about the opportunities in private practice and decided to turn my sights to the world of politics. After all, I was in Washington, DC. What better place to pursue a political career? So I sent my résumé to a number of political organizations. Several months later, I was watching the Republican National Convention on TV when my phone rang.

"This is Paul Butler," announced my caller. Only a benign providence kept me from responding with, "And this is Madame Curie." Paul Butler was chairman of the Democratic National Committee. "I have the résumé that you sent to the Committee," he said. It was indeed Paul Butler. Immediately, visions of myself as a woman politico danced in my head. Political conventions, fund-raising dinners, invitations to the White House—all swam before my eyes.

"The Committee doesn't currently need anyone," Mr. Butler continued, "but they thought *I* might be interested. You see, I'm planning to leave the Committee and open my own law office here in Washington."

The dream changed. I would be Paul Butler's law partner. I saw myself sharing an office with him, surrounded by secretaries and constantly ringing telephones, meeting prominent business people and politicians, all of whom were seeking my advice.

"But I won't be able to be in the office every day myself," he continued. "So, I'll be needing a receptionist to take phone calls. Do you think you might be interested in something like that?"

I didn't ask Butler why he thought a Phi Beta Kappa graduate from Cornell and a *summa cum laude* graduate of law school would be interested in working as a receptionist. I simply turned down the job.

That was the end of my political career. Since I wasn't doing so well in the East, I decided to follow Horace Greeley's advice and go west, even though it, like most career advice, had been directed to men. I secured a transfer to the NLRB's Los Angeles office and headed for California.

After I'd been with the NLRB's LA office for over a year, I got an offer from my friend, Robbie*. Robbie and his wife, Rose*, were my best friends in the Los Angeles area. Robbie had left Washington three years before I had for a legal position with the State of California. After 1½ years in that job, he had secured a job as an attorney with an entertainment conglomerate. Now he planned to go into private practice in Beverly Hills and was looking for a partner. Robbie himself was assured of all the business his wealthy father-in-law, the rest of his in-laws, and his friends could give him, but he needed a partner to share expenses. I was immensely flattered at his confidence in me, and a new dream materialized before my eyes. I saw myself ensconced in a plush Beverly Hills office, wined and dined by Hollywood potentates, and—swathed in furs—escorted to the latest Hollywood premieres. It was very heady stuff. But a Beverly Hills office and its accouterments cost money, more money than I had.

I wired my father, explained the situation to him, and asked him to send the necessary funds by return airmail. To my surprise, the return letter did not contain a check. This was odd as my father rarely refused me anything. But this time he suggested that I turn down Robbie's offer of a partnership and return to Washington to pursue the less glamorous business of furthering my government career. Dad had the peculiar notion that an offer to share expenses but not business wasn't the opportunity of a lifetime.

Regretfully, I told Robbie about this turn of events. "It would have been a perfect opportunity for you," he said. "After all, as a single woman, you'd have been able to put in lots of overtime without having to draw much money from the firm for living expenses." My father had been right.

And so, with another dream gone, in 1963, I returned to Washington. I finally realized that the exciting world of private practice was not for me. I'd have to find my niche elsewhere.

23.

SEX MANIAC

In 1965, when I entered the office of Charles T. Duncan, the first general counsel of the Equal Employment Opportunity Commission (the EEOC), he pointed to the papers strewn across his desk. "You see these papers?" he asked. "Those are all résumés sent in for the one opening I have in the general counsel's office. I don't know why," he continued, looking at me, "but I'm going to hire *you*." That's how I entered the field of women's rights, which became the focus of my life.

I date the beginning of the modern revolution in women's rights—referred to as the Second Wave of the women's movement—to December 14, 1961. On that date, President Kennedy established the President's Commission on the Status of Women, with Eleanor Roosevelt as chair, to review, and make recommendations for improving, the status of women. In 1963, that Commission issued its report, *American Women*. On November 1 that year, three weeks before his assassination, President Kennedy signed an Executive Order establishing the Interdepartmental Committee on the Status of Women and the Citizens' Advisory Council on the Status of Women to facilitate carrying out the recommendations contained in *American Women*.

During the early sixties, while I was working as an attorney at the NLRB in Washington, DC, I was unaware of these developments. Early in 1963, however, I became involved in women's rights by chance. A colleague mentioned that he did volunteer work for the American Civil Liberties Union (the ACLU) and suggested that I might be interested as well. When I volunteered, Larry Speiser, the director of the ACLU's Washington office, gave me an immediate assignment—to prepare testimony for him to deliver before a committee of the House of Representatives in favor of a bill requiring equal pay for men and women for equal or substantially equal work.

When Larry saw how involved I became in the subject matter of his testimony, he suggested that I deliver it myself. On March 26, 1963, at the age of thirty-four, I testified before the House Committee on Education and Labor.

Later that year, the Equal Pay Act was signed into law, after which I assumed my involvement with women's rights was over. Since I wanted to explore the West Coast, I transferred to the NLRB's Los Angeles field office. I moved to Hollywood and for a while enjoyed the California life and the friends I made there. But after a year-and-a-half, I was ready to return home. I didn't like the fast freeway driving, the distances between friends in LA's far-flung community, and the fact that California was the locus of one natural disaster after the other: sandstorms, forest fires, and earthquakes. I was simply not a Californian. Besides, my parents were unhappy with my living so far away and wanted me to come back east. So, at a time when hundreds of thousands of Americans were heading west, I returned to the East.

Early in 1965 I was back at the NLRB's Washington headquarters, working as a legal assistant for Gerald Brown, a fine man and a liberal member of the Board. But after several months on the job, much as I admired Gerry and appreciated his offering me the job that enabled me to return from LA, I again felt driven to seek other employment. There was something else I was supposed to do. I didn't know what it was; I only knew what it wasn't. It wasn't writing decisions at the NLRB.

My only resource at the time was Art Christopher, a short, squarely built, fiftyish African American trial examiner at the NLRB. He liked spending time with young women, and he dangled the many contacts and connections he had as an incentive for me to join him for lunch. I had numerous luncheons with him, none of which produced a single job lead.

But, finally, indirectly Art *was* responsible for my finding another job. In the summer of 1965, I complained to my friend, Jackie Williams, who had formerly worked at the NLRB, that I had just had another fruitless luncheon with Art. Jackie, a young African American woman lawyer, responded by saying, "You want another job? Why don't you go across the street and see Charlie Duncan at the EEOC?" Duncan, an African American lawyer, had been Jackie's professor at the Howard University Law School. Now he was the general counsel of a brand new agency, and Jackie arranged an interview for me with him.

The EEOC had been established to implement a new law that prohibited employment discrimination, Title VII of the Civil Rights Act of l964. That law prohibited discrimination based on race, color, religion, sex, and national origin by employers, labor unions, and employment agencies. Later, age discrimination and discrimination based on physical and mental disabilities were added. Title VII was much broader than the Equal Pay Act. It prohibited discrimination not only in pay but in all terms and conditions of employment, including recruitment, promotions, and employee benefits. The Act had just become effective that summer.

As originally drafted, Title VII did not prohibit sex discrimination, but on a wintry day in February 1964, 81-year-old Congressman Howard W. Smith introduced an amendment to do so. He was chairman of the House Committee on Rules, which was then preparing to consider the civil rights bill for clearance to the floor. The suggestion that he introduce an amendment to add the category of sex discrimination to Title VII's prohibitions came to him from Alice Paul, founder of the National Woman's Party, and her lieutenants. His motives in doing so were apparently mixed. He was a Virginia segregationist and the principal opponent of the civil rights bill. He may have viewed the amendment as a tactic to delay or forestall the bill's passage. On the other hand, he may have favored the amendment because he didn't want African Americans getting rights at the expense of white women. In any event, after some wrangling, the bill became law with the prohibition against sex discrimination in it.

Actually, I had an ideal background for the EEOC, having spent six years at the NLRB, the agency that enforced the National Labor Relations Act, the model for Title VII. Beyond that, however, my coming to the EEOC was not solely a matter of chance. As a Jew who had escaped from Germany, I naturally had an interest in the rights of minorities. Furthermore, I had been concerned with the rights of African Americans from childhood when I was struck by the segregated buses, water fountains, restrooms, and benches and the racist headlines and articles in southern newspapers as my family traveled through the South en route to Miami Beach for the winter.

In addition, from the age of ten, I had felt there was a purpose to my life, a mission I had to accomplish, and that I was not free as other girls and women were simply to marry, raise a family, and pursue happiness. This feeling arose from three factors in my life: I had been born only because my mother's favored abortionist was out of the country, my immediate family and I had escaped the Holocaust, and I was bright. To me, that meant that I had been saved to make a contribution to the world. But I had no idea what it was to be.

Unfortunately, as I was growing up, there was no one with whom I could discuss such thoughts. As far as I knew, I was alone in having them. I felt that if I ever expressed such thoughts to anyone, my ideas would seem unbelievably arrogant. So, I kept them to myself and grew up essentially a lonely child. Years later, through the women's movement, I learned that there were other girls and women like me who wanted to play a role in society. But as children, we were alone and considered ourselves misfits.

Before I could begin work at the EEOC, a short period of time was needed to process the necessary paperwork. While waiting, I received a call from Charlie Duncan, asking me to come to his office as he had to talk to me "confidentially" about something right away. I could not imagine what it might be.

When I arrived, he began by asking: "Have you ever been married to or had any relationship with . . . "

An eternity elapsed before he finished that question. I wondered whose name might come next. I was thirty-seven years old and hadn't reached that age without having had a number of relationships. Which one would Charlie ask me about? What would I say, and how would it affect my career?

"Lee Pressman?" he concluded.

I breathed a sigh of relief. Lee Pressman, a graduate of Cornell and the Harvard Law School, had held a number of prestigious positions in and out of government and had made significant contributions to the labor movement. He had, however, achieved notoriety through his involvement with Communists in the 1930s and 1940s. He was old enough to be my father, but he was not related to me.

"No," I said to Charlie, "I'm not related to Lee Pressman."

How ironic this was. Had my father been one of the most brilliant labor attorneys in the country, I probably would not have been hired at the EEOC. Since my father was instead a largely illiterate Jewish immigrant, I was deemed qualified.

There was one additional hurdle. Charlie said that I would need to provide a reference from a member of Congress. At first, I was stymied by this request, but then I remembered a tenuous connection to a senator.

Many months earlier, I had attended a function where one of the speakers was a senator who referred to his immigrant parents. Following his talk, I wrote him that my parents and I were also immigrants and asked for his help in advancing my career. Shortly thereafter, I received a phone call from the senator's administrative assistant inviting me to come in for a meeting, which I did. We had a pleasant chat, but no job prospects opened up as a result of it. We did, however, maintain a sporadic correspondence thereafter.

When Charlie asked me for a congressional reference, I remembered this connection. By this time, the senator's aide had returned to his home state to pursue his own political career, so I wrote him asking whether he could secure the senator's endorsement for me. To my surprise, he answered with a phone call, saying he was flying to Washington on business soon and asking me to meet him for a drink at the Mayflower Hotel. I thought this was an odd way to get a reference, but I agreed to meet him.

The senator's aide and I met in the Café Promenade, had drinks, and danced. We chatted while we danced, and he mentioned his young wife and baby son. He said he'd be happy to get me the senator's reference—and then invited me up to his room. I declined, and he then gave me the most unusual excuse I'd ever heard for a man's making a pass: "Man is a delicate seismological instrument."

I bade him good night and caught a cab home. While in the cab, I berated myself. All my life I'd read biographies and autobiographies of famous women, many of whom had advanced their careers by bedding famous men. Evita Peron was an outstanding example. What was wrong with me? Why had I turned the senator's assistant down? He was certainly attractive enough. Why did I have to be so strait-laced? I had destroyed the possibility of getting the most challenging job I'd ever been offered.

But the senator's assistant was true to his word. Charlie received a reference for me from the senator, and I joined the EEOC as the first woman attorney in the general counsel's office.

Thus I found myself in 1965 in a brand new job in a brand new agency with responsibility for fighting discrimination, including that based on sex. At that time, few Americans were aware that there was such a thing as sex discrimination. Words like "sex discrimination" and "women's rights" hadn't yet become part of our national vocabulary. In my early speeches for the EEOC, any reference to women's rights was greeted with laughter.

At that time, men and women basically lived in two different worlds. By and large, a woman's place was in the home. Her role was to marry and raise a family. If she was bright, common wisdom had it that she was to conceal her intelligence. She was to be attractive—but not too attractive. She was not to have career ambitious, although she could work for a few years before marriage as a secretary, saleswoman, schoolteacher, telephone operator, or nurse. It was expected that she would be a virgin when she married. When she had children, she was to raise them differently so that they, too, would continue in the modes of behavior appropriate to their sex. If she divorced, which would reflect poorly on her, she might receive an award of alimony and child support—although it was unlikely that she would receive the monies for more than a few years. If she failed to marry, she was an "old maid" relegated to the periphery of life.

Married women could work outside the home only if dire household finances required it. Under no circumstances were they to earn more money than their husbands.

Women were not to be opinionated or assertive. They were expected to show an interest in fashion, books, ballet, cooking, sewing, knitting, and volunteer activities. Political activities were acceptable as long as they were conducted behind the scenes.

Of course, not all women were able or wanted to fit into this pattern, and there were always exceptions. But most women did what they were told because society exacted a high price from deviants.

Men, on the other hand, were the decision-makers and activists. They were the ones who became presidents, legislators, generals, police chiefs, school principals, and corporate executives. They were the heads of their households, and wives and children deferred to their wishes. Men were expected to take the initiative in dating, to have sexual experiences before marriage, to propose marriage, to bear the financial burden for the entire family, and to have little or nothing to do with running their households and raising their children. It was assumed that they would be insensitive, uncaring, and inarticulate—and interested in activities such as sports, drinking, gambling, extramarital affairs, and making money.

Most men did what they were told, too.

This picture of our society was true for most of the population. There were, however, other dynamics at play in minority communities. Historically, for example, more African American women than men attended college. But for most Americans, this was the climate in which the Commission and I, as a staff member, were supposed to eliminate sex discrimination.

Not only was the country unconcerned with sex discrimination, so were most of the people at the Commission. They had come there to fight racial discrimination; they did not want the Commission's time and money sidetracked into sex discrimination.

But the country and the EEOC were in for a shock. In the Commission's first fiscal year, about 37 percent of the complaints alleged sex discrimination, and these complaints raised a host of new issues that were more difficult than those raised by the complaints of race discrimination. Could employers continue to advertise in classified advertising columns headed "Help Wanted—Male" and "Help Wanted—Female"? Did they have to hire women for jobs traditionally reserved for men? Could airlines continue to ground or fire stewardesses when they married or reached the age of thirty-two or thirty-five? What about state protective laws that prohibited the employment of women in certain occupations, limited the number of hours they could work and the amount of weight they could lift, and required certain benefits for them, such as seats and rest periods? Did school boards have to keep teachers on after they became pregnant? What would students think if they saw pregnant teachers? Wouldn't they know they'd had sexual intercourse? Did employers have to provide the same pensions to men and women even though women as a class outlived men?

Although the EEOC was responsible for deciding these questions, no one really knew how to resolve them. There had been no nationwide movement for women's rights, like the civil rights

movement, immediately preceding the enactment of the sex discrimination prohibitions, and there was scant legislative history.

As for me, when I came to the EEOC, I was blithely unaware
of the legislative history of the Act. I just read the law and thought
it prohibited sex discrimination in employment. For that heretical
notion, Charlie Duncan called me a "sex maniac."

My bêtes noires at the Commission were Luther Holcomb,
the vice-chairman; Herman Edelsberg, the executive director; and
Richard (Dick) Berg, the deputy general counsel. All three were
opposed to women's rights. It pained me that two of them were
Jewish.

Holcomb was a former Baptist minister from Dallas and the
Commission's most conservative member. Through their shared
Texas backgrounds, he had a personal relationship with President
Lyndon Johnson and kept him informed of developments at the
EEOC. I sat behind Holcomb when he testified before Congress
shortly after the Act became effective and asked that the prohibition of sex discrimination be removed. Later, he asked Charlie to
remove me from the assignment of writing the lead decision in the
stewardess cases because I was in favor of women's rights. To him
that meant I was prejudiced. Charlie refused. Later still, when the
tide had turned in favor of women, Holcomb had the effrontery to
ask me why women's groups turned to me rather than him for
counsel.

Edelsberg had an impressive background. Before coming to
the EEOC, he had served as an attorney for the Congress of Indus-
trial Organizations (CIO) and, for almost twenty years, as director
of the Washington, DC, office of the Anti-Defamation League
(ADL) of B'nai B'rith. At his first press conference at the EEOC,
however, he told reporters that he and the other men at the Commission thought men were entitled to have female secretaries.[3]
The following year, he publicly labeled the sex discrimination pro-
vision a "fluke . . . conceived out of wedlock."[4]

In an article published in 1964, before the EEOC had com-
menced operations, Dick Berg described the sex discrimination

amendment as an "orphan" and recommended that the exclusion of women from jobs "involving strenuous activity, hazardous working conditions, or close contact with fellow workers or customers" and from "certain hazardous occupations, principally mining" remain lawful.[5] He argued that an employer who refused to assign overtime or night work to women because of state law or to hire them for jobs requiring overtime or night work should not be found in violation of Title VII. Berg believed that a woman's place was in the home.

In addition to Holcomb, the other commissioners were Franklin D. Roosevelt, Jr., the chairman; Aileen Clarke Hernandez; Dick Graham; and Sam Jackson.

Roosevelt had no real interest in the Commission and wasn't there long enough for his views on women's rights, whatever they were, to matter. His sights were set on running for governor of New York, and he resigned from the EEOC in 1966 to announce his candidacy. The only remark of his I remember involved the decor of his office: "This place looks like a French whorehouse."

Hernandez, the first African American woman commissioner and the first woman commissioner, had served as assistant chief of the California Fair Employment Practices Division before coming to the EEOC. Graham was a business executive who had served as director of the Peace Corps in Tunisia. Both were ardent feminists.

Jackson, an African American lawyer who had been president of the Topeka, Kansas, branch of the NAACP, was sympathetic to the fight to end discrimination against women; he viewed it in the context of discrimination against African American women. But he felt that discrimination against African Americans deserved the Commission's greater attention.

Roosevelt, Holcomb, and Hernandez were Democrats; Graham and Jackson, Republicans.

In the area of sex discrimination, the EEOC moved very slowly and conservatively or not at all. I found myself increasingly frustrated by the unwillingness of most of the officials to come to grips with the issues and to come to grips with them in ways that would expand employment opportunities for women—which was, after all, the purpose of the prohibition against sex discrimination.

I became *the* staff person who stood for aggressive enforcement of the sex discrimination prohibitions of the Act, and this caused me no end of grief. At the end of one day, after a particularly frustrating discussion with Edelsberg, I left the EEOC building with tears streaming down my face. I didn't know how I had gotten into this position—fighting for women's rights. No one had elected me to represent women. Why was I engaged in this battle against men who had power where I had none?

While I knew that Commissioners Aileen Hernandez and Dick Graham felt as I did, they were commissioners; I was just a staff lawyer. I did not think I had the option of making common cause with them. At the Commission, I was basically on my own.

But outside the Commission, I developed a network of support. Through my work, I came in contact at various government agencies with midlevel staffers like myself who were concerned with improving the rights of women. Together, we formed an informal network for support and information sharing. I passed on to this network information on women's rights cases that were developing at the EEOC, which the members of this network would then pass on to Marguerite Rawalt, a trailblazing feminist attorney. Marguerite, in turn, would relay this information to her network of feminist attorneys. These attorneys would then represent the complaining parties in precedent-setting sex discrimination lawsuits.

During my early days at the Commission, a writer came to the EEOC. She had become famous through writing a book in 1963 called *The Feminine Mystique*, which dealt with the frustrations of women who were housewives and mothers and did not work outside the home. Now, she was interviewing EEOC officials and staff for a second book. Her name was Betty Friedan.

When we met, Betty asked me to reveal problems and conflicts at the Commission. As a staff member, however, I did not feel I could publicly speak out about the Commission's dereliction, and I did not tell her what was happening with regard to women's issues. But when she came a second time, I was feeling particularly frustrated at the Commission's failure to implement the law for women, and I invited her into my office. I told her, with tears in my eyes, that the country needed an organization to fight for women like the NAACP fought for African Americans.

Subsequent events reinforced this conclusion. In June 1966, at the Third National Conference of Commissions on the Status of Women in Washington, DC, the attendees wanted to pass a resolution demanding the reappointment of Commissioner Dick Graham and the enforcement of Title VII for women. They became enraged when the leadership told them that they did not have the authority to pass resolutions. As a result, at a luncheon at the Conference, Betty Friedan and a small group planned an organization that subsequently became NOW. Its purpose, as written by Betty on a paper napkin, was "to take the actions needed to bring women into the mainstream of American society, now, full equality for women [*sic*], in fully equal partnership with men." By the end of the day, everyone at the Conference who wanted to join had tossed $5 into a war chest and NOW had twenty-eight members. Those twenty-eight were NOW's original founders.

Another twenty-six, of whom I was one, were added that fall at an organizing conference in Washington, DC. We met in the basement of the *Washington Post* and adopted a statement of purpose and skeletal bylaws. Most of us did not know each other. One of the realities of those days was that there was no national network whereby women and men interested in women's rights could come to know each other and work together. What we had in common was a frustration with the status of women and a determination to do something about it. The concept of women's rights was an idea whose time had come.

After its founding, NOW embarked upon an ambitious program of activities to get the EEOC to enforce Title VII for women. It filed lawsuits, petitioned the EEOC for public hearings, picketed the EEOC and the White House, and generally mobilized public opinion.

I became involved in an underground activity. I took to meeting privately at night in the Southwest Washington apartment of Mary Eastwood, a Justice Department attorney and founder of NOW, with her and two other government lawyers: Phineas Indritz, also a NOW founder, and Caruthers Berger. At those evening meetings, I discussed the inaction of the Commission that I had witnessed during that day or week with regard to women's rights, and then we drafted letters from NOW to the Commission demanding that action be taken in those areas. To my amazement, no one at the Commission ever questioned how NOW had become privy to the Commission's deliberations.

As a result of pressure by NOW, the EEOC began to take seriously its mandate to eliminate sex discrimination in employment. It conducted hearings and began to issue interpretations and decisions implementing women's rights. The Commission ruled that employers could no longer advertise in sex-segregated advertising columns. With narrow exceptions, all jobs had to be open to men and women alike, and members of both sexes were entitled to equality in all terms and conditions of employment. I had the great pleasure and privilege of drafting the lead decision finding that the airlines' policies towards stewardesses were unlawful.

The Commission ruled that a woman could not be refused employment or terminated because of the preferences of her employer, coworkers, clients, or customers or because she was pregnant or had children. State laws that restricted women's employment were superseded by Title VII; those that required benefits for women were equally applicable to men.

Men also used the remedies provided by Title VII, although to a much lesser extent. They complained when they were excluded from traditionally female jobs, such as nursing, or were prohibited from wearing beards, mustaches, or long hair on the job.

The EEOC for the first time in this country began the collection of statistics from employers on their employment of women and minorities in various categories of employment.

NOW was the first organization formed to fight for women's rights in the mid-1960s, but many others followed. Traditional women's organizations, which had initially refused to join in the struggle, did so later, and new organizations were formed. Among them were the Women's Equity Action League (WEAL), a spin-off from NOW, and Federally Employed Women (FEW), both founded in 1968, and both organizations of which I was a founder. Through my activities in FEW, I learned that men in the federal government had opportunities to attend training programs that were not, as a practical matter, available to women. One of the sites for these programs was the Federal Executive Institute (FEI), a residential facility operated by the Civil Service Commission (CSC), now the Office of Personnel Management, in Charlottesville, Virginia. While there were various programs at FEI, the core program was an eight-week course for federal employees in the three top grades, GS-16, -17, and -18 (now called supergrades). Since women rarely reached those grades, they rarely had an opportunity to get this training.

As a result of my letter of complaint to CSC and similar complaints from others, CSC developed a one-week program for a small group of women—the first time in its history that there would be a special program for women at FEI. Tina Hobson, director of CSC's Federal Women's Program, selected ten or twelve women to attend this program from among women who had expressed an interest in getting FEI training. She and I attended this historic and exhilarating week. Thereafter, CSC began for the first time to actively recruit women for attendance at FEI.

Unions, most of which were initially hostile to women's rights, became involved in the struggle. They were in fact in the forefront of the pay equity struggle, the fight to secure equal pay for women for work of comparable worth or value to that of men. The various levels of government also became more active: Presidents signed executive orders, federal and state laws and municipal ordinances were passed, and court decisions issued.

New government agencies were created to fight discrimination, such as the Office of Federal Contract Compliance Programs (OFCCP) in the Department of Labor. The OFCCP requires contractors and subcontractors of the federal government to do more than simply not discriminate. They are required to take affirmative action to hire and promote women or risk the loss of millions of dollars in government contracts.

Discrimination based on sex or marital status in the sale and rental of housing and in the granting of credit was prohibited. Title IX of the Education Amendments of 1972 prohibits educational institutions, from preschools through colleges and universities, that receive federal funds from discriminating on the basis of sex against students and all employees, including administrative personnel and faculty members. One of the effects of Title IX has been the requirement for equality in expenditures for school athletic programs.

Legislation in 1972 gave the EEOC the power to enforce its orders in the courts. The Pregnancy Discrimination Act of 1978 codified the EEOC's guidelines on pregnancy and leave in connection with pregnancy. In 1991, for the first time, women were given the right to secure limited monetary damages for harassment and other intentional sex discrimination. About two weeks after taking office, President Clinton signed the Family and Medical Leave Act. This law requires employers to provide their employees with up to twelve weeks of unpaid, job-protected leave each year in connection with the birth or adoption of a child or the serious illness of a child, spouse, or parent. Due to all this activity, the American public became aware that there was a new national priority: equal rights for women.

Our society has undergone a massive change. Women are now found in large numbers in professional schools and in the professions, and, to a much lesser extent, in executive suites and legislatures. They work at a host of technical and blue-collar jobs previously closed to them. In 1976, women were admitted to West Point and our other military academies, a development that was unthinkable before the women's movement. The percent of women in the military rose from 1.6% in 1972 to 13% by 1990, and, since the 1980s, the variety of their assignments has increased substantially. Women-owned businesses are now one-third of all businesses in the United States and employ one out of five American workers. Over six hundred colleges and universities have women's studies programs.

When I first began giving talks on Title VII, I said that the Act involved only employment. That was literally true and I believed it, but I was naive. The effects of Title VII spilled over onto every area of our society. Laws have changed women's rights with regard to abortion, divorce, alimony, child custody, child support, rape, jury service, appointments as administrators and executors of estates, sentencing for crimes, and admission to places of public accommodation, such as clubs, restaurants, and bars. Our spoken language has changed, and work continues on the development of gender-neutral written language in laws, textbooks, religious texts, and publications of all sorts.

Eighteen years after the founding of NOW, a woman ran for Vice President of the United States, and nine years after that, a woman became attorney general.

A little-known law, a relatively small organization, the developments that followed in this country, and similar movements worldwide have completely changed the face of this country and are well on their way to changing the face of the world. Eli Ginzberg, a Columbia University economist and chairman of the National Commission for Manpower Policy, said that the increase in the number and proportion of women who work is the single most outstanding phenomenon of our century. In August and September 1995, 50,000 men and women attended the UN Fourth World Conference on Women in Beijing, China.

In the early 1980s, when my daughter, Zia, was about eleven years old, we spent a week in Chautauqua, New York, where Betty

Friedan was lecturing. Betty invited us to her room for a drink, and as we were going there, I said to Zia, "You're going to meet a woman who's changed the lives of women all over the world."

"China too?" she asked.

"China too," I answered.

We've achieved a lot, but much remains to be done—and new problems face us. Women are still subject not only to sex discrimination, but if they are older women, women of color, or have disabilities, they may be the victims of multiple discrimination. Women are still far from being represented equally in political life. They comprise a mere 12 percent of the members of Congress; no woman has ever served as President, Vice President, speaker of the House of Representatives, or majority leader of the Senate—and only rarely has a woman served as full committee chair of either body of Congress. Only three states have women governors. Women are still underrepresented in corporate boardrooms and executive suites and in top positions in academia and unions. They still do not receive equal pay for equal or substantially equal work. The Equal Rights Amendment (ERA) has yet to be ratified, and the US has not yet joined the overwhelming majority of the world's nations in ratifying the United Nation's Convention To Eliminate All Forms of Discrimination Against Women (CEDAW). Complaints of sexual harassment are one of the fastest-growing areas of employment discrimination cases at the EEOC. Student-to-student sexual harassment at all levels of education is on the increase. We have a disproportionate number of women in poverty, and women in poverty means children in poverty. There are increasing numbers of women and children among the homeless, and we need more safe houses and services for battered women. The battle for reproductive choice goes on. Millions of women do not have health care coverage. Women have to deal with new realities, such as combining a demanding position with marriage and raising a family, and finding affordable, quality household help and childcare. Women increasingly find themselves in the sandwich generation—

having to be the caretaker both for their children and their parents.

When we look beyond the US to the rest of the world, the status of women is often shocking. In Third World countries, culture, religion, and law often deprive women of basic human rights and sometimes relegate them to almost subhuman status. Violence against women is a worldwide problem. Female genital mutilation continues, as do child marriages, the selling of young girls into prostitution, and the use of rape and forced impregnation as political weapons.

Nonetheless, the changes we've seen in the past thirty years have been breathtaking.

In thinking about where we've been, where we are, and where we're going, I can't say it any better than the anonymous African American woman Dr. Martin Luther King was fond of quoting:

> We ain't what we oughta be,
> We ain't what we wanna be,
> We ain't what we gonna be,
> But, *thank God*, we ain't what we was.

This chapter is dedicated to Mary Eastwood and to the memory of Catherine East and Phineas Indritz, my three closest colleagues in the struggle for women's rights—and to all the others.

24.

THE CORPORATE WORLD

At the EEOC, it was my dream to someday become an EEOC Commissioner, but that was not to be. By 1973, I had gone as far as I was going to go at the agency. I was a grade 15, earning $30,000 a year. The next step up was a supergrade, GS-16, and I saw no possibility of that. Charlie Duncan had gone on to become Corporation Counsel of the District of Columbia. Though he had promised to take me with him to that organization, he found he could not do so. Any available higher grades in the Corporation Counsel's Office had to go to employees within that office. There was no future for me at the agency I loved so much and none with the Corporation Counsel's Office. It was time to move on.

By this time I was imbued with the spirit of public service and gave no thought to leaving government, but my applications to federal agencies produced no job offers. One day, an ad from an employment agency in the *Washington Post* caught my eye. The agency was named Today's Woman, and the ad was for a corporate legal counsel at a salary of $24,000 a year. I pointed the ad out to my husband, Roberto. "I like the name of that agency," I said. "But, I'm making more than that now. Besides, how could I work for a corporation?" Corporations were bastions of Republicanism. As a liberal Democrat, I could not picture myself in that environment.

Roberto suggested I write to Today's Woman, setting forth my interest and qualifications, but pointing out that I was looking for a higher salary. I did so, and, to my surprise, not much later, I received a letter telling me that I had an appointment with George Shertzer, general counsel of the GTE Service Corporation, in New York City.

Due to my lack of interest in corporate work, I was reluctant to keep the appointment, but Roberto encouraged me to do so. I went, the general counsel offered me $40,000 a year, and I took the job as senior attorney.

On June 18, 1973, I began work at GTE, formerly the General Telephone & Electronics Corporation, in Stamford, Connecticut. That day was not only my first day but also GTE's first day at its new headquarters in Stamford. With 200,000 employees worldwide, GTE was the second largest telephone company in the United States.

I was the highest-paid woman at headquarters and the first woman in the Legal Department. George Shertzer, a tall, handsome, elegant man, was one of the few Democrats and one of the few liberals at the upper levels of the company. He hired me because the changing climate toward women in the United States required that the company increase its employment of women at higher levels and because of his own liberal views, but it was certainly not a change understood or welcomed by most of the thousands of employees at company headquarters. On my first day at GTE, as I stood at the elevators on the ground floor, a security guard directed me to the section for secretaries.

After I'd worked at the company for several weeks, George called me into his office and told me I was going to be admitted to the previously all-male sanctum sanctorum of GTE: the executive dining room. George told me I'd be the Jackie Robinson of the dining room. I was dismayed.

"I don't know the first thing about baseball, George," I said, somewhat facetiously, to mask my dismay. "How can I be a Jackie Robinson?" Coincidentally, the real Jackie Robinson's home, where his widow Rachel lived, was only a few miles from my home on Winesap Road in Stamford. The executives at GTE were no more comfortable with me than the white baseball officials and players had been with the real Jackie Robinson, perhaps even less so, because my employment involved sex, an issue even more sensitive than race. The executives at GTE had been working in what was essentially a male club; now, a female was being placed in their midst. They were used to women as wives and mothers at home, not as equals in the office and the even more sacrosanct executive dining room. It was as if they were told by fiat that a gorilla would be living in their homes.

Shortly after I came aboard, I learned how men tend to overvalue their abilities while women tend to undervalue theirs. George asked me to accompany the office's antitrust specialist, Simon Colton*, to a meeting in New York City to discuss an antitrust litigation matter facing GTE and the company with whose representatives we would meet. I was petrified; I knew absolutely nothing about antitrust and very little about litigation. Simon, on the other hand, was confident about his ability to handle the situation.

At the meeting, when the issue was raised, I was reminded of a similar problem that had arisen in civil rights cases and mentioned the technique that had been used successfully in those cases. The others were unfamiliar with it, but agreed that it should work in this situation, too. My suggestion carried the day.

After I'd been in the headquarters Legal Department for over a year, it was reorganized. Company-wide legal sections, such as Antitrust, Patent Law, and Human Resources were created, but general corporate legal work remained in the overall department. I had the choice of remaining in the broader entity or, because of my background in labor law and EEO, transferring into the Human Resources Section. I was torn by this decision. I knew I wanted to do human relations work, but common wisdom had it that lawyers who did general corporate legal work were the ones who rose to the top of the corporate ladder. So, initially, I chose to remain in the overall Legal Department. However, I was not comfortable with this decision and discussed it with a friend who had a social work background. She pointed out that one did not find happiness in life by doing the "shoulds" but by going in the direction of one's heart. I told George that I wanted to change my decision and transfer into the Human Resources Section, and he graciously allowed me to do so. In that section, I enjoyed doing general labor law and EEO work, and I represented the company in arbitrations.

I had difficulty adjusting to corporate life after sixteen years with the federal government, especially in view of the role I'd played in my almost-eight years at the EEOC. There, I had frequently made speeches to employer groups essentially laying down the law for them. The import of my talks was: this is the law, and if you don't fall in line, the EEOC and the courts will zap you. But things were different at GTE. There, after I gave corporate executives my opinion of what the law required, they'd say, "We'll include that as a factor when we make our decision." Basically, it was the executives' position that unless a federal agent had a gun at their throats, they did not have to comply with the law. They were able to get away with that approach to the sex discrimination provisions of Title VII because in those early years the import of those provisions had not yet been decided by the US Supreme Court.

While these top corporate executives thought they were playing hardball and displaying tough macho stands, not only were their decisions contrary to the law being enunciated by the EEOC, they were poor business practice. One of the issues was the company's policy towards pregnant employees. The EEOC had ruled that employers could not lawfully terminate women because they were pregnant provided they could perform the duties of their jobs. In addition, employers were required to provide the same leave and benefit policies to women who requested time off for pregnancy, childbearing and childcare as they applied to employees in general who requested leaves for illness or other reasons. This was not GTE's policy. As a result of the company's stance, however, it was embroiled in litigation, with the concomitant legal costs, throughout the country. The bottom line was that when the Supreme Court upheld the EEOC's position, the company had to change its policies after all.

One of the eye-openers for me at GTE was the incompetence of many corporate officials. Women had traditionally been excluded from executive positions in business and industry because they weren't considered competent to make decisions in the economic and business realms. At GTE, when I witnessed first-hand the many inept business decisions made by men, I realized how totally baseless women's exclusion had been.

While my time at GTE was rocky, after a number of years, it became intolerable. To ease my sense of isolation, I had formed a support group with about five other women at GTE. We met for dinners and formed a network to share experiences and information within the company. But we had to keep the existence of the group and our meetings secret for fear of recrimination.

In my years at the company, the treatment of women executives had not improved. Furthermore, my marriage had collapsed, I had gotten divorced, and I found it painful to see Roberto every week when he came to take Zia out. It was time to leave Stamford as well as GTE.

I began to look for another position in another community. I was now past fifty, a woman with a young daughter, looking for a top corporate position. My prospects were bleak.

Several years passed, and no job offers had come my way. I was thus dejected when I went to pick Zia up at the home of friends one day, where she'd been playing with their daughter. Ed Fein was a lawyer who had been a vice president at Hearst Publications; now he was a free-lance consultant in publishing. He asked me how I was doing and, in response, I began to cry. I explained that I'd been trying for several years to find another job, and it seemed hopeless. I hadn't gotten a single offer.

"If it's a job you want," Ed said. "That's easy. One of my free-lance activities is counseling people who want to change jobs. If you promise to do everything I tell you, *exactly* as I tell you to do it, I guarantee you'll find another job. And I'll do it for you at no cost." This was an astounding offer. I did not, of course, believe for a minute that Ed would be able to fulfill his promise. But what did I have to lose? Just some time and effort.

For the next three months, I spent every free minute following Ed's instructions. I compiled a list of three hundred top corporations in the United States for which I'd be interested in working. My list included the corporations' names and addresses and the names of their chief executives. Ed said I would be writing a form letter to each of these chief executives, telling them why they should interview me for a job with their companies. Under no circumstances was I to send a résumé to any company; that was for lower-level positions. We spent most of three months composing this letter, which eventually ran to 1½ pages. The last few weeks were spent selecting the right quality, size, and color of the stationery. Ed also advised me on negotiating with any employer who made me an offer. His philosophy included the caveats that under no circumstances was I to reveal the salary I was currently earning or the one I aspired to before the employer made me an offer.

When I was just about ready to begin the mailing, I got a call from Jay Siegel. Shortly after I had begun work for GTE, I had made it my business to become acquainted with Jay, the outstanding labor lawyer in Connecticut. Then, after I'd been with GTE for several years, when Jay and I were both panelists at a labor law program at the University of Bridgeport, I told him that I was interested in making a job change. He promised to keep that in mind, a comment that was about to bear fruit.

Jay said he had had a call from Bob McCarty, vice president of Employee Relations of TRW, Inc., at its Cleveland, Ohio, headquarters. Bob told Jay, who represented TRW, that he was looking for a new director of compliance management. Bob asked Jay whether he knew someone who was both an attorney and an expert in EEO. Jay looked into his Friends Looking for Jobs file and found me. He suggested I call Bob.

I didn't know what to do; I had no interest in going to Cleveland. The Midwest had always seemed like terra incognita to me.

I certainly couldn't picture myself living there. But the possibility of being director of compliance management with responsibility for equal employment opportunity and affirmative action for a major corporation sounded like a dream job. I called Ed Fein and asked his advice. He suggested I call Bob as the experience would serve me well when I mailed my letter out and engaged in real job hunting.

I phoned Bob and he invited me out to Cleveland for an interview. When I met with him, the job sounded nearly tailor-made for me; and, in those areas where it wasn't, Bob was willing to fashion the job to suit me. I would be in charge of the company's affirmative action and equal employment opportunity programs nationwide; I would have a manager reporting to me; and the job would entail as much travel as I chose. Bob asked me to send him a résumé on my return home.

When I returned to Stamford, I discussed the interview with Ed Fein. He told me that under no circumstances was I to comply with Bob's request for a résumé. Instead, this was a good opportunity to try out the letter we had spent months designing. Since I still wasn't keen on going to Cleveland, I felt I had nothing to lose by sending Bob that letter.

After receiving it, Bob called and asked what I was earning. He said the company had a fixed salary for this position, and if that was less than I was currently earning, there was no sense in continuing our discussions. I said I'd get back to him and again asked Ed what to do.

"Don't tell him your present salary and don't discuss your future salary until he makes you an offer," said Ed, repeating what he had taught me. "He'll back down if you refuse."

"I don't want to discuss salary at this point, Bob," I said when I called back. "I'm more interested in discussing the challenges of the job." Not only did Bob back off, as Ed had predicted, but he never again said there was a fixed salary for the position.

When Bob later made me an offer on the phone, I asked for time to consider it. During this time, I realized that if I accepted

TRW's offer, I'd be losing my GTE pension rights. By that time, I had been working at GTE for more than eight years; in less than two years, I'd be vested with a GTE pension. I did a rough calculation and figured out the present value of that pension. It is axiomatic that one's best negotiating posture is at the time of hire, when the company most wants you. I wrote to Bob and asked whether the company could make up for the loss of my pension. Bob responded with a four-page offer of employment that included a one-third increase over my salary at GTE. In addition, he offered me a lump sum to make up for the loss of my pension and a first year mortgage differential payment. Furthermore, the company would buy my house in Connecticut at the market price, handle my moving expenses, and arrange advantageous terms for me to get a mortgage on a Cleveland house. I would be the highest-paid woman at the headquarters staff level. What could I do? I took the job. I became director of compliance management at TRW in Cleveland. The letter Ed and I had worked so hard at fashioning had served its purpose.

TRW had begun when the Pentagon chose two engineer-entrepreneurs, Simon Ramo and Dean Woolridge, to manage the development of an intercontinental ballistic missile (ICBM) on a parallel basis with the Air Force. The purpose of this ICBM was to deliver a hydrogen bomb (H-bomb) to counterbalance the Soviet threat of dropping an H-bomb on the United States. Ramo and Woolridge founded the Ramo-Woolridge Corporation in 1953, and, five years later, it merged with Thompson Products, Inc., an automotive parts manufacturer based in Cleveland. The company name was changed to the Thompson-Ramo-Woolridge Corporation, which later became the TRW Corporation.

In January 1982, when I joined the company at its Euclid, Ohio, headquarters, TRW was a 90,000-employee multinational corporation. In addition to its involvement in the manufacture of auto parts and space and defense equipment, it had subsidiaries in data processing and credit reporting.

I found that working in a highly visible top level position for

TRW had its advantages. After I'd been there for a couple of years, I was selected by the Republican National Committee as one of twenty women in corporate human resources work to attend a special briefing in Washington, DC. The group had lunch with the Secretary of Labor and met with various senators and members of Congress. In February 1984, I was featured in the *New Cleveland Woman Journal* as one of Cleveland's six top executive women. Nonetheless, I was uncomfortable in the corporate world. It was not the place for an outspoken, independent, liberal, Jewish woman who wanted to change the way things were done. As I'd previously seen at GTE, success in the corporate world required more than performance; it required buying into the company philosophy. This I was unable to do. After I'd been with TRW less than three years, I submitted my resignation.

That was the end of my corporate career. It took me a while to find another job, but 1½ years later I happily returned to Washington, DC, for a position with HUD, my final job before retirement.

25.

IF YOU LIVE LONG ENOUGH

In the Introduction to Business program in which I enrolled at the beginning of high school, I took a course in typing, in which I quickly became proficient. At first, I found it a useful skill, but it soon became a necessity. I had become proficient not only in typing but also in thinking at the typewriter. At the same time, I lost the ability to think in longhand. Furthermore, writing anything of any length in longhand was much too slow and laborious a process for me. Years later, when I was getting ready to take the Florida Bar, I secured permission from the Board of Examiners to take the bar examination on a typewriter so I could answer the essay questions.

My affair with the typewriter, like all relationships, went through various phases. In my first jobs out of college as a secretary in the early '50s, proficiency in typing, along with shorthand, was a requirement. Later, when I began my first job as a lawyer at the Office of Alien Property in Washington, DC, proficiency in typing was not, of course, a requirement. But since a typewriter had become a necessity for me, my first request on starting the job was for a typewriter.

When I was working as a corporate lawyer for GTE in Stamford, however, other considerations came into play. Actually, Roberto brought them to my attention. "You can't continue to let people see you typing in your office," he began. "It makes you look like a secretary. You're a corporate attorney now. You've got to look the part." His comments made sense. My male colleagues often stopped by my office, attracted by the swift clickety-click of my fingers on the typewriter keys. "Oh, we've got a new secretary," they would say, with a mixture of sarcasm and humor.

So, I had the typewriter removed from my office. Now, I was in a dilemma. I couldn't type at the office, but I was unable to work in longhand. So I took to bringing work home and working on my typewriter at home nights and weekends.

This went on for a good many months. I was no longer giving my colleagues the impression that I was a secretary, but neither did I have any free time at home. As a working wife and mother, my nights and weekends had already been overly full. Now, they were impossible. Much as I agreed with Roberto, I found this way of life impossible; so I had the typewriter returned to my office.

The 1980s witnessed a revolution in office equipment. Personal computers were introduced, along with word-processing software. Offices converted from typewriters to computers; and secretaries, to a large extent, disappeared. Executives and lawyers were expected to produce their own work on their own computers, at least for first drafts.

I did not actually learn to operate a computer until 1988 because, prior to that time, while the offices where I worked had computers, I did not have one assigned for my personal use. But that year, while on the payroll of the legislative counsel's division at HUD in Washington, DC, to get legislative experience, I spent several months with Senator Howard Metzenbaum's Subcommittee on Labor. There, I had a computer at my desk. My office mate taught me how to operate it, and I took a word-processing course given for Senate staffers. I was quickly able to transfer my proficiency at the keyboard of a typewriter to the keyboard of a computer.

When I returned to my regular job at HUD, I brought my computer proficiency with me. I was able to put it to good use when, shortly thereafter, HUD installed personal computers at lawyers' workstations. Again, my male colleagues were impressed with the fast clickety-click of my fingers on the keyboard. But now they said, "Boy, I wish I had your skill." I was reminded of the Yiddish expression, "*Az men lebt, derlebt men alts.*" ["If you live long enough, you will live to see everything."]

PART VI

26.

THE OPPOSITE SEX

As the years passed, and I created a persona for myself as a witty, sophisticated, shapely woman, I began to exude a quality that made me very attractive. I had only to go to a reception, party, wedding, or any other place where people congregated, and people would be drawn to me, as moths to a flame. Unfortunately, these people were always women. From the age of ten, I was attracted to men, but it remained throughout my life largely a one-way street.

Of course until contact lenses and later cataract surgery and implants in my eyes eliminated the need for eyeglasses, I was not particularly attractive. When I was eight years old, my elementary school in Woodridge provided eye examinations for all students. The result in my case, although I'd never had any problems with my vision, was that I was told that I needed glasses for myopia. So I began wearing eyeglasses at a time when few of my classmates wore them, and when the availability of attractive frames still lay in the future. It didn't take long before I was highly myopic and astigmatic and wearing thick glasses. Dorothy Parker, who was herself Jewish and myopic, was right: men didn't make passes at girls who wore glasses.

Also, I had no sense of style and no particular talent with makeup, hairdo, or clothes until much later in life. Perhaps, this was because I had no sisters, or because we always lived outside of town and were always moving. So, I was never part of a close circle of girlfriends from whom I might have learned how to maximize my assets.

In addition, I did not get braces until just before I left for college. So, when I began college, ordinarily a happy hunting ground for husbands, I did so wearing thick eyeglasses, braces on my teeth, and with the savoir-faire that one could acquire in the Catskills.

That is not to say that there weren't men in my life. But I never had the luxury of dating more than one man at a time, and my romances tended to be unorthodox. At Cornell, for example, I was madly in love with one of my classmates in the Graduate School of Business and Public Administration. There were, however, two strikes against that relationship. Cliff* was an African American and he was already married.

After college, I did have a relationship with a most suitable man named Cal. I met him at Tamiment, one of those hotels in the Poconos where young men and women in the '50s went to meet. Cal was a handsome, tall engineer who paid no attention to me during the week we were at the hotel. But at the end of the week, he asked for my telephone number and, to my surprise, called and began to take me out. The relationship was moving along beautifully until one night, after we'd been to the movies, when we were having ice cream at an ice cream shop. I told him that I always ordered vanilla ice cream and asked him what he did. He said he liked to try different flavors. I was terrified. I interpreted this to mean that Cal would not be a faithful husband but would be interested in sampling the charms of a variety of women. I never saw him again.

While men generally did not find me attractive in the United States, as soon as I left the country, my attractiveness quotient shot right up. On my first trip to Israel in the mid-'60s, I had not one, but two, romances. The first, however, lasted only a few minutes. It occurred when I went into a jewelry shop with the rest of my tour group. As soon as I entered the store and began to look at the jewelry in the case, the proprietor, who stood behind the counter, asked me to marry him. When he saw the look of amazement on my face, he said, "Don't worry. You won't have to leave your country. We can live half the year in Israel, and half in the United States." Due to the short time of the stopover, I was forced to turn him down. Since that encounter, I've wondered from time to time whether he was just an Israeli desperate to get to the United States or a man struck blind by my attractiveness. I've always chosen to believe the latter.

My second romance, of somewhat longer duration, was with our Israeli tour guide. This one was somewhat dampened in mid-tour, however, when his wife joined us on the bus.

I went to Mexico twice, first to Acapulco and then to Cancun, and had a totally unsuitable romance each time. On my first trip, my would-be lover was my taxicab driver. He was shocked when I refused to have sex with him one night in his cab. "You mean you don't want my baby?" he asked. He was flabbergasted that a single woman with no children would pass up such an opportunity. Several weeks later, he even followed me to LA, where I was then living. But whatever cachet he'd had in Acapulco clearly did not follow him to Los Angeles, and we parted soon thereafter.

My second trip to Mexico took place some fifteen years later when I went to Club Med in Cancun to recuperate from my divorce. There, I had a most romantic interlude on the beach with a thirty-year-old businessman from Manhattan. Since I was fifty-two at the time, this was good for my ego but not for anything else.

Then came Egypt, where I fell madly in love with the manager of the boat on the cruise I took down the Nile. He was half-Egyptian, half-Lebanese, and all gorgeous. I ingratiated myself with him by telling him about the passengers' reactions to various activities on board ship and offering suggestions for improving the voyage. But we parted forever when the boat docked in Cairo after ten glorious days.

In London, while attending a month's course in Yiddish at the University of London's Queen Mary & Westfield College, I had a flirtation with one of my classmates, Michael. He was handsome, unemployed, penniless, and seventeen years my junior. As if that wasn't enough, he had one other strike against him. Three years earlier, he had decided to change his affiliation from Conservative to Orthodox Judaism, and he was deep into Orthodoxy. To him, that meant he could not go to the movies and the theater with me since there might be portrayals of men and women together who were not married to each other. When he came to my apartment, which consisted of a kitchen (which I shared with another student) and a bedroom, he stayed in the kitchen when I went into the bedroom. Needless to say, this put quite a crimp into our romance.

In China, where I represented the American Cancer Society at the First International Conference on Women's Health in March 1993, I had a mild flirtation with a physician at one of the hospitals I visited in Shanghai, Chen Huibing*. It was an accomplishment merely to pronounce his name. However, since he was Chinese, married, the father of three, and forty-five years old (to my sixty-four), this flirtation did not have a lot of promise.

In the States, one of the ways to meet men, of course, was on blind dates, but I never had much success with them. For example, one evening, when we were living in Long Beach, I got a call from Frances, the unmarried niece of my sister-in-law. Frances had a date that evening with a man who had an unattached friend; would I be interested in joining them for the evening? I wasn't, but my parents prevailed upon me to go, and so I reluctantly agreed.

When my date Ray* arrived, I was pleasantly surprised to see a tall, attractive man. But that was both the beginning and the end of my pleasure that evening. The four of us went to a movie first and then for ice cream sodas. At the movie, Ray turned his back to me, and when we had ice cream, he failed to say anything to me. As he was driving me home, his negative body language was so strong, I finally turned to him and said, "What is it about me? You seem so hostile."

"It's not you," he responded, "I was supposed to get married this weekend, and my girlfriend broke it off. I hate all women." I consoled myself with the fact that at least *I* was not at fault.

On another occasion, I had a blind date who remained blind—at least to me. I never got to see him. It started as many of my blind dates did. A woman who knew my parents couldn't understand "how come a girl like you never got married." So, she racked her brain and came up with an eligible male. Several days later, Lenny* called. He offered to take me out the following Saturday—after midnight. He worked in a store that didn't close until midnight on Saturdays.

I hadn't wanted this blind date in the first place; I certainly wasn't going to wait for Lenny until after midnight. "I don't think that will work," I said. "It's much too late for me to go out." But I hadn't reckoned with my mother. As always, she hovered in the background and let her thoughts be known. "What did you say that for?" she asked. "What's so bad about midnight?" This from a woman who, under other circumstances, would have looked askance at any social activity beginning at that hour. "You take a little nap in the day," she continued, "and before you know it, the fellow's here. After all, it's not for forever." Then, she capped it with, "No wonder no one wants you." I accepted the date.

That Saturday morning, Dad was home, Mother was ironing, and I was just lazing around the house when the doorbell rang. I opened the door and saw a man I presumed was a repairman come to fix something in the house. I was not completely wrong; he was a plumber. But what he had come to fix was not something in the house.

"Is this the Pressman residence?" he asked. When I told him it was, he marched in and announced himself. His name was Putterman* and he was Lenny's father. He had learned of his son's date with me and had come by train from Manhattan to look us over: Mother, Father, and me. Putterman started by questioning us all—what my father did for a living, how come my mother wasn't working, whether I drove a car. I expected my father to throw him out. But on one of the few occasions in my recollection,

Father displayed a sense of humor. He treated Putterman with all seriousness even though I could see he had trouble keeping his tongue in cheek.

Putterman then proceeded to tell us that thus far all his attempts with his son had failed. He had tried to make a businessman out of him, but "the boy" just had no head for business. Instead, he was interested in becoming a doctor. "But," Putterman said, "I've done all I can with him. I put him through college. "Now," he continued, turning to my father, "it's up to you. If you want a doctor for a son-in-law, *you'll* have to send him to medical school and open up a practice for him later on. I don't have any more money." My father never blinked an eye. He said he'd be happy to consider it.

When Putterman left, the three of us erupted into laughter. I was even allowed to break my after-midnight date. Lenny obviously wasn't my *basherter*—my destined one, my mother concluded.

After that fiasco, Mother agreed to a special arrangement with me for future blind dates. Since she knew my taste in men, when a blind date came to the door, if she thought I wouldn't find him attractive, she would ask him to wait a few minutes and come into my bedroom to warn me that I'd find him unattractive. I would immediately hop into bed, and Mother would return to tell the date I had suddenly been taken ill, that he could come by my bedroom to say, "Hello," but that, unfortunately, I would be unable to spend the evening with him. This didn't produce any attractive men, but at least it fended off the unattractive ones.

Then there was the date that went awry because of my father. This was unusual because my father never had anything to do with my dates. Mother would fuss and putter about trying to be hospitable—"You'll take a piece Danish, gentleman?" But not Father. It was his feeling that these men came and went, like trains that passed in the night, and there was no sense *his* bothering with them. If there was somewhere he could go, he would leave the house when the date was expected. If not, he would try to be as unobtrusive as possible.

"Hey," said one of my dates to me one evening. "Did you know your gardener is still out there?"

"That's no gardener," I'd say. "It's my father."

Or, "Did you know," asked another, "someone's sleeping on your front porch?"

"I know," I'd say. "That's my father."

But once in a while, some young man, determined to preserve the amenities, would insist on engaging Father in conversation. The results were always disastrous. On one such occasion, we were living in an apartment in Miami Beach: Mother, Father, I, and Father's supply of fishing equipment. My escort, noticing the fishing rods and related paraphernalia lined up against the four walls of the living room, thought he had hit upon a topic that would get my father talking. "I take it, Mr. Pressman, those are your fishing rods," he began, fated never to continue. "No," said my father, as he continued to oil one of his rods. "Dey are not." That ended the conversation. Mother looked as if she was about to have an apoplectic fit, and I hastened to get my wrap.

I don't remember too much about that date; I was too struck by my father's denial to really notice what was going on. Why on earth had he denied ownership of his fondest possessions? I couldn't wait to ask him.

"OK, Dad," I said at breakfast the following morning. "Come clean. What's the story? Why did you tell my date those fishing rods weren't yours?" He looked surprised at the question—but he had the answer ready. "Look," he said, with his own inimitable brand of logic, "if that fellow was too dumb to figure out those fishing rods were mine, why should I tell him?"

That wasn't the only relationship of mine ended by my father. There was also *Tseyndl*. Mark Adler was a handsome singer who worked the smaller Miami Beach hotels. It was romantic sitting in the audience knowing that Mark was singing his romantic ballads especially to me. Dad, however, saw no future in his daughter's involvement with a second-rate crooner in Miami Beach's seedier establishments. So he took to referring to Mark as *Tseyndl*—Little Tooth—a derogatory reference to the fact that one of Mark's front teeth hadn't developed properly. This soon cooled my ardor for Mark.

At about that time, I left home to begin my government career in Washington. That's when I had my Ethiopian affair, which combined the worst elements of the blind date and the foreign romance. It began innocuously enough at the apartment of my friend, Harriet. I had known Harriet for a number of months and was having dinner at her apartment when she turned to me and said, "You know, Sonny. There's a fellow I'd like to introduce you to. I think you two would really hit it off." Then Harriet went on to extol this fellow's virtues. His name was Barry* and he was with the International Cooperation Administration, a part of the State Department. He was tall, he was Jewish, he had had a nice apartment when she knew him, and he was an excellent cook (a definite plus for me). What else could anyone want? She assured me that she had had only a platonic relationship with him, but she thought he'd be great for me.

"So, go ahead," I said. "Introduce me if you think he's so terrific."

"I can't right now," she answered. "He's in Ethiopia." I groaned. The story of my life. I hear of an attractive man, and he's unobtainable.

"Not right now," continued Harriet. "But he's due to get back to Washington in several months. I'll do it then." It was then February and Harriet expected him to be back in Washington around July. That was almost half a year away. Since patience was never my strong point, I sought another way.

"I'm not going to wait five months, Harriet. Anything could happen during that time. I'll write him now."

"What do you mean" she asked, "you'll write him now? What will you say?"

"Don't worry," I answered. I'll think of something."

And so it came to pass that I sat down and wrote to Barry in Ethiopia. I told him that I was planning to come to Addis Ababa, Ethiopia's capital, shortly on a job, and that our mutual friend, Harriet, had mentioned his being there. I asked him whether he could send me any information on living and working conditions in Addis Ababa.

Several weeks later, I received an answer from him, which began, "The best way to learn about Ethiopia is to talk to someone who's been there." He went on to say, "And since I'll be coming back to Washington on a visit in March, I'd be happy to discuss it with you. By the way, what sort of job are you coming out on?"

Now, there was a stumper. But as a firm believer in the theory that there's a solution to every problem, I knew there was an answer to this one, too. I just had to find it. I answered Barry's letter by telling him I'd be delighted to speak with him when he came back, and I implied that the job that was taking me to Ethiopia was with the CIA; therefore, for security reasons I could not share any of the details with him.

I spent several weeks boning up on Ethiopia and Addis Ababa. So I was prepared when Barry called one Sunday in March, told me he was in Washington, and suggested coming over to my apartment with a friend of his that evening. I agreed. As I was awaiting their arrival, I had visions of my life in Addis Ababa with Barry. I saw myself clad in exotic Ethiopian garb entertaining the local potentates—going shopping in the ancient marketplaces—teaching English to the local children—perhaps doing social work among the poor.

I was in the midst of these reveries, when the doorknocker sounded, and I opened it to admit one of the most unattractive men I had ever seen. Barry was indeed tall, but he was also homely, with large, stained yellow teeth, filthy horn-rimmed spectacles, and a threadbare overcoat hanging over his shoulders. Behind him was the friend he had brought along, presumably for protection.

Upon seeing these two, I had an almost irresistible urge to shut the door in their faces. But, of course, I could not do that.

Instead, I invited them in, took their coats, brought them a couple of drinks, and asked Barry questions about Ethiopia. He described the climate—three months or so of the rainy season—the swamp-filled streets, the boredom. And then, looking around my modern air-conditioned apartment, he asked, "How come you want to go to Ethiopia?" He had me there for a while, until I was able to mutter some phrases such as "advance my career," "see the world," and "need for a change." Barry seemed to accept that. After all, he had gone to Ethiopia himself.

He and his friend had another drink and, finally, stood up to leave. We shook hands, and I promised to contact Barry when I got to Addis Ababa. Fortunately, that day never came.

Then there was the knit suit incident. In the late sixties, while I was living in Arlington, I flew down to North Miami Beach for a long weekend with my parents. I had no sooner arrived than one of their friends arranged a blind date for me. My father insisted that for this date I needed a new knit suit. I protested: I had other suitable outfits with me; I had lots of knit suits up north; I would probably never see this date again; and I had only a few days to spend home and did not want to spend one of them shopping. All to no avail. I was forty years old, but Father insisted that I needed a new suit, and that he needed to accompany me on the round of stores we'd have to make so he could buy me the best suit we could find.

Since I was adamantly opposed to buying a knit suit, I managed to find something wrong with each one I tried on, and although we spent an entire day going from store to store, much to my father's chagrin, we did not make a purchase. That blind date came and went, and I never heard from him again. Father was certain a new knit suit would have made the difference.

Blind dates did, however, work well for me on two occasions but not with the men who were my dates. The first blind date led me to Hal and the second to Roberto.

I met Hal in Miami Beach on New Year's Eve. As usual throughout my life, I did not have a date for New Year's Eve. So at about

10:30 PM, I put my hair up in curlers and prepared to go to bed—when the phone rang. It was my friend, Bonnie; she was downstairs with her date, another couple, and a date for me. Was I interested? No, I said, my hair's up in curlers and I'm getting ready for bed. "I'll come up," she said, "and get you ready." She came up, fixed my hair, helped me dress, and shortly thereafter, we three couples went out on the town. I have absolutely no recollection of my date that evening, but the next morning, when I went downstairs for my mail, standing in the lobby was Hal, the male half of the third couple of our New Year's Eve group. It seemed his aunt and uncle lived in my apartment building, and he had come by to visit them. There followed a relationship of several years' standing with a most unsuitable man. Hal was in the direct mail business in New Haven, Connecticut, but his real loves were betting on horses and flying kites. He had a system that involved betting on the favorites listed in the *New York Daily Mirror* in increasing amounts until he won. If the favorite didn't win in the first race, you bet enough money in the second to make up for the loss and win some money, and so on. It was a foolproof system, he told me. All one needed was enough money so one could keep betting until one won. Unfortunately, in the several years that I went to the tracks with him in Florida and New York State, he never had enough money to really test the system.

His kite flying grew out of one of the items in the mail order catalog that he marketed. It was a special kind of box kite, and Hal liked to go around the country flying it. I often went with him, but the nagging thought that this was not an appropriate type of outing for two adults never left me. Ultimately, that relationship, like all the others, ended.

And then I met Roberto on a blind date. One afternoon in Washington, after I had given a speech on women's rights, a woman who had been in the audience came up to the lectern and introduced herself. Her name was Anita De Lemos, and she was a minor league Perle Mesta, the legendary Washington, DC, hostess. Anita was an exotic woman, with a background that included the

Dominican Republic and various European countries. She had had a number of husbands, a daughter with whom she had a rocky relationship, and a son who had vanished in the mists of time. She was constantly throwing parties, many to benefit the City of Hope Hospital in Los Angeles, but others just to bring interesting people together. She collected such people. Shortly after I met her, she invited me to a picnic she was giving in Virginia and told me she was also inviting a banker whom she thought I'd like. Unbeknownst to me, she had also invited my friend and colleague at the EEOC, Patsy, to the picnic and had arranged for a Hispanic friend, Roberto Fuentes, to drive Patsy to the picnic.

I saw Patsy and Roberto as soon as I arrived at the picnic but gave him only a passing glance. He was a handsome, well-built man in his early forties, dressed in a T-shirt and slacks. He looked like the proverbial "Latin lover," with his dark hair and mustache—decidedly not my type. Besides, I was there to meet a banker, and Roberto was with Patsy. I was never one to attempt to snare a friend's beau. So I set off to meet the banker. When I met him, we spent about thirty seconds greeting each other and went our separate ways. Neither of us had the slightest interest in the other.

The day would have been a total bust if the entire picnic group hadn't gone en masse to another party. There, I met Luigi*, a handsome Italian, to whom I was immediately attracted and with whom I spent the night.

The result of all that was that a year later—at the age of forty-two—I finally married. I married Roberto.

27.

MARRIAGE

Shortly after I began to date Roberto, he let me know that he did not want to marry again. He'd been married before, and he simply "couldn't go through another divorce."

After we'd dated for about six months, however, I told him that *I* was interested in marriage and a family. If he was not, that was OK with me, but then we needed to start seeing other people. Not that there were then any other people interested in seeing me, but he didn't know that. Roberto, passionate Latin male that he was, wouldn't hear of my seeing anyone else. He couldn't bear the thought of losing me, but he also couldn't bring himself to contemplate marriage again. So he asked for time to decide, and I agreed. I gave him three months.

Shortly before the end of the three months, we attended the wedding of a friend of mine in New Jersey. On the drive home, Roberto said, "I want to break that glass." This was a reference to the traditional breaking of a glass underfoot by the bridegroom at the end of the Jewish wedding ceremony. That was my marriage proposal.

Some months after Roberto's proposal, we began to make wedding plans. Our biggest difficulty was finding a rabbi who would marry us. Although Roberto did not actively practice his religion, he had been born a Protestant. In 1970, there were hardly any rabbis in the Washington, DC, area who would conduct a Jewish wedding ceremony between a Jew and a non-Jew. Finally, we found a Reform rabbi who would, and we made an appointment to see him.

Shortly before the date set for the appointment, I was having lunch with a colleague at the EEOC, Herb Hammerman. The discussion naturally turned to my forthcoming marriage, after which I talked about the child I planned to have and the Jewish upbringing that child would receive. With regard to having a child, the fact that I'd be forty-two years old when I got married was irrelevant. Mother and Dad had raised me as a "nice Jewish girl" and nice Jewish girls got married and had a child, even if they were somewhat long in the tooth.

"Have you discussed with Roberto the fact that you want to raise your child Jewish?" asked Herb.

"No," I answered. "What is there to discuss? Roberto doesn't practice any religion. Obviously, I'll raise my child Jewish." Under Jewish law, any child of a Jewish mother is automatically Jewish.

"Well," continued Herb, "I think you should discuss it with Roberto." I saw no problem with that. The following Sunday Roberto and I were going to see the rabbi whom we had found to conduct our wedding ceremony. I could discuss it with Roberto en route.

As we were riding to the rabbi's home in suburban Maryland, I broached the subject of our future child's Jewish upbringing. "I have no objections to your raising our child Jewish," said Roberto. "But I do not want any more children." He had already had three children with his first wife, who were, at that time, ten, twelve, and fourteen. He'd been through all the stages of raising children, including changing diapers in the middle of the night, and he did not intend, at forty-four, to go through them again. He pointed out that when any child of ours would be ready for college, with the consequent expense, *we'd* be going on Social Security. No, what he wanted now was a lover and a companion.

I was stunned. At the age of forty-two, I had finally found someone who wanted to marry me (albeit reluctantly) and someone I wanted to marry, and now it would not come to pass.

Perhaps I shouldn't have been as nonplused as I was. Roberto had made it clear early in our relationship that he was uninterested in marriage, a house, and children. However, since I felt so strongly that I wanted these very things, I didn't give sufficient weight to his feelings. Furthermore, when he agreed to get married, I assumed the rest went with it. But I had assumed incorrectly.

"Well, there's no sense driving to the rabbi, Roberto," I said. "I have no interest in getting married if we're not going to have a child. Why don't you just turn the car around?"

"No sense doing that now," he answered. "The rabbi's expecting us. And we're almost there. We may as well keep going."

In that state of affairs, we arrived at the rabbi's house. The rabbi turned out to be a tall, balding, pleasant fortyish man. He must have seen something in my face because we'd no sooner seated ourselves in his living room when he said, "Sometimes couples have a wonderful time while they're dating, but when they begin to contemplate marriage, the fun goes out of their relationship." At that, I began to cry.

"What's wrong?" asked the rabbi. "Does your family object to your marrying a non-Jew?"

"No," I answered, through my sobs. "My mother, brother, and sister-in-law are crazy about Roberto."

"Is it *your* family then that is unhappy with this match?" asked the rabbi, turning to Roberto.

"No," Roberto answered. "They're all fond of Sonia. My sister, Norka, said she's never seen me this happy since my divorce."

"Are there any other problems?" the rabbi asked.

"No," answered Roberto. "No problems."

Through all this, I kept sobbing. For some reason, I was unable to tell the rabbi what had happened in the car. Instead, I said, "I don't think I'm ready to get married yet, rabbi."

The rabbi ignored my statement. He took out a small notebook and, looking at it, said, "Have you thought of a date for your marriage?"

"We'd thought about October," I answered, "but that's irrelevant now. I'm just not ready to get married."

"I have either October 17 or October 24 available," continued the rabbi, again ignoring my comment. "Which date would you prefer?" When I just kept sobbing, he said, "Well, let's just say October 24."

"Anyway," he continued, "I always see couples twice before I marry them. So, how about next Sunday—same time?" Still crying, I nodded my head. It was ridiculous, but I agreed to come again on the following Sunday, and Roberto and I left.

As soon as we were outside, I said, "Roberto, I've never been abroad; I've always concentrated on my career. All my friends have traveled. Why don't I go to Europe for six months, and when I return, we can see how we feel about each other?" Roberto said nothing. We got into his car to go home.

"Why do you suppose the rabbi does this?" I mused as we were driving home. "He sees couples twice and then performs the marriage ceremony, all for $75. It hardly pays. I wonder why he does it."

"He does it for the laughs," answered Roberto.

"For the laughs?" I asked. "What do you mean?"

"Don't you think it's funny," he chuckled, "for a 42-year-old woman to say she thinks she's too young to get married?" At that, we both laughed uproariously, and all the tension of the last hour was released. Without another word, we both understood that we were going to be married after all.

28.

A PLACE TO LIVE

After we'd been dating for some months, Roberto moved into my one-bedroom apartment at Potomac Towers. Several months later, when we decided to get married, we also decided to look for a bigger place. We liked Arlington and decided to look for a two-bedroom apartment there.

We were standing in one such apartment talking to the manager of the building one day when she turned to Roberto and asked, "Are you an American citizen?" Because of his Spanish name, Latin looks, and slight Hispanic accent, she had become concerned about his citizenship. Ironically, Roberto had been a US citizen at birth. Although he had been born in the Dominican Republic, he had acquired US citizenship through his father, who was born in Puerto Rico. I, on the other hand, was an American citizen through naturalization. But the manager had no similar question for me. I looked and sounded like an American. We did not rent that apartment.

Next, we found an apartment we liked at Timberland Place*, and I signed the application form. Shortly thereafter, the resident manager sent me the lease, which Roberto and I both signed and mailed back.

Some weeks passed without notification that the lease had been approved. When I called the manager, she said approval of the agreement had been held up because she needed a second application form signed by Roberto. "No problem," I said. "I brought a copy of the form home with me. I'll have him sign it when he comes home from work tonight and mail it to you tomorrow."

When Roberto came home that evening, he bristled at the requirement that he sign the application form. He had become sensitized to discrimination through my activities, and this time, he was more sensitive than I was. "Why do they need my signature?" he asked. "If *I* had been the one to sign initially, would they now be asking for *your* signature?" I didn't know but thought it would be worthwhile to ask.

I called the manager and asked why she needed Roberto's signature. "We always get two signatures when a married couple will be living in the apartment," she said. I asked if she would have asked for my signature if Roberto had signed the application. "Yes," she said. I then asked why she needed two signatures on the application form. At that point, she contradicted her prior statement and said that Timberland Place did not require a signed application from the wife where one had been obtained from the husband. But when the situation was reversed, "We need to get the signature of the head of the household."

"You don't understand," I told her. "I'm a feminist. My husband will not be the head of the household; we will head our household together." I explained that I was in the field of women's rights; that we planned to have an egalitarian marriage; that I'd been employed as a federal government attorney for thirteen years and planned to keep working; and that we both planned to contribute financially to the support of the family unit.

"I don't care if you make more money than he does," she then screamed at me. "He's *still* the head of your household."

We didn't rent that apartment either.

We went to Fairfax County next. But there was a problem with the apartment we found there. The building did not have a desk that provided services as Potomac Towers did. I was concerned that there would be no one to accept deliveries of packages and expressed my dissatisfaction to the manager. But by this time we were so tired of apartment hunting, we nonetheless applied for the apartment.

Shortly thereafter, I received a notice saying that our application had been denied. I could not believe it.

I called the manager, who confirmed that the company had denied our application but gave no reason. The only explanation I could think of was that Roberto, about whom I really knew relatively little, must have had a problem with a rental agent, manager, or landlord in the past, and *this* manager had discovered that in checking his record. I called Roberto immediately and asked him. "No," he said. "I've never had a problem." This did not make sense.

As fate would have it, I had no sooner completed my conversation with Roberto when my friend, Hank Schmerer, called from Ft. Lauderdale. "What's new?" he asked. I told him about our being turned down for the apartment. He thought about it for a few minutes. Then he asked, "Did it occur to you that it might be because you're Jewish?"

"No," I answered. "That never occurred to me."

"Well," he continued. "Did you see the names of any of the other tenants?" As a matter of fact, I had. As we were passing the various apartments, I had looked at the names on the doors.

"Did you notice any Jewish names?" he asked.

"Come to think of it," I answered. "I didn't."

"That's it, then," said Hank. "That building doesn't want Jews."

Hank told me that HUD enforced the Fair Housing Act that prohibited discrimination in the sale and rental of housing based on race, color, religion, or national origin. He strongly urged me to file a complaint of discrimination with HUD.

I discussed it with Roberto and we decided to file a complaint. For good measure, we included a complaint of discrimination based on national origin. Perhaps the manager was also prejudiced against Puerto Ricans.

Some time later, a HUD official told us the results of the agency's investigation. We had not been turned down because I was Jewish or Roberto was Puerto Rican, but because I was "uppity." The manager did not want to rent to a "troublemaker," a woman who was presumptuous enough to raise questions about building services.

We decided to buy a house.

29.

AND BABY MAKES THREE

Sister Jean Marie

Although Roberto had agreed to our having a child, he still didn't want one. So he gave me a deadline of six months after our wedding: either I'd become pregnant within that time, or we'd forget the whole thing. I agreed to his condition, thinking that if I didn't meet the deadline, I could always ask for an extension.

It usually takes a couple from six to twelve months to conceive. Roberto assumed that with a 42-year-old woman who'd never had a child, his chances of avoiding fatherhood for six months would be pretty good. His chances got even better when, six weeks before our wedding date, I checked into the Georgetown University Medical Center for the removal of ovarian cysts. This was not the ideal time for a gynecological operation. I didn't know whether I'd be physically able to stand up for the ceremony, much less engage in marital relations thereafter.

When I had settled myself into my hospital bed, I noticed a large wooden cross hanging on the wall above my bed. I buzzed for a nurse, and, when one appeared, I said, "Please remove that cross." The nurse was dumbfounded.

"This is a Catholic hospital," she said.

"I know that," I said, "but I'm Jewish. Please remove that cross."

"No one's ever made such a request before," she told me. That was the wrong thing to say to me. I have always bristled when given that rationale as a reason for not doing something.

"I'm making it now," I said. "Please take down the cross." The nurse reluctantly removed the cross and placed it in the drawer of my night table.

Although I was anxious to have a child, I was concerned about the risks associated with pregnancy in an over-thirty-five woman. And I was not just over thirty-five; I was over forty. Before going into the hospital, I had looked into the problems of the older mother and learned that there were two leading geneticists in Washington, each associated with a university medical center: one, with Georgetown and the other with George Washington (GW). Now that I was at Georgetown, I had an opportunity to meet the geneticist there sooner than I'd planned.

While I was recovering from the surgery, which also resulted in the removal of three-quarters of my right ovary, I asked to see this geneticist. When he entered my room, I realized he was both a geneticist and a priest. He came with an acolyte and asked my permission for the young man to remain while he spoke to me. He then spent two hours regaling me with the horrors that loomed when the mother was older. For the mother, they were: deep venous thrombosis, gestational diabetes, hypertension, postpartum pulmonary embolism, prolonged labor, preterm delivery, Caesarean section, placental abnormalities, and maternal mortality. For the child, they were low birth weight, fetal macrosomia (excess weight), fetal distress, late fetal death, and Down's syndrome. It was a nightmare. The dreams of a lifetime were shattered in those two hours. When the geneticist-priest left, I was a basket case.

He had barely shut the door, when I heard a timid knock. "Come in," I said. The door opened slightly, and I glimpsed a wisp of a woman in a black street-length uniform. She introduced herself as Sister Jean Marie, a nun who visited patients. "How are you doing?" she asked. There was such compassion in her voice that I began to sob uncontrollably and to pour out the story of the geneticist-priest and his catalogue of horrors. Sister Jean Marie listened until I had finished sobbing and talking. Then she began to talk to me soothingly about the situation— about the risks and the options I had. She said she'd pray for me, and she did not say that in a perfunctory manner. She asked if I wanted to go to the hospital chapel and pray with her. I said I did, and the two of us went to the chapel and prayed, each to her own God. The tension of the past few hours eased, and I remembered there was another geneticist in town. Maybe his prognosis wouldn't be quite so dismal.

Sister Jean Marie visited me daily after that, and we became fast friends. As a result, toward the end of my hospital stay, I again buzzed for a nurse. As fate would have it, I got the same nurse who had reluctantly removed the cross from the wall of my room. "Put back the cross," I said. This time she was even more dumbfounded than before, but she said not a word. Obviously, the Lord worked in mysterious ways. She returned the cross to its place on the wall.

Becoming Pregnant

After Roberto and I were married, I went to see the other leading geneticist in the Washington area, Dr. Cecil Jacobson, a professor at the GW Medical Center. He took an altogether different approach. He said there were only two dangers for the older mother: Down's syndrome, a congenital disease characterized by mental deficiency, a broad face, and slanting eyes; and problems during labor.[6] He said the first could be detected by amniocentesis and monitoring the fetal heartbeat could guard against the second. If the fetal heartbeat revealed possible problems, a Caesarean section would be an option.

Amniocentesis, a new diagnostic procedure at that time, involved removing a sample of the amniotic fluid and studying the fetal cells it contained for genetic disorders. If genetic disorders were revealed, abortion would be an option.

When I discussed amniocentesis with Roberto, he was reluctant to have me undergo the procedure if I became pregnant because of the risk involved. Insertion of the needle used to extract the fluid could cause lethal injury to the fetus. Dr. Jacobson suggested that Roberto and I come to his office so he could discuss the procedure with us. We did, and he went over the procedure in detail, explaining that through the use of a sonogram, he could determine the position of the fetus and avoid harm to it when inserting the needle. Roberto was assured of the safety of the procedure and dropped his objection.

Now all I had to do was become pregnant. I was forty-two years old, newly married, with one-and-a-quarter ovaries, a husband who didn't want a child, and a six-month deadline. Three months passed with no sign of pregnancy when my friend, Shannon O'Connor*, invited me to lunch. She was a close friend from the days when we were fellow attorneys at the NLRB, had two children, and was a strong proponent of motherhood.

"What are you doing about getting pregnant, Sonny?" she asked.

"Doing?" I asked. "Nothing special. Just sleeping with my husband."

"Sonny," she asked, "whenever you've wanted a new job or anything else in your life, did you just sit back and wait for it to come to you?"

"No," I answered, "Of course not. I went out and hustled for it."

"This is no different," she said. She reminded me of the efforts she and her husband, Ronnie*, had made before she conceived their first child. "What doctor are you seeing?" she asked. I told her I was seeing Dr. Thomas Gilday, who'd been my gynecologist for years. Dr. Gilday, however, had subtly discouraged my getting pregnant, I presumed because of my age. I thought it ironic that he was discouraging my having one child when he had eight. When Shannon heard this, she said, "I think you should see my doctor, James Sites. He's chief of Obstetrics and Gynecology at GW." Ronnie was an anesthetist at that hospital and well connected there. I knew that any doctor Shannon chose would be first-rate and I made an appointment to see Dr. Sites.

When I entered his office, Dr. Sites asked me why I was there.

I told him that I had been married for three months and was not yet pregnant. He was amused.

"We don't usually do fertility studies on couples who have been married only three months," he said.

"I understand that," I said, "but I only have three more months." I explained my agreement with Roberto. Dr. Sites examined me and saw no problems. "You're built like a teenager," he said. He suggested I have intercourse with Roberto on the most fertile days of my menstrual cycle. Then, if I didn't get pregnant within the next three months, and if Roberto agreed to an extension of my six-month deadline, he would run some fertility tests on us. As I was leaving, I mentioned that Dr. Gilday had said that if I got pregnant, he'd put me on DES [diethylstilbestrol]. "What for?" asked Dr. Sites.

"To prevent my losing the baby because of my age," I said.

"I see no need for that," said Dr. Sites. [7]

I went home, followed the doctor's instructions, and at the end of three more months I was pregnant. Roberto was chagrined. He had never imagined that I would indeed get pregnant. But there was nothing he could do. I had become pregnant within the deadline.

Amniocentesis and Tay-Sachs

When I was 4½ months pregnant, Dr. Jacobson performed the amniocentesis. Several weeks later, his office told me that the fetus was female and that the child I was carrying would not have Down's syndrome. I was, of course, thrilled.

One more trial awaited me. I was listening to the radio when I heard a reference to pregnant Jewish women. It seemed there was a disease called Tay-Sachs caused by the congenital absence of a vital enzyme. The gene that causes this disease is present in about one in twenty-five Ashkenazic Jews in the US, Jews descended from Central and Eastern European Jews. Tay-Sachs, which develops in infancy, leads to blindness, dementia, convulsions, extensive paralysis, and death, usually in two to four years.

The announcer stated that free tests for Tay-Sachs were available at a local clinic. I grabbed my coat and was dashing out the door when the announcer added that testing was recommended only where both parents were Jewish; both had to be carriers to pass the disease on to their child. I took off my coat. It was gratifying that my intermarriage, which was supposed to cause so many problems, had this unexpected benefit.[8]

Delivery

After I was pregnant for some months, I convinced Roberto to join me in taking Red Cross and Lamaze classes. The only lesson that made an impact on me in the Red Cross course involved large posters on easels showing the various bilious shades of green of infant feces. We were required to study these so as to be ready to identify the nature of our child's feces. After Zia was born, I checked her feces but never saw any the color of those in the Red Cross posters. I never determined whether there was something was wrong with Zia or the posters.

In the Lamaze classes, I practiced the breathing I was to do at the onset of labor pains. All went well until Saturday, January 29, 1972. Roberto and I had not yet completed our Lamaze classes at the time. I had worked the preceding day as usual, and Roberto and I had gone out that evening. On Saturday morning, as Roberto was about to leave for Baltimore to see his three teenage children, my water broke. I called Dr. Sites' office and spoke to his associate, Dr. McKelvey, who told me that if I didn't go into labor within twenty-four hours, he would induce labor. Roberto wanted to go on to Baltimore anyway, but I prevailed upon him to stay home. Finally, after almost nine months of my asking him to get Zia's room ready, he busied himself with laying the carpet on her floor and setting up her crib.

Except for the breaking of my water, there were no other developments, and I went to bed around midnight. Roberto didn't join me as usual because he was engrossed in watching *To Kill a Mockingbird* on TV, which I'd already seen. Around 2:30 AM, I was awakened by abdominal pain and saw the "bloody show," the telltale sign that labor is imminent.

"I'm in pain, Roberto," I said. "And I just saw the 'bloody show.'"

"Go back to sleep," he said. The movie had just ended and he was ready for a good night's sleep. "It could be hours away."

"I can't sleep," I said, "I think I'm having labor pains."

"Do the breathing," he ordered. He was really tired.

"The Hell with the breathing," I said, "I'm in pain."

Those breathing exercises were great at the Lamaze classes when all of us prospective parents did them together in an atmosphere of calm and well being, but this was different. Also, I was worried because my labor pains weren't coming in intervals of decreasing length as we'd been told they would. I just had continual severe pains.

Getting up, I said to Roberto, "I'm going to call the doctor."

"You can't call the doctor now," he said. "It's 2:30 in the morning."

"You're going to tell me I can't call the doctor?" I said, in my most imperious tone. And, so saying, I called Dr. McKelvey and explained my physical condition. Go to the hospital," he said. "I'll meet you there."

Roberto finally realized he wasn't going to get any sleep that night and got up. Frantically, we packed a small bag for me and drove off to GW. En route, my pains were unbearable. I wondered why I had gotten myself into this situation and vowed never to do it again. Since I was 43½, I knew this wouldn't be a difficult vow to keep.

My pains disappeared as soon as the doctor administered an epidural injection. I was conscious throughout the delivery, Roberto was with me, and at 9:09 AM Zia was born, a healthy six-pound ten-ounce girl.

Nursing

A day or so after the delivery, I was walking in the hospital corridor when I recognized a young Hispanic man who also lived at Potomac Towers. "What are you doing here?" I inquired. It turned out that his 24-year-old wife had just delivered a baby, too, and was recuperating in the room directly across from mine.

During my pregnancy, I had joined the La Leche League, a support group for women who breast-fed, and had determined to breast-feed Zia. I had only nursed her a few times when the nurse brought her into my room one morning for her 2 AM feeding and placed her in my arms. As I looked down at the suckling baby, I realized for the first time that I didn't like her face: she had a homely nose.

I looked at her closely. Oh my God! I didn't like this kid. And she was going to be living with me for at least the next seventeen years. There was no way out. But that nose was so unattractive. Well, what could I expect? She had a Jewish nose. But *I* didn't have a Jewish nose. Why did she? Maybe she had Roberto's nose. Everyone always said he looked Jewish. But he had a beautiful nose. Why did she have such an ugly one?

At that point, I was about to shift the baby to my other breast when the nurse returned. "I'm so sorry, Ms. Fuentes, she said. "We brought you the wrong baby." And, so saying, she scooped the baby up in her arms and left. Shortly thereafter, she brought another baby in for me to nurse, who she said *was* Zia.

I was stunned, and then I began to worry. I worried that the baby I had fed might be allergic to the mother's milk I had given her. I wondered whether the doctors would tell that baby's mother what had happened. I determined to talk to the mother. Later that morning, I asked the nurse to tell me whose baby I had breast-fed. She told me it was the baby of the woman across the hall, the wife of the Hispanic man I'd met in the corridor. I went to her room. She was lying in bed, pale.

"Did they tell you I had breast-fed your baby?" I asked.

"Yes," she said. "That's the only mother's milk my baby will get."

"Why is that?" I asked.

"Because I'm unable to breast-feed," she said.

We chatted a while, and she said to me, "You're lucky you can walk around." Again, I was mystified by her comment.

"Why is that?" I asked again. She explained that she'd had a Caesarean section and wouldn't be able to walk for four or five days.

I left her room feeling sad about her situation but grateful for mine. Here was a woman about half my age who hadn't been able to deliver normally or breast-feed. So far, it looked as if I'd be able to cope with the difficulties of being an over-35 mother.

But I never did get over having the wrong baby brought to me. There's always been a corner of my mind where I wonder if I got the right baby after all. Periodically, for reassurance, I go down to the basement and look through Zia's baby book for the little hospital bracelet I cut off her wrist when I brought her home. It always says, "Female, Ms. Sonia Fuentes, 9:09 a.m., 1/30/72."

Zia Monina

When I had gotten the results of my amniocentesis, I was thrilled to learn I'd be having a girl. My lifelong desire for a child had always been for a girl. Now all we had to do was find a girl's name. Roberto and I ran through a number of names, but neither of us was taken with any of them.

Then, as I was driving the car one day, the name just popped into my head: Zia Monina Fuentes. Zia would be in memory of my father, Zysia. And Monina was Roberto's late mother's name. Both our parents would be memorialized, and, furthermore, the name had a mellifluous sound to it.

When I got home, I excitedly told Roberto what had happened in the car and asked what he thought of Zia Monina as a name for our baby. "I can live with it," he said, which was about as enthusiastic as he ever got. So, Zia Monina it was.

Weaning

I was elated when I brought Zia home; my dream of a lifetime had been realized—I had a baby. I planned to remain home with her for six weeks and then return to work. But I wondered how I'd be able to leave her in six weeks; she was so adorable, and it was so wonderful to hold her in my arms.

For the first few weeks, I felt as if she and I were in a world of our own, in our own cocoon. We had no need of anyone else. But as the weeks went by, our closeness became suffocating. I was with Zia all day long, kept in the house by my nursing schedule. I had heard that some women used a breast pump and stored their milk so as to be free of the demands of the nursing schedule, but that idea didn't appeal to me. And so I remained in the house all day— nursing Zia, bathing her, changing her, watching her sleep, and watching her wake.

I began to crave adult company and conversation. So, I de-cided to give a series of small dinner parties. This would give me a chance to kill several birds with one stone: I could hone my culi-nary skills, get some adult company and conversation, and accede to the requests of my friends to see the baby.

Unfortunately, it didn't work out quite as I had hoped. My friends were delighted to come. And so I found myself spending my days not just in the endless round of nursing, diapers, and bathing Zia but also in planning my constant parties, shopping for groceries in between nursing, and cooking. By the time my friends came in the evening, I was so exhausted from this routine, I couldn't enjoy their company. Furthermore, the conversation wasn't the stimulating conversation I had sought; it was largely confined to the baby.

Roberto's life, on the other hand, hadn't changed all that much. He had the best of both worlds. He still went to work every morning, but now when he came home, he came home not only to a wife but also to a baby—a baby who was clean, fed, and otherwise cared for. When I watched him leave for work jauntily every morning, I began to hate him. And I began to hate the four walls that were closing in on me. This was supposed to be the happiest time of my life. Why was I feeling so depressed? Didn't I have everything I'd always wanted? I had been home for less than five weeks.

In the middle of that fifth week, Roberto came home from work one evening and announced, "You're going back to work next week."

"What are you talking about?" I asked. "I planned to be home for six weeks."

"I don't care what you planned," he said. "You've become impossible since you've been home. You're returning to work next week."

"I can't do that," I said. "There's something called weaning. I'm not sure how it works, but you have to do that before you can stop nursing a child."

"Well, find out what it is and do it," he grumbled. "This can't go on."

I called Dr. McKelvey and explained the situation to him. "What's weaning?" I said.

"Give her a bottle," he said.

"But what about weaning?" I repeated. "Don't I have to do that?"

"Just give her a bottle," he repeated.

The next day, I bought baby bottles and formula and prepared Zia's milk. She took to the bottle as if she'd been doing it all along, and I returned to work the following Monday. Happily, my days as a full-time mother were over.

A Matter of Concern

When Zia was four months old, I took her for a special visit to the pediatrician, Dr. Javedan. My visit and the anxiety he saw on my face puzzled him.

"Why are you here again, Ms. Fuentes?" he asked. "You were here two weeks ago."

"I'm very worried, doctor," I began. "Zia isn't doing anything. I've always been considered bright; all my life I thought I'd have a bright child. My husband is bright, too. Zia's four months old, and she doesn't do anything. She eats and sleeps, of course, and soils her diapers, but, beyond that, she just lies there on her back staring at the ceiling. I'm terribly worried. I don't know how I'll adjust to having a child like this. What's wrong with her, doctor?"

"I've never found anything wrong with her," Dr. Javedan said. "She's only four months old. What did you expect her to do?"

"I don't know. I thought she'd show me something, doctor," I said. "Some indication of brightness. She hasn't shown me anything. She just lies there."

"I think she'll be OK," said the doctor. He was only partially able to repress a smile. "Why don't you take her home and give her some more time? If you still feel that way in a few months, come back again and we can look into it further."

I took Zia home and thereafter she seemed to be all right. These days she's working as an executive for Ameritech in Chicago—and they haven't noticed anything wrong.

A Laundry Problem

Zia did have a problem though. Whenever she ate anything, she would spit up a considerable amount of her food. Lorena, the young woman who took care of her during her first six months, took to seating her on the kitchen sink when she fed her. That way she could spit right into the sink after a meal.

I took Zia back to Dr. Javedan and inquired about this condition. "It's a laundry problem, not a medical problem." He said. "It will stop when she reaches eight months." And, precisely when Zia reached eight months, she discontinued this awful habit.

But before that, Sister Jean Marie came to see her at our home.

She held Zia in her arms, gave her her bottle, and was the recipient of a hearty upchuck of food onto her habit. I was aghast to see my daughter spitting up on a nun. But Sister Jean took it in stride, as if an infant's spitting up on her habit was an everyday occurrence. She and I remained close friends until the day she died some years later.

A $100,000 Baby

After we'd brought Zia home, we worried about our financial ability to raise her. Since we were both in our forties, we'd need to get life insurance to care for her in the event either or both of us died before she reached maturity. We decided to estimate the cost of raising a child for food, clothing, transportation, housekeepers, babysitters, nursery school, medical and dental bills, and college. We came up with the astounding sum of $100,000.

"We must have made a mistake, Roberto," I said. "We're only planning to have *one* child; most people have two or three. They don't have $200,000 or $300,000. We must have miscalculated. Let's do it again."

We calculated again and came up with the same figure. We had a $100,000 baby!

Actually, that amount was far below what it actually cost to raise Zia. And she was born in 1972. Today it would be more like half a million dollars. So, Zia came cheap.

Hired Help

Who would care for Zia when I returned to work? There were no family members upon whom I could rely. Both my parents were dead, and Hermann and his family lived on Long Island. I had no neighbors who were available. I could not co-op with friends; they had all had their children years ago.

Working part-time or taking a leave of absence were not options for me. Part-time employment for lawyers was not available at that time. Furthermore, as a founder of NOW and other women's rights organizations, I had to set an example to show that women could both work and raise a family. Therefore, I needed to hire help.

While I was pregnant, I hired a practical nurse for the two weeks following Zia's birth and even found a backup in case anything went wrong. This arrangement would give me time to find more permanent help later.

Zia was a model baby at the hospital, but she shrieked without letup her first night at home. Roberto and I hovered over her crib all night but could not determine what was wrong. Not to worry, we finally thought, the practical nurse would arrive in the morning and know what to do. In the morning, Zia stopped crying, but the practical nurse never appeared and we were unable to reach her by phone. The alternate, whose name and telephone number I had carefully kept, had suddenly become ill, and was unable to come.

After frantic hours on the phone and with some trepidation, I hired an 80-year-old woman through an employment service that referred senior citizens. Ms. Claus, the German widow of a doctor, was available for a month. She turned out to be a godsend. She was capable and had infinite patience, carrying Zia in her arms all day, thereby freeing me to do other things. When she left, I found a 20-year-old college student through an ad in the paper. Lorena, who had contracted mononucleosis and taken a leave of absence from school, would be available for several months until her next semester started. She was a lovely, caring, young woman who had done a great deal of baby-sitting—but never for a baby. She was as inexperienced around a newborn as I was. The two of us shook with fear whenever we bathed Zia: we were afraid we would drop her in the water and she would drown

Almost every evening when Roberto came home, I'd say, "Roberto, I almost dropped the baby today."

"Almost doesn't count," he'd answer.

After Lorena returned to school, we had a succession of housekeepers, each of whom I hoped would remain with us permanently, and none of whom did. First, I hired Ms. Reynolds*, a middle-aged woman who, though lame, had been highly recommended. On her first day, she tripped several times while holding Zia, almost dropping her each time. We both realized her disability would not allow her to continue. Shirley* had recently arrived from Trinidad. She was so homesick that she cried throughout her preparations for our first dinner and then decided to leave. Jeanette's* previous employer told me that after a year, Jeanette just disappeared one night. "But that year she was terrific," she said. "I'd hire her if I were you. She'll be wonderful as long as she stays." Two weeks after I hired Jeanette, I was awakened by a thud at 2 AM: Jeanette was lying, clad in only a bra and panties, at the foot of the steps. She'd gone out that evening, come home drunk, gone upstairs for something to eat, and fallen down the steps going back to her room. Fortunately, she was unhurt, but it did not bode well.

Several mornings later, I needed to get to the office early as I was expecting a visitor, Joan Davies, one of England's leading feminists. When Jeanette hadn't appeared by breakfast time, I went down to her room—and found it bare. She had left during the night and taken all her belongings. It was 8:00 AM, I was expecting Ms. Davies at 9:00 AM, and Roberto was in Canada on business. I quickly called his hotel room. "You've got to come home," I said. "Jeanette's gone."

"Don't be ridiculous," he said. He had just arrived and was there for an international conference. I'd have to deal with the matter myself.

Hurriedly, I prepared Zia's food for the day, gathered her clothes, diapers, and bottles, and took her to the apartment of Ms. Gomez* in Potomac Towers. She took in children by the day and had cared for Zia in the past when we'd lived there. Somehow, I made it to the office by 9:30 AM, almost in time to greet my visitor.

From then on, my backup arrangement became permanent.

Every morning, I packed Zia up, along with her food and clothing for the day, and dropped her off at Ms. Gomez's apartment en route to work; every evening, I picked her up on the way home.

But I resumed my search for a permanent housekeeper. I called friends and employment agencies and read book and magazines. I learned that there was an employment agency in Washington that specialized in bringing housekeepers to the States from abroad. It would require a long period of form filling and documentation, but the end result would be worth it. I was assured that foreign housekeepers stayed at their posts. They did not disdain live-in work as Americans did.

I spent over a year mired in the necessary paperwork to get government approval to bring Myung Soon Kim* from Korea to this country as my housekeeper. Just when it looked like I had surmounted all the hurdles, Myung Soon wrote that she had a husband and three children, couldn't leave them, and asked if she could bring them along. Since I had no room for a family of five, even assuming we could have gotten the necessary government authorization, I returned to looking for an American housekeeper.

I found Mary Jackson*, hired her and all went well until she returned home one holiday weekend—drunk and argumentative—in the midst of a party we were giving. Roberto insisted I fire her on the spot—she refused to leave and cried, "My baby, my baby," as she held onto Zia. I called the police, who came and took Mary out of the house. The party was over, and I was devastated. I told Roberto I could not go through the phoning, interviewing, training, and leaving procedure again. We returned to our arrangement with Ms. Gomez.

That worked fairly well until I changed jobs and we moved from Arlington to Stamford. I had no Ms. Gomez there, but I found a live-in housekeeper, Gladys*.

Gladys had been with us for six months when I was diagnosed with a ruptured disk and confined to bed. Gladys promptly announced that she had found a clerical job and would be leaving in two weeks. Now I needed not only a housekeeper but also someone to tend to the needs of a bedridden patient. No one would take such a job, so I resorted to hiring temporary help through an employment service. During the next few weeks, I had a new house-keeper every day or two. To each one, I explained Zia's schedule, my own, and the household routine. Some weeks later, when I was finally taken to the hospital for a laminectomy, it was a relief to escape from the almost daily turnover of housekeepers. During my hospitalization, Zia stayed with my niece in Long Island.

While I was recuperating at the hospital, I hired a young woman, sight unseen, from an employment service that recruited college students from around the country as mothers' helpers for the summer. Her name was Sharolyn Hales, she was a heavy-set blond young woman, and she turned out to be a mother's dream as well as a mother's helper. She was one of six children from a Mormon family in Utah; at eighteen, she knew more about childcare, housekeeping, and cooking than I did at forty-six. She also played the piano and had a lovely singing voice. That sum-mer, our house sparkled and echoed with the sounds of beautiful music. We were truly blessed to have her.

When September came, I was again in the market for a perma-nent housekeeper. Flora*, a young woman from Columbia, an-swered our ad in the *Stamford Advocate*, and Roberto and I drove to downtown Stamford to interview her. She was beautiful, intelli-gent, personable, experienced in housework, fluent in English and—most important of all—immediately available. She was also twenty-four years old. "Are you sure you want a live-in position?" I asked her. "A beautiful young woman like you? It can be confin-ing." She told us that she had just broken up with her boyfriend, John, in New York City; had come to Stamford to get away from him; knew no one in town; and would be completely happy living in. We hired Flora.

Two weeks later, she announced that she was getting married. "How could that be?" I asked. "You just broke up with your boy-friend and know no one in Stamford." She had run into John at a party in New York City on her day off; they had reconciled and decided to marry. "Don't worry," she said. "I'll still work for you." She did not want to leave us and would see John on weekends. I was astonished that a newlywed would live with us rather than her husband, but that's just what she did—for a year. Then, she learned that John was having an affair. Flora and John separated and she was a sad presence in our home for a number of months thereafter. Then flowers began arriving for her; John wanted her back. In time, they reconciled on her promise to live with him full-time. Flora, Zia, and I were in tears when she left us.

By this time, it was 1979. My marriage had unraveled and Roberto and I separated; less than two years later, we divorced. Shortly after that, I took a job with TRW, and Zia and I moved to Cleveland.

The next few years saw a succession of housekeepers—so many, in fact, that we sometimes had to distinguish among them by resorting to roman numerals. There was Jenny I*, who left us when her husband started hanging around the house and she realized he was obsessed with me. Jenny II* worked for my friend, Jane Picker, and could only help us on an interim basis. Yetta* had dirty, unkempt fingernails, which repulsed us when she prepared and served our meals. I fired her in short order.

Betsy* came next. Zia was happy with Betsy. Betsy watched TV all day and let Zia join her. This did not leave Betsy any time to clean the house or do the dishes, and Zia began to get bleary-eyed from so much TV. I let Betsy go. Jewel* was a model housekeeper during her first year. In her second year, her social life got out of hand. She was dating several men, including her ex-husband, and her late nights interfered with her coming to work. I had to let her go.

Then I resigned my job at TRW and could no longer afford a housekeeper. Fortunately, I wouldn't need one because I could be home with Zia. That worked well for over a year until I found a position with HUD in Washington, DC, and returned to the Washington area. For my first six months, until the house I bought in Potomac, Maryland, was built, I stayed with a friend in Bethesda, and Zia remained in Cleveland with the mother of one of her classmates so she could complete the school year there.

In June 1986, Zia joined me and we moved into our new home. Zia was now fourteen—and I was liberated. I no longer needed housekeepers or babysitters to take care of her. Now all I had to worry about was college tuition.

30.

LA CASA GRANDE

In 1973, after Roberto and I had lived in our house in Arlington for 1½ years, I got a job with GTE in Stamford. Roberto and I flew to the New York area and took a train to Stamford to look for a house. We had allotted four days to accomplish this. GTE gave us a list of five recommended realtors, and we chose one called Carriage Trade Realtors owned by Arlene Feldstein. Arlene assigned a very competent and experienced realtor named June Rosenthal to us, and we spent several days looking at houses with her. During this time, Roberto was reading the classified section of the *Stamford Advocate*, and one day he noticed an ad for a house headed, *La Casa Grande*—the big house. "Why don't we call the realtor?" he said. "With a heading like that, he sounds like my kind of guy."

"Don't be ridiculous," I answered. "June's a perfectly competent realtor—and the firm's been recommended by GTE. Why get confused with another realtor? I'm sure June will find us something soon."

Roberto persisted, however, and I called the *La Casa Grande* realtor. He turned out to be a nice Jewish guy named Jerry Kranz who ran a company called Northeast Realty. I asked him why he ran an ad titled, *La Casa Grande*.

"Why not?" was his response.

Roberto and I spent an afternoon with Jerry looking at houses, none of which met our specifications.

The next day June found us a lovely house on Newfield Avenue, the street where the Jewish Community Center, the Jewish

Federation, and Jewish Family Services were located. You couldn't get much more Jewish than that. We liked the house, chatted with the elderly couple who were selling it, and returned to June's office to make an offer, which June was to transmit to the sellers the next day.

The next morning, we went to June's office to inquire about the reaction to our offer. "They're not ready to sell yet," she said. We were astounded. We'd discussed our interest in buying the house with the sellers just the day before. "They've just taken the house off the market," June continued. It seemed the sellers owned a lamp store in Stamford, which they planned to sell since they were aging. Instead, they planned to operate their lamp business from a new, smaller home. But so far they'd been unable to get zoning permission to operate a business in the residential area where they planned to buy. Until that happened, they could not sell their current home.

By that time, the four days we had allotted for house hunting were up, and we had to return to Arlington.

The following Sunday, while my mother was spending a week with us, we got a call from Jerry Kranz. He had found a house he thought we'd like. Would we fly up to see it? I told him I'd think about it, but I had no intention of going. The houses Jerry had shown us the previous week hadn't interested us. Besides, my mother was visiting, I didn't have any cash in the house to take along on a trip, the banks were closed, and it would take time to arrange for Zia's care. We'd have to plan a future trip to Stamford to look for houses again, but I certainly wasn't going to fly up every time a realtor had one house he thought we'd like.

Roberto, however, urged me to go. He said he could remain in Arlington with my mother, who could lend me some cash for the trip and take care of Zia. I returned to Stamford alone.

Just as I had expected, I didn't particularly care for the house Jerry showed me. But I gave it some thought and went through the rooms again. I'd seen so many houses by this time, perhaps I needed to compromise. While I was doing this, the phone rang—someone else had bought the house.

Jerry was driving me back to the airport when he said, "You know there's another house that just came on the market. I didn't mention it to you because it's outside of town, and you said you didn't want to be far from the business district."

"Well, as long as I'm in Stamford," I said. "I might as well see it."

Jerry turned the car around and told me the house was at 133 Winesap Road, on the outskirts of Stamford, almost at the New York State line. But en route he checked the mileage and time; it took less than five minutes from the Merritt Parkway, which was the end of the business district, to the house.

I fell in love with the house on sight. It was only 1½ years old, spacious, and beautifully appointed with cathedral ceilings on a tree-shaded residential street. But it was priced at $69,000. Our house in Arlington had cost $47,000 and for three months after I bought it, a voice in my head constantly repeated: "I own a $47,000 house; I own a $47,000 house; I own a $47,000 house." The financial responsibility was a terrible burden. During the time we'd owned the house, we'd sunk another $15,000 into remodeling costs. How could I now buy a house for almost $70,000?

I called Roberto from Jerry's office. "I found a house," I said.

"Good," he said.

"But the seller is asking $69,000. That's too much money."

"Don't buy it."

"But we've seen so many, and I like this house."

"Buy it. It'll be all right." Money never bothered Roberto.

I decided to offer $65,000. Jerry called the seller, who turned it down and refused to make a counteroffer. The house was fairly new and he had just put it on the market. He had no intention of taking anything less than his asking price at this time.

I'd never heard of anyone who didn't bargain on the price of a house. Aside from the price, I could not buy a house from someone who refused to negotiate; it would be a loss of face.

I called Roberto again. "I can't buy the house; the buyer won't negotiate."

"Don't buy it," he said. "Come home. We'll go back together another time."

I was on my way out of the office when Jerry picked a small black book up from his desk and opened it. "Look here," he said. "The difference in your monthly payments over the thirty-year period of the mortgage is miniscule. It's less than $30 a month."

I called Roberto again. "I'm thinking of buying the house. Jerry looked it up, and there's less than a $30 difference in the monthly payments between what they're asking and what I offered."

"Fine," he said. "Buy the house."

I bought the house.

31.

SURVIVING

In 1974, I was in the Stamford Hospital awaiting an operation for a ruptured disk in my back. This was to be my second operation in two years for the same ruptured disk, the one at my fifth lumbar region, and this time I was worried. Last time the neurosurgeon had performed a laminectomy, which resulted in removal of part of the disk that was pressing on a nerve. This time I might need more serious surgery: a fusion of the vertebrae on either side of the damaged disk. If such surgery were required, I would need the services of an orthopedic surgeon as well as a neurosurgeon; I would be under the knife longer; I would need a blood transfusion; there would be a greater possibility of complications; there would be a longer recovery period; and the mobility of my back would be reduced for the rest of my life.

I would not know before the surgery whether or not a fusion would be required. The orthopedic surgeon would be standing by during the operation and would determine at that time whether a fusion would be necessary. I had a two-year-old daughter, a husband, and a job that awaited me. I needed to be able to walk.

In the early evening of the night before my surgery, my cousins, Freddy and Berta Fischel, came to visit. Freddy was the son of my father's sister, Reizel, and Berta was his wife. They were Holocaust survivors, Polish Jews who had met in Germany after the war and then come to the United States. Hermann had picked them up on their arrival at Kennedy Airport, then known as Idlewild. They had settled in Long Beach where Hermann and his family lived. I had known them for years but knew very little of their experiences during the Holocaust.

As we chatted, I began, as usual, to tease Freddy about his eating habits. For example, for breakfast he liked to eat rye bread on which he had rubbed raw garlic. Freddy, like my father, was a man of few words; in the past, he had never responded to my gibes about his eating habits, but this time he began to talk. He told me the Germans had picked him up in Poland in 1940, after which he had been shifted from one concentration camp to another, ultimately spending time in five of them. He talked about the lack of food and how he had learned to survive by eating whatever was available. His peculiar eating habits had developed during this period. Before the Holocaust, he had had parents and three brothers. He alone survived.

Berta joined in the conversation and told of her experiences. She had initially joined the partisans, but as the Germans continued to round up Jews in Poland, her partisan friends suggested she go to Germany. The Germans were recruiting Poles to go to Germany as laborers. With her fair skin and blond hair, they thought she might be able to pass as a non-Jewish Pole.

With false papers, Berta was able join a work transport train to Germany, and she spent the war years working as a domestic on the farm of a German family. The farmer was the brother of one of the top aides to Heinrich Himmler, Reichsführer—head—of the SS, or *Schutzstaffel*—the protection squad, the elite guard of the Third Reich as well as its main instrument of terror. During the SS official's frequent visits to the farm, Berta was terrified, but her identity was never questioned or discovered. The farmer and his family were happy to have another hand to help with the chores.

In May 1945, when she learned the war had ended, Berta walked to the nearest US Army base and declared herself a Jew, but the American officials did not believe her. She was fair-skinned, blond, and had survived the war in Germany. What made her think she could pass herself off as a Jew now?

When Freddy had been liberated from his last camp, he had

found work as a handyman at that Army base. An Army official called him out now and asked him whether he could verify Berta's claim of Jewishness. He began to talk to her in Yiddish, and she responded. They had a brief conversation, which convinced Freddy that Berta was indeed Jewish. The Army official then asked Freddy to help Berta find accommodations. He did so, and three months later they married. After they had been married for nine years, during part of which time they lived in Israel, they came to the United States. And twenty years after that, they stood by my hospital bed and told me their stories.

By the time they finished, evening had fallen, and it was dark. Berta and Freddy kissed me, wished me well, and left the room. I picked up the phone and called Roberto. "Berta and Freddy were just here," I said, "and they told me what happened to them during the war." I briefly recounted their stories to him. "I'm no longer worried about my surgery," I concluded. "If they survived *that*, I'll survive *this*." And I did.

32.

A PUSHY MOTHER

In 1976, when Zia was a little over four years old, I got a call from the psychologist at Briar Brae, her nursery school. "All of Zia's classmates are completing nursery school this June," she said, "and starting kindergarten. But Zia's too young for kindergarten in the Stamford public schools." Stamford's entrance requirement, which had been in effect for thirteen years, required that a child entering kindergarten in September be five years old by the following January 1. Zia wouldn't turn five until January 30. Ironically, prior to the January 1 requirement, the date on which a child had had to reach age five had been January 30.

"Should she repeat nursery school?" I asked.

"No," she said. "Zia's ready intellectually, psychologically, and emotionally. Why don't you call the school principal and see if he'll admit her?"

I called the principal of the Northeast School and explained the problem. He told me that the Stamford Board of Education was currently working on this very problem. They wanted to admit children like Zia who were somewhat short of meeting the age requirement but had gone to good nursery schools. However, they wanted to be able to exclude children coming from other communities whose nursery schools might not meet local standards. Thus far, the Board had been unable to come up with language to do this. He regretted, therefore, that he would be unable to admit Zia to kindergarten until she was five.

I decided to explore other possibilities. I was motivated by two factors. The first was the psychologist's telling me Zia was ready for kindergarten. The second came from my past. When I arrived in the United States, I was almost six years old. I started kindergarten then, was older than my classmates, and remained that way throughout my school career. One of the reasons I had initially shied away from college was that I thought I would be too old on graduation—twenty-two. I didn't want Zia to have the same handicap.

When I looked into other options, I learned about the New Canaan Country Day School. This was a private school nearby that had a fine reputation as a school but not such a fine reputation with regard to admitting Jewish students in the past. However, I had heard they were now anxious to change their reputation vis-a-vis Jewish students. I called the principal and told her the problem with Zia's age. She said if Zia passed an IQ test, she'd be happy to enroll her. Zia took an IQ test, scored well, and was enrolled at New Canaan.

All went well until just before Christmas when Zia rushed into the house one day, bursting with excitement. "I'm going to be an angel and get to walk by the Baby Jesus," she said. It appeared she had been cast as an angel in the school's Christmas pageant. "What?" I exclaimed. "A Christmas pageant? You're Jewish. You're not going to be in any Christmas pageant." I immediately called the principal and remonstrated with her. "What do you mean by putting my daughter in a Christmas pageant? She's Jewish."

"This is our annual Christmas pageant," said the principal. "It's a tradition at our school. Every child is in it."

"You've had a reputation for not enrolling Jewish children in your school. I understood you were trying to change that. Why are you putting on a Christmas pageant?" I asked.

"We've always done that," she said. "No one's ever questioned it before."

"I'm questioning it now, " I said.

"We also celebrate *Chanukah*," she said. "We bring *latkes—*

potato pancakes—into the classroom."

"I don't care," I continued. "I don't want my daughter in a Christmas pageant."

"Well, you're free to pull her out of the pageant," she said. "That's no problem."

"No problem?" I asked. "The entire student body is in a pageant, and my daughter will be pulled out? How do you think she's going to feel about that? If that's your only solution, then this will be Zia's last year at New Canaan."

"I'm sorry you feel that way," she said. "But if you change your mind, we'd be happy to have Zia back."

"Thank you," I said.

I had burned my bridges behind me. I didn't know of another private school in the area. Besides, even if I could find another private school, that might mean I'd have to send Zia to private school for her entire elementary, middle, and high school education. But I was a proponent of public school education when an area had good public schools. I was also saving to send Zia to college; I hadn't anticipated private school tuition, too.

The following spring, I called the principal of the Northeast School again. Zia would be ready for the first grade in the fall. Had the Stamford Board of Education been able to develop language yet that would enable her to start first grade? "No." he said. "They're still working on it."

"I'm in a spot," I told him. "I've told the New Canaan Country Day School that I'm not sending her back there, and the Board of Education won't allow her into the public school. What can I do?"

"I'll tell you what," he said. "Why don't you bring her to the school for a reading test, and, if she passes, I'll admit her."

"Great," I said.

A few days later, I dropped Zia off at the school for the reading test. Several days later, I called the principal to see how she had done. He didn't tell me her score but said he'd enroll her for the coming fall semester. He asked me to come in to do the paper work.

I was elated and came to the school the next day. After I completed the paper work, an aide working in the school office looked at it and said, "Your daughter's too young."

"I know," I said, "But the principal said he'd admit her if she passed the reading test." The aide called the principal out of his office and questioned him about admitting Zia. He asked me to speak to him in his office. "I didn't know Zia was too young," he said. His remark stunned me. I could only assume that he had been acting without authorization when he had agreed to admit Zia based on a successful reading test score. Now that the aide had confronted him, he backed down.

"What do you mean you didn't know she was too young? What do you think all this has been about?" I asked. "If she weren't too young, why would I have called you?"

"Tell you what," he said. "I'll raise Zia's case with the superintendent of schools. Maybe he'll make an exception for her."

"Thanks," I said and went home.

The principal sent a memorandum to the superintendent, pointing out that I had taught Zia to read when she was three, and that she had achieved a high score on her reading test. He recommended that the age requirement be waived in her case and that she be admitted to the first grade.

Several days later, the principal called me. "I'm sorry," he said. "The superintendent turned me down. The Board of Education is still working on the language for admission, and they don't feel they can make an exception at this time."

I was back to square one. I couldn't return Zia to New Canaan, and Northeast wouldn't admit her. What could I do now?

As fate would have it, the very next morning when I picked up the *Stamford Advocate*, the front page headline read: "Parents Vow To Fight School." The article, the lead story that day, was about a Mr. and Ms. Philip Catlett* and their son, Peter*. Peter, like Zia, had gone to kindergarten at a private school because he did not meet Stamford's age requirements; he missed the requirement by *one day*. Now he wanted to attend the first grade in the Stamford school system so he could attend the same school as his older brother. His father had requested a hearing, which the superintendent of schools had denied.

I called the Catletts, told them we were in a similar position, and invited them for coffee at my house the following week. They agreed to come. When I got home from work after talking to the Catletts, I reviewed the books on education Roberto had stashed in a closet. He was a member of the Connecticut State Board of Education, which had only general supervision over elementary and secondary schools and direct supervision over state regional vocational-technical schools. But Roberto had brought home educational materials dealing with all levels of the school system.

In one of the books, I found a Connecticut statute that I thought might be helpful, section 10-186 of the Connecticut Laws Concerning Education. It required every town or regional school district to provide school accommodations for every child over five and under twenty-one. If a town or school district did not do so, the parent or guardian could request a hearing before the appropriate Board of Education, which would have to be conducted within ten days of the receipt of the request.

When the Catletts arrived at my house, I suggested that we use that law to wage a campaign to get Peter and Zia admitted to the first grade. The Catletts agreed. Later that evening, I drafted a letter to the chairman of the Stamford Board of Education. I argued that the meaning of the statute was that *appropriate* school accommodations had to be provided and that the appropriate class for Peter and Zia was the first grade.

I then got another set of allies, my friends, Ronnie and Ed Fein. Their daughter, Meredith, one of Zia's best friends, also missed the age requirement by a short period of time. Ronnie entered the battle with me.

I began to research the subject of age requirements for admission to public schools. I learned that having a rigid age requirement, though easy to administer, was not educationally sound. Not only did it exclude children like Zia, Peter, and Meredith who were academically ready for the grade involved, it also required the admission of children who met the age requirement even though they might not be academically or emotionally ready. Children born prematurely often fell into this latter category. For them, too-early admission was often the start of a school career fraught with difficulties. Enlightened Boards of Education were testing children close to the age requirement and admitting those who were academically and emotionally ready.

With this information in hand, Ronnie and I decided to lobby the Stamford Board of Education. We began with Ellen Camhi, a board member we both knew. Ellen told us there were nine members on the Board and suggested we call each one. We did so and learned that Board Member Sarah Silveira had been trying to get the policy changed for four years and had most recently raised the issue just a few weeks earlier at the Board's May 31 meeting. She had, however, been unable to get the requisite number of votes.

As a result of our calls, board members invited us to attend a working session on June 21. At that meeting, the superintendent of schools supported maintenance of the current age standards. He cited budgetary considerations and the difficulty of testing children individually. The board scheduled another meeting for June 28.

In the meantime, I did additional lobbying. At my request, the executive director of the State Commission on the Status of Women wrote to the chairman of the Stamford Board, pointing out that recent studies showed that young girls might be ready for the first grade before Stamford permitted them to start. Therefore, she concluded, the Stamford policy might have an adverse impact on girls. She added that the policy might also adversely impact young boys with higher than average attainments.

Ronnie and I attended the next Board meeting on June 28. To our amazement, the Board voted unanimously to admit Zia, Meredith, Peter, and any other children who did not meet the age requirement if they passed a series of tests. Ronnie and I were elated—until the school system's director of research and evaluation arose. He explained that the psychologists who administered tests in the schools were already gone for the summer, and that these children would not be able to be tested until after the start of the 1977-1978 school year. He suggested that Zia, Meredith, and Peter be admitted to the first grade in September, that they be tested about a month later, and that a final decision about their grades be made six weeks after admission when their test results had been evaluated. If they passed the tests, they would remain in the first grade; otherwise, they'd be returned to kindergarten.

I was astonished. "Are you kidding?" I asked. "*You're* an educator, *I'm* not. But what do you think it would do to my daughter if she were placed in the first grade and then told six weeks later that she hadn't made it and would be returned to kindergarten? How would she feel in front of her first grade classmates? How would she feel upon being sent back to kindergarten? She's already had a year of kindergarten. That solution is totally unacceptable."

Again, to my amazement, the Board of Education agreed with me. They said Zia, Meredith, Peter, and any other children in their situation would be tested that June and, if they passed, would be admitted to the first grade in September. The headline in the *Stamford Advocate* for June 29 told the story, "School board alters policy on age for entering kids."

In June, Zia, Meredith, and Peter were given two weeks of psychological and academic testing by the school psychologists, who had magically become available. A few weeks after that, Ronnie, Ms. Catlett, and I were asked to meet with the school psychologists. The chief psychologist began by thanking us for waging the struggle to have children tested in connection with school admission.

"You're thanking us *now*?" I asked, fuming at the struggle we'd had to wage. "We're lay persons. You're professional psychologists. Where were you and your colleagues all these years when children who were qualified were kept out of the schools because they didn't meet the age requirements? Why did *we* have to wage this battle?" The chief psychologist did not respond to my question. Instead, she explained the process of testing and told us that Zia and Meredith had passed the tests and were deemed eligible for the first grade. But she recommended that Peter, who had also passed, remain in kindergarten. Since boys tend to lag behind girls in emotional development, she thought it best if he waited another year before entering the first grade. Ms. Catlett acceded to the recommendation.

Thus ended the saga of Zia's admission to the Stamford school system. She, of course, did not appreciate any of this. She hated being the focus of attention. For years afterward, she complained that not only did she have the oldest mother of any student in her classes, but also she was always the youngest student. All would have been well if she just hadn't had such a pushy mother.

But she was unable to make me feel guilty. Years later, she graduated from Winston Churchill High School in Potomac as a National Merit Scholar, and at the University of Michigan, where she was one of four Jewish members of her 120-member sorority, she was elected president of the sorority. Now twenty-seven, she's a senior manager at the headquarters of a leading corporation. It doesn't appear that I did her any permanent harm.

33.

JEWISH BLOOD

In the summer of 1980, when Zia was eight, we were home alone one day in Stamford when there was a knock at the door. I answered it to find two men in their twenties dressed in dark suits. They identified themselves as Mormons; they had come to convert us. I was about to shut the door when one of them mentioned that Sharolyn Hales, the wonderful mother's helper who had spent a summer with us, had sent them. When I heard her name mentioned, I could not refuse to let them in. It turned out they were missionaries who were devoting two years of their lives, as young Mormon men were encouraged to do, to proselytizing. They were there to teach us the Gospel of Jesus Christ, convert us to the Mormon faith, and discuss our future baptism.

They seated themselves in the living room with Zia and me and began to extol the virtues of Mormonism. They started by telling us that Mormons were probably descended from one of the ten lost tribes of Israel, so we were all of the same religion to begin with. Then, one of them said he had spoken to God. This aroused my intense interest. I began to press him for details. When was this? Was it on a Wednesday? What time of day or night was it? What was God wearing? What did God look like? Was God male, female, or some sexless spectral form? My questions were endless.

Faced with all these queries, to my disappointment, the young man backed off. He admitted that he himself hadn't actually spoken to God; another Mormon man had, however, and had told him about it. God hadn't actually referred to Zia and me by name, but He clearly implied that He wanted people like us to become Mormons.

The two young men stayed about half an hour, at the end of which I told them that if Zia and I decided to convert to Mormonism, we'd certainly credit them with the conversion.

When they left, I said, "Zia, do you know what those young men wanted us to do? They wanted us to convert, to change from Judaism to Mormonism."

Zia said, "But, Mommy, we can't change from Judaism. We have Jewish blood."

I explained to her that the term "Jewish blood" had no grounding in reality, that it was just an expression used in connection with Jews, and that everyone had the same type of blood. "You mean *everyone* is A positive?" she asked.

That did it. I went right out and bought her a book on the circulatory system. She learned that we didn't have Jewish blood. But we didn't convert to Mormonism either.

34.

CLEVELAND

I've moved from Berlin to Antwerp to the Bronx to the Catskills to Long Beach to Ithaca to Miami Beach to North Miami Beach to Washington to Arlington to Pittsburgh to Hollywood to Stamford to Beachwood and, finally, to Chevy Chase and Potomac. Of them all, the most difficult move I ever made was from Stamford to Beachwood, a suburb of Cleveland near the better known and tonier Shaker Heights.

Zia, who was almost ten, and I arrived in Beachwood at the end of December 1981. We spent a few days at the Beachwood Marriott Hotel until we could move into our new home. Then on January 1, in the midst of a snowstorm, we moved into our house on Halburton Road. Present with the two of us were my new housekeeper, Jenny I, whom I had hired sight unseen through an ad in the *Cleveland Plain Dealer*, and the two married couples who worked for the moving company.

I looked around the large empty house and felt dreadful; it would be up to me alone to create a life in this house. This was the first time I had moved with Zia, without Roberto's assistance. I knew no one in Cleveland except for the officials at TRW who had hired me, and Lana Moresky, the former Ohio state chairman of NOW.

As the movers started bringing in my furniture and Jenny I was bustling about, I decided to use the phone to make a connection to *someone*. But the phone was dead. It didn't occur to me that this was due to the snowstorm that was raging outside. I thought the line had simply gone dead, so I told Jenny I that I would go next door to a neighbor's to call the telephone company. I couldn't bear to be in this empty house cut off from all contact. "Don't go in the midst of the snowstorm," Jenny ⅃ said. "Besides, the movers are bringing the furniture in, and you need to tell them where it goes." But, unheeding, I ran out. I was running from that empty house and the empty life I needed to fill.

As I ran, I slipped on the snow but kept going until I was right in front of my neighbor's house. And then I slipped again and fell to the ground, landing on my right hand, in front of the massive wooden door of the house. The pain was intense, and, although I'd never had a fracture before, I knew I had broken something in my right hand.

I couldn't stand up, so I began to scream, "Help," to the two young couples who were moving my furniture into the house. Because I could see them easily, I was surprised when they did not respond to my screams. The howling wind that accompanied the snowstorm was covering my shrieks. "Oh my God," I thought. "I'm going to die here alone in Cleveland where I know no one."

I kept screaming for help, and then the heavy wooden door opened slightly, and my neighbor stood looking down at me. She helped me to my feet, brought me inside, and introduced herself as Arlene Silverman. "Hello," I said. "I'm Sonia Fuentes, your new neighbor, and I just broke my right arm." This was too much information for Ms. Silverman to take in all at once, and for a moment she simply stood there, looking at me.

Then she said "Uh, maybe it's not broken."

"Look, Ms. Silverman," I said. "You don't know me. But if I tell you I have a broken arm, you can believe it."

She believed it and called an ambulance. Then she told me she thought she had heard something, but her nine-year old daughter, Abby, was home from school watching television, and Ms. Silverman assumed the noise came from the TV show. When she heard it again, she decided to check, opened the door—and saw me.

Shortly thereafter, an ambulance came with two medical technicians. When they saw the swelling at my right wrist, they put a contraption on it with plastic that blew up like a balloon to keep my wrist in place.

"It looks like you've broken your arm," one of them said.

"I know that," I said, "Can you get me to a hospital?"

The two attendants then named two local hospitals and asked me which one I wanted to go to. I told them I didn't know one hospital from the other and asked them to take me to either one. As they were taking me out to the ambulance, I pleaded with one of them to tell my daughter what was happening to me. He left to do that and, on returning, told me he had done so. Actually, he had told one of the young women movers that her mother was going to the hospital. I was fifty-three at the time, and seeing a twentyish woman outside my house, he logically assumed that she was my daughter. The young woman decided it was a case of mistaken identity and went on about her business.

Zia, seeing the ambulance parked next door, said to Jenny I, "Oh, someone must be sick next door." Thus, no one in my home knew I was en route to the hospital.

When I got to the hospital, I called Ms. Silverman and asked her to please go next door and make sure Zia was all right. She told me she'd already done that, and that Zia was at that moment happily playing in her house with Abby.

The hospital then put me in a waiting room for a while. Also in that room was a young man, and we began to chat. He was a lawyer, like me, and his name was Dominic Antonelli. He said he had injured his foot in a sports accident and was at the hospital to determine whether he had broken anything. After some time, an intern, a native of India, came in, and examined me.

"You have a broken arm," he said at the conclusion of his examination.

"I know that," I said. "Can you help me?"

"Do you have a born doctor?" he asked.

"A born doctor?" I repeated. "What's that?"

He asked again, "Do you have a born doctor?"

"I don't know what that is," I said, close to hysteria. "What are you asking me?"

He just kept repeating the question until I finally figured it out. He was asking me if I had a bone doctor, an orthopedic surgeon.

"No," I said. "I just arrived in town. I don't know anyone."

"That's OK," he said. "Dr. Becker* will be here in three hours." I thought I must have misheard him. "What did you say?" I asked.

"Dr. Becker, the born doctor, will be here in three hours," he said again.

"Are you kidding?" I asked. "I'm sitting here in pain, and you expect me to wait three more hours for a doctor?"

"Dr. Becker will be here in three hours." he repeated. "But if you'd like to see him sooner, you can go to his office."

I did want to see him sooner. I thought I'd call Lana or Arlene Silverman to see if they could help me. As I picked up the receiver, Dominic Antonelli was at my side. He'd overheard my conversation with the intern.

"There's nothing broken in my foot," he said. "And my wife, Debbie, is coming to pick me up. She'll drive you to the doctor."

Shortly thereafter, Debbie appeared, and the three of us went off in their car. The snowstorm had gotten worse and was now a full-scale blizzard. Dom mentioned that Debbie intended to get snow tires for the car but hadn't yet had a chance to do so. "Not to worry," he added. "We'll get you there." And they did.

When we arrived at the office of Dr. Becker on Cedar Road, I realized that if I had to make a call or do anything else that required money, I didn't have a cent with me. I had not, of course, taken my handbag when I went next door to use the telephone. "Could you lend me some change in case I need to make a call?" I asked Dom and Debbie. They immediately gave me seventy-five cents. I looked down at the money. What had happened to me in a few short hours so that I found myself standing in the midst of a blizzard in a strange city asking total strangers to lend me a few cents?

I went upstairs to Dr. Becker's office, where I saw a number of people with metal appliances attached to various parts of their bodies. "What's that?" I asked a tall man who had metal rods attached to his head. He explained that he'd fallen off a ladder at work and had to have those rods inserted in his head. I was sorry for him but glad I didn't need anything like that.

Dr. Becker examined my arm and told me I had a Colles' fracture, a fracture of a tiny bone in my right wrist, and that he would set it in a plaster cast. He told me I'd have to have x-rays regularly to determine whether the cast was continuing to hold the hand in place. He then proceeded to regale me with jokes to lighten my mood. When he got no reaction, he said, "You don't have much of a sense of humor, do you?" I explained that breaking my right wrist upon moving to a new city as a single parent with a nine-year old daughter as I was about to start a new job had, for some unknown reason, deprived me of my sense of humor.

I called Arlene, who came to Dr. Becker's office and drove me home. Next, I telephoned my new boss at TRW, Bob McCarty, told him what had happened and that I wouldn't be able to start work for another two weeks.

Then, although I was back home, there was not much I could do. Outside, it was still snowing. Inside, I was without the use of my right hand, the hand with which I wrote, typed, dressed—did everything. I began to get depressed.

Several days later, I was on a long distance call with a friend when Zia ran in. She shamefacedly told me that she had been playing with Socks, the Silvermans' dog, when he grabbed her mittens and tore them to shreds. I had bought those mittens for her just before we left Stamford as I knew how cold the weather in Cleveland was. Now those mittens were gone, and I could not replace them—I could not drive a car to go and buy her another pair. It was all too much. At that moment, I lost it. I hurled the receiver against the wall and began to scream at the top of my voice. Zia, terrified, ran from the room into the arms of Jenny I. When I calmed down, Zia returned to my room. Due to my becoming hysterical, she'd been unable to finish her story. She then told me that the mittens had in fact been replaced. It turned out that our new neighbors owned seven department stores in the Cleveland area named Silverman's. After Socks had destroyed her mittens, the Silvermans immediately took her to one of their stores, where she picked out a lovely new pair of mittens, which she proudly showed me.

After that, things started to improve. Jenny I's husband, Bill, a handsome, well-built, strong man who had been hurt in a work-connected accident four years earlier, had never returned to work. Although he had fully recovered, he planned to spend the rest of his life living on Workers' Compensation. For a reasonable fee, he offered to drive me to do my shopping and to work. I was thus able to start my new job, but every two weeks I went to Dr. Becker's office for the follow-up x-rays. After one such visit, Dr. Becker's office asked me to return. I wondered what this might be about. When I saw Dr. Becker, he told me that the x-rays indicated that the fracture wasn't healing properly, and, if he didn't fit me with a different type of cast, I'd have a misshapen arm for the rest of my life. He would fit me with the kind of device I had seen coming out of the head of the man in his office who'd fallen off a ladder. Dr. Becker said the device was made of the lightest metal possible, titanium. He did not say, but I learned later, that a veterinarian had developed these monstrous contraptions for use on horses. Now one of them would be used on me, and its insertion would require surgery.

I left the job I'd started late and been on for less than three weeks and checked into the hospital for the surgery. When I awoke after the surgery, I covered my right arm; I could not bear to look at it and screamed for a social worker. One came and began to calm me down. With her help, I removed the blanket from my arm. What I saw was enough to frighten anyone. Six metal pins had been inserted into my right hand starting to the right of my thumb and extending up to my wrist. Above those metal pins and attached to them was a long metal bar.

I looked at this monstrous device attached to my arm, and wondered how I would ever face people again—and how I would ever get into my clothes. But both turned out to be manageable. I remembered reading about a company that designed clothes for people with disabilities but did not know how to contact it. However, my friend, Ruth Shapiro, from Philadelphia came to my assistance. Years earlier, when she was pregnant and expecting a baby in February, she had made a woolen cape to wear during the final months of her pregnancy. She said she would put that on a Greyhound bus in Philadelphia and Bill could pick it up for me at the Cleveland bus station. That's how I got an outer garment that I could wear for the long, cold Cleveland winter.

But what to do about getting into other clothes? After much thought, I gathered up a number of my sweaters and dresses that had seams down the arms. Bill drove me to a local tailor, who sewed triangular inserts into the right sleeves of those outfits so I could insert my arm with the titanium appliance.

And that's how I lived and worked for eight more weeks. I did, of course, get unusual looks and reactions wherever I went. But there were also advantages to the contraption: it was a terrific ice-breaker and, more importantly, it enabled me to write and type comfortably again. I had not been able to do that with the cast. That reminded me of a Yiddish expression and a short story I had read. The Yiddish expression is, *As men geveynt zikh tzu di tsores tanst men mit zey in freyden.* Literally translated, it means, "When you get used to your troubles, you dance with them with joy." The story was titled "Piggotty's Parcel of Shortcomings." Piggotty, an Irish cleaning woman, through a series of events, gets stuck with a parcel and has to tote it around all day. After the initial inconvenience, the parcel serves her well in a variety of ways during the course of the day.

When that metal appliance was removed, my wrist was rigid.

But three months of physical therapy righted it, and I regained the use of my right hand.

Four years later, I left Cleveland.

35.

ZIA GOES TO COLLEGE

When Zia was a sophomore at Winston Churchill High School in Potomac, I began to think about college for her. I went about the project in my usual organized manner: I read books on the subject; I looked at articles in periodicals, such as "America's Best Colleges" in *U.S. News & World Report* and "Ten Great Tuition Deals for Your Dollars" and "How To Grade a College" in *Money* magazine; I attended a meeting for parents of would-be college students at Churchill and a lecture by an educational consultant who specialized in college consulting; I spoke to friends whose children had gone to college and others whose children would soon be going; I reviewed information online—and when I was through, I had lots of information—but I didn't have the slightest idea of how to proceed.

In desperation, I called the college consultant I had heard, Shirley Levin, who lived in nearby Rockville and ran a company called College Bound. She said for a reasonable fee she would work with Zia, starting in her sophomore year, to assist her in selecting appropriate colleges and working through the application process. I leaped at the opportunity to have expert advice in what had become, for me, an overwhelming project.

Our first meeting with Shirley was not propitious for me. Shirley began by giving Zia a questionnaire entitled "Why Are You Going to College?" Zia checked: "To get further away from my mother."

Things improved after that, however. Shirley suggested that Zia apply to seven colleges in three categories: "safety schools," those where Zia's chances of acceptance were practically assured; "realistic schools," those where her chances of acceptance were good; and "reach" or "longshot schools," those where the selection process was very competitive.

I told Zia that in spite of her desire to get further away from me, I would not send her anywhere west of the Mississippi. As a single parent, I knew that in the event of an emergency I would have to fly to her college, and I did not want to be in the position of having to travel suddenly to California or Texas.

The seven schools we agreed upon were Cornell, Northwestern, Washington University in St. Louis, Miami University in Ohio, and the Universities of Massachusetts, Virginia, and Michigan. The latter three were state schools, whose fees would be considerably lower than those of the private colleges, even for an out-of-state student like Zia.

Northwestern was of special interest to Zia. During our time in Cleveland, she had qualified under the Midwest Talent Search for Northwestern's Summer Program for Academically Talented Adolescents. Starting in 1985, after completion of the eighth grade, she had spent three summers at their Center for Talent Development. She really found herself in that program and fell in love both with Northwestern and Chicago. Also, Northwestern had recently instituted a special intensive program called Mathematical Methods in the Social Sciences, which was limited to forty students a year. Zia's best subject in high school was math, she was on the school's math team, and she wanted to study math in college.

Shirley said she would arrange for Zia to visit a number of these seven colleges; to some she ran tours, and at others she had the names and telephone numbers of students she had assisted in the past. Zia could stay in the dorms with those young women and discuss the colleges with them. It seemed an ideal way in which to select a school.

The procedure was not, however, without concern for me. Universities were difficult to get into in the '80s; one of my friends said that even though Zia was a National Merit Finalist, all seven universities might turn her down. Her attendance at Churchill might both help and hurt her. It would help her because Churchill was recognized as one of Maryland's premier high schools, and many of its students were academic achievers. It might hurt her because a university might not want to accept too many students from one high school.

When Zia was in her senior year, I decided that if both a state and a private university accepted her, and if she did not dislike the state school, I would send her to the state school because the difference in costs was considerable. When I told Zia this, she said, "Well, then, why did I apply to private universities?" I told her I hadn't thought this through at the time we began the process, but since she had already applied, we would wait and see what happened. Perhaps some of the private universities would offer her scholarships that would make up the difference.

Zia's visits to the universities were telling. She came back from each trip with a clear impression of the school and whether she wanted to attend it. When she returned from the University of Virginia, she said she'd be happy to go there but still wanted to explore other schools.

It was different when she returned from Michigan, where she had been accepted into the Honors Program. She was exuberant. Her first words were: "That's it!" She had fallen in love with the university and wanted to mail her acceptance in immediately. By that time, she had received acceptances from all of the universities to which she had applied except Northwestern. "Hold on," I said. "You know how you feel about Northwestern. Let's see what we hear from them." Reluctantly, she agreed to wait.

Within the week, we heard from Northwestern. She had been accepted. We were thrilled. If Northwestern would offer Zia a scholarship, that would be her university of choice. She was glad she had waited.

The next day, I called Northwestern and inquired about scholarship assistance for Zia. I was told there was none. When I saw Zia that evening, I told her Northwestern would not offer her a scholarship. I then did the financial calculations and realized it would cost me $17,000 more over the four-year period to send her to Northwestern rather than Michigan. I didn't know what to do. So I did what I always did when unable to make a choice: I decided to get additional information. I told Zia I'd spend as much time as necessary the next day calling experts throughout the United States to inquire as to whether I should spend the extra money to send her to Northwestern. "Mommy," she said. "It means a lot to me that you're even considering Northwestern."

I spent much of the next day at work on a pay phone. My first call was to Shirley Levin. She felt that Zia would get an excellent education at Michigan and that Northwestern did not warrant the additional expense. Friends in the academic community and professors of mathematics at universities around the country unanimously expressed the same sentiment. In fact, one professor felt that putting Zia into the intensive Northwestern program might be harmful for her educational development in the long run. She pointed out that undergraduate school was the time for a broad educational experience and that intense concentration was best reserved for graduate work. Several mentioned the more liberal political atmosphere at Michigan. This was a factor of importance to both Zia and me.

I typed up everyone's comments; they ran to four single-spaced typed pages. That evening, as we were sitting at the kitchen table, I told Zia about my calls to experts around the country and gave her the write-up I had prepared. When she finished reading the material, I said, "Well, what do you think?"

"It looks like I'm going to Michigan," she said. Then she folded her arms on the table, put her head down on them, and began to cry. I tried talking to her, I tried hugging her, but I could not stop her sobbing. Forty-five minutes later when I went to sleep, I could still hear her sobs throughout the house.

The next morning she was sullen, and from then on, she had little to say to me. I tried explaining to her, but it was to no avail. "My friends' parents are sending them to Brown and Yale," she said. "And you are sending me to Michigan. Why did I have to knock myself out all these years trying to get good grades when this is what I get for it?"

A week went by, then two. Zia rarely spoke to me. Nor did she mail her acceptance in to Michigan. Not much time was left. I began to question my decision. Seventeen thousand dollars wouldn't change my life. I called Shirley. "Why don't you send her to Northwestern" she said, "if that's where she wants to go?" I thought about my parents. They had totally opposed my going to college but had never said a word about the cost of sending me to Cornell. I, on the other hand, would have been devastated if Zia *hadn't* wanted to go to college. Why then why was I balking at seventeen thousand dollars? I wished I had a husband to discuss this with, but I did not. My decision had seemed right at the time, but now I wasn't so sure. Nonetheless, I decided to stick to my guns.

At the last minute, Zia mailed her acceptance in to Michigan. The rest of the summer passed in uneasy silence between us. At the end of August, we shipped her things to Michigan and flew there. I got her settled in the dorm and left for home, filled with misgivings.

It wasn't until Zia came home for Thanksgiving that I learned the denouement of this story. Not directly, of course. Zia rarely told me anything directly. I overheard her talking to a friend on the phone. "I love it," she said. "From day one. It's the greatest school."

Postscript. While at Michigan, Zia switched her major from economics in the College of Literature, Science and the Arts to marketing in the Business School. Shortly before graduation, she got a job with a corporation in Michigan. Later, she transferred to the company's Chicago headquarters. There, she finally got to go to Northwestern. She went to Northwestern's Kellogg School of Management at night and got her MBA in June of 1999. I prevailed initially, but Zia prevailed in the long run. And we both won.

36.

A SCHOLARSHIP FOR ZIA

When Zia was accepted into the University of Michigan Honors Program in the College of Literature, Science and Arts, she was awarded a $3,000 academic scholarship. The university told me that no further scholarship money would be available for her since we did not qualify on the basis of financial need.

Undaunted, I decided to seek additional scholarship funds. Zia's tuition and room and board for the first four years, without regard to other expenses, would come to about $65,000. I was over sixty years old and did not relish the idea that a substantial part of my life's savings was going to go for her undergraduate education. I knew that money for graduate school, a wedding, a house and children all loomed in the future—at a time when I'd be retired.

I began to explore additional possibilities. I called and wrote to organizations and individuals across the country—all to no avail. There was no scholarship money available for a bright young woman with outstanding academic credentials—and a Puerto Rican heritage—when she wasn't in financial need.

Unbeknownst to me, one of my letters did hit a target. Since Zia was outstanding in math, I had written to the president of a women's math and science organization. It turned out that she knew a math professor at the University of Michigan, Hugh Montgomery, and had forwarded my letter to him. He called to say he had received some scholarship money from an alumnus, most of which he had already awarded, but he had $2,000 left, which he would like to give to Zia. I was delighted.

Also unbeknownst to me, he then passed Zia's file on to Professor Maxwell Reade at the Liberal Arts College. One morning, I was home doing laundry when the phone rang. I was irritated at being interrupted but answered, and the conversation went like this:

Professor: Hello. I am Professor Reade at the University of Michigan. Is this the home of Zia Fuentes?

Me: Yes. (Pause. The sound was barely audible from the cordless phone.) Would you mind if I took this call upstairs? I can't seem to hear you.

Professor: (Trying to be funny) Have you been paying your telephone bills?

Me: Certainly.

Professor: Are you related to Zia?

Me: Of course, I'm her mother.

Professor: Is Zia planning to go to the University of Michigan?

Me: (Very angry. I had recently gone through a mix-up caused by the University's mistakenly failing to register Zia in the Honors Program.) What do you mean, "Is she going to Michigan?" She's had her application accepted, submitted the form stating that she's attending, turned down offers from other colleges and universities, is about to go to Orientation Week— and, *now*, you ask if she's planning to attend?

Professor: I'm sorry. I didn't know. I'm not on the Admissions Committee; I'm on the Scholarship Committee. Sometimes students get accepted and then don't attend.

Me: (Not realizing the import of what he had just said): How come you're calling about Zia's going to Michigan?

Professor: Someone left her file on my desk. They know I'm always looking for bright students. (Pause) You know, Michigan's an expensive school.

Me: *I know that.* But other schools are more expensive.

Professor: Can you afford to send her there?

Me: Look, if I couldn't afford to send her there, she wouldn't be going.

Professor: (Not giving up) Could you use some help?

Me: (He had finally pushed the right button.) Are you kidding? My ex-husband isn't contributing ten cents to her college education.

Professor: Well, I'd like to give her $2,500 a year for the next four years. I wish it were more, but if she does well, she can apply for more.

Me: (Totally flabbergasted) Well, thank you so much. That's just wonderful.

Professor: What does "Zia" mean?

Me: It doesn't mean anything. It's just a name I made up so she could be named after my father, whose name was Zysia.

Professor: But what does it *mean*?

Me: It doesn't mean anything. In the Jewish religion, we like to name our children after a deceased person who meant a great deal to us. In that way, the person who is gone lives on in the child.

Professor: I see a number of Asian students on campus—and they have names like Wong and Han. When I ask them what those names mean, they always tell me it means something like flower, river, and so on.

Me: Let me tell you something, Professor Reade. Jewish isn't Asian. "Zia" means nothing.

I later remembered that "Zia" does mean something, at least the Yiddish version of it, *Zisel*, does. *Zis* means "sweet," and *Zisel* is the diminutive. I wrote Professor Reade, correcting my past statement. But by that time he'd given up in defeat and just deposited the scholarship money in Zia's account.

PART VII

Sonia Pressman Fuentes and her parents, Hinda and Zysia Pressman
Berlin, Germany, about 1931.

Sonia Fuentes, Norderney, Germany, June 14, 1932.

Sonia and her brother, Hermann Pressman
Antwerp, Belgium
March 31, 1934.

Sonia with her parents,
Zysia and Hinda Pressman,
Graduation from Cornell University, 1950.

Photo courtesy of Vincent J. Graas.
Founding of NOW, Washington, DC, October 1966.
Sonia, front row, third from the right (facing picture), two
seats to the left of Betty Friedan.

Wedding of Sonia and Roberto Fuentes
National Lawyers Club, Washington, DC
October 24, 1970.

Sonia's cousins, Berta and Fred Fischel, in front of Sonia's
Stamford, Connecticut, home, 1970s.

Sonia (center) at her retirement party at HUD, Washington, DC, May 1993.

Sonia with University of Miami (Florida) Law School professors, Richard Hausler and Minnette Massey Coral Gables, Florida, 1990s.

Sonia, standing, with Sarasota, Florida, friends, seated
from left to right (facing picture):
Phyllis McGlyn, Geri Bowman, and Dee Fanella, 1990s.

Photo courtesy of Evelyn England, SAGE, Sarasota, Florida.
Sonia, Sarasota, Florida, 1997.

Sonia and Zia Fuentes, Plainfield, Illinois, 1998.

37.

ALL IN THE FAMILY

Dad

The Peaked Child

As a child and a teenager, I was of normal build—even a little chubby. But, by Piltzener standards, this was unacceptable. My parents saw me as mere "skin and bones." How would "such a skinny thing" ever attract a husband? "A man wants a woman who's *zaftik*—juicy," said my father.

So every year, they took me to the family doctor—Dr. Fernhoff, when we lived in Woodridge; Dr. Breakey, when we lived in Monticello; and Dr. Alterman, when we lived in Long Beach. "What's wrong with her, doctor?" they would ask. "She's so terribly thin."

The doctor would dutifully give me a thorough examination and pronounce me perfectly fit. My parents would shake their heads, but the decision of the doctor had to be accepted. All they could do was wait till next year and try again. Maybe one day the doctor would find out what was wrong.

Will My Real Parents Please Stand Up?

As many children do, I fantasized that my parents weren't my real parents. There had to have been some mistake. Anyone could see we weren't suited to each other. I was an American, interested in books and the world at large. They were uneducated Europeans, whose only interest was taking care of their immediate family. I was certain that one day my real parents would come for me, and I would have to leave.

One day, I told my mother that if my real parents came for me, I would have to regretfully say good-bye to her and Father and go to my rightful home. Mother thought about the consequences of such a turn of events.

"You know," she said to me. "If I found out you weren't my real daughter, I'd still want you to stay with us. We love you. What does it matter whose child you are? What do you say, Daddy?" she asked my father.

"She'd be out in a minute," he answered. "What for do I need to raise a strange child in my house?"

My real parents never came. So, I never found out whether my father would actually have given me up.

Nothing To Be Afraid Of

In my 36-year career as an attorney and executive in various federal agencies and in two multinational corporations, I had occasion to meet a number of powerful men and women. I never experienced any fear before such meetings because I'd been well trained by my father.

As a child, whenever I expressed anxiety about meeting someone in authority with whom I had an appointment, my father would say, "What's the worst he can do to you? Eat you up. And if he does, you'll come out the other end." Not a pretty image, but it stood me in good stead through the years.

And then he taught me a little Yiddish song to sing in moments of stress: "*Ikh bin Gola, der groyser held, far mir tzitert di gantse velt.*" ["I am Gola, the big hero, the whole world trembles before me."] Sounds simple, but to this day, I have but to hum that tune, and I march forward fearlessly to whatever awaits.

Not His Fault

My father wasn't articulate in any language, but he was most comfortable with Yiddish. He didn't, however, limit his Yiddish-speaking to Jews. It was his preferred form of communication with everyone, the coin of his realm. "Dad," I remonstrated with him once, after hearing him give orders in Yiddish to contractors working on our bungalow colony, "you were talking in Yiddish to those men. They don't understand Yiddish, they're *goyim*"—gentiles.

"Yiddish is my language," he answered. "It's not my fault if they don't understand it."

Lots of Land

In the early '40s, whenever Dad took me driving in the Catskills and we passed a stretch of empty land, which was often, he'd always wave toward the land and say, "Look at that land. Why couldn't they let the Jews in to live here?"

I was young and it was a time when I still had the utmost confidence in the wisdom and good faith of my country's leaders. I told my father people far more educated and wiser than we were setting this country's immigration policy and they must know what they were doing.

Of course, I was wrong.

I return to the Catskills from time to time and most of those stretches of land are still there. But the people who could have lived on them no longer are.

The Whorehouse

In the spring of 1947, during my freshman year at Cornell, Mother
and Dad drove up for a visit. We spent a pleasant Saturday touring
the campus. In the evening, we chatted in my room and ate the
kosher dinner Mother had brought along.

The next morning, the screams and shouts of the residents of
my dorm, Balch Hall, awakened me. The screams came closer and
closer. Finally, my father charged in, followed by Mother, who
looked very distressed. "Pack your things," said my father. "You're
going home with us. You're not staying another minute in this
whorehouse."

I was dumbfounded. What had happened since I had bid my
parents good night the previous evening? What produced this in-
sane behavior? And what was my father doing in Balch Hall, which
was strictly off-limits to men?

Mother explained. When they had left Balch the evening before, it had been midnight. On Saturdays, coeds had to be back in
their rooms by midnight. Thus, when my parents walked through
the wide deck at the back of Balch Hall as they were leaving, it was
full of entwined couples kissing good night. Father was aghast at
this display. He'd never seen anything like it. Balch was nothing
short of a whorehouse, and he certainly wouldn't permit his daughter to remain there.

I didn't know how to respond. Should I begin to pack my
things? What would happen to me if I left Cornell? As I was wondering what to do, the housemother, Miss Armor, a no-nonsense,
battleship-type of woman, steamed in. The young women in the
dorm—who had been in various stages of undress when my father
had stormed up the steps to my room—had alerted her to his
presence. She told him he'd have to leave immediately.

"I'm happy to go," he said, "but my daughter's going with
me. She's not staying in this whorehouse."

"What on earth are you talking about?" asked Miss Armor.

When he told her, her lips turned upwards in one of her infrequent smiles. "This isn't a whorehouse, Mr. Pressman. Please don't use such language here. This is a strictly regulated freshman dorm. What you saw was simply young men kissing their girls good night. I admit there were a lot of them, but that still doesn't make it reprehensible. Your daughter's perfectly safe here. Why don't we talk about it further over a cup of tea?"

Miss Armor took us to her private quarters, where she prepared tea. Over tea and cookies, she explained to my father the rules and regulations of Balch Hall, all of which were designed to safeguard her young charges. Father began to calm down, and nod his head. He understood. I was permitted to remain at Cornell and continue my college career. It's as close as I ever came to being in a whorehouse.

Don't Give Her an Education

Although my father was unschooled, he had lots of smarts, and people frequently came to him for advice. Usually, it was on matters of business, but on one occasion it was on something completely different. We were living in North Miami Beach. I had graduated as valedictorian from Monticello High School, Phi Beta Kappa from Cornell, and was attending the University of Miami School of Law, from which I would later graduate first in my class.

On the afternoon in question, one of our neighbors came to visit, a widow with her ten-year-old daughter. She came to ask my father for advice on raising her daughter since she had to do so alone.

"There isn't much I can tell you," began my father. But then he remembered that I was twenty-nine years old, was intent on a legal career, and had no marriage prospects in sight. "But one thing I can tell you," he continued. "Whatever you do, don't give her an education."

Not a Hotel

When I was growing up, I sometimes wished I could have been born into one of those American families I saw in the movies. This ideal family was always large, and their home was usually brimming with company. People would drop in, sometimes invited, sometimes not, but they were always welcome and there was always food for them. The life of this ideal family was filled with cocktail parties, dinners, and other festive occasions.

My home was not like that. When I was ten, Hermann married and left home. From then on, my family at home consisted of my mother, father, and me. Most of the members of my parents' families had been killed in the Holocaust, and my parents did not have many friends. Those they did have were never invited for cocktails (a word not within my parents' ken), lunch, dinner, or any other meal. A really good friend might be offered a glass of *shnaps*—whiskey—or "a piece cake." But that was it. My parents were totally devoted to their immediate family; everyone else was beyond the pale.

If I didn't know this before, I learned it when Steve Lacheen came to the house. When I was preparing for the Florida Bar Exam, I thought it might be helpful to study with a classmate. I picked Steve, one of the brightest students in my class, and he came to study with me one afternoon.

We were still studying together when Mother announced that it was six o'clock: time for dinner. Even though I knew my parents' aversion to inviting company for meals, I did not see how I could tell Steve to go home. Furthermore, I knew there was plenty of food. So I invited him to join us for dinner, and he accepted.

After dinner, we studied a few more hours, and then Steve left. He'd no sooner shut the door than my father came into the den. "Why did he have to eat with us?" he asked. "Doesn't he have a home of his own?"

"I'm sorry, Dad," I said. "I didn't know what else to do. He was here at dinnertime, so I felt I had to invite him."

"OK," he said. "But, remember. For the future. This is not a hotel."

Eating Out

I love to dine out and do it every chance I get. I have no doubt it's because my family so rarely ate out. It was customary for us to eat at home. My mother didn't seem to mind cooking three meals a day; after all, it was for her family, the focal point of her life. And my father loved eating at home.

I can't recall an occasion when my parents and I were invited to dinner at someone's home—other than for *simkhes*—celebrations—at the home of my brother and his wife. In my parents' set, people ate at home.

Once in a while, however, on a rare occasion—a Jewish holiday or when we were out of town—the family would eat at a restaurant. It was always a disaster.

We'd sally forth to the restaurant, but none of us would be happy about it. My father was unhappy because he didn't like spending money for restaurant food; my mother was unhappy because my father was unhappy; and I was unhappy because we were going to a kosher restaurant, to eat the same kind of food I got three times a day every day of my life. I wanted to taste shrimp, lobster, and Chinese food, but those were not kosher and, therefore, forbidden. "*Verem,*"— "worms," was the word my mother used derogatorily to refer to shrimp. "If I served you something that looked like that at home, you'd never eat it," she'd say. "But in a restaurant, it's good."

During and after the meal, something always went wrong. The food didn't taste right. It wasn't cooked sufficiently. The bill was too high. My father would refuse to leave an adequate tip; my mother would be embarrassed and they'd wrangle about it. I'd want to escape through a hole in the floor. Or my father would get sick days after the meal and point to the restaurant as the culprit.

On one occasion, in the middle of the dinner, my father developed a nosebleed, and we had to leave our meals half-eaten and rush home so he could lie down. It only proved what he'd known all along. It was always a mistake to eat out.

My parents were similarly wary of eating at other people's homes and rarely did so. As I grew up, however, I would receive dinner invitations from friends from time to time. Mother, with typical Jewish angst, would say to me, "Eat first—you don't know what they'll give you." She wanted me to have a complete dinner at home before going out. She knew that each course of the meal she prepared would be fresh, kosher, and *geshmak*—tasty. Who knew what one might get on the outside?

Asking Directions

In this age of books explaining the stereotypical differences between men and women, we all know that women like to ask directions and men don't. Deborah Tannen described one couple in her best seller, *You Just Don't Understand*, as follows:

> A man and a woman were standing beside the information booth at the Washington Folk Life Festival, a sprawling complex of booths and displays. "You ask," the man was saying to the woman. "I don't ask."[9]

My parents had their own way of conforming to this stereotype. We'd be driving along, say, on the way to Long Beach to visit Hermann. I'd be in the back seat, poring over maps; Mother would be up front with Father, holding in her hand the written directions Hermann had sent us in advance. We'd just have come from a gas station, where we had double-checked the directions, and we'd just have passed a sign pointing to Long Beach, when mother would spy a man up ahead standing at the side of the road.

"Let's ask that man, Daddy," she'd say, "if we're on the road to *Lung* Beach."

"Why should I ask him?" Father asked. "I know I'm on the

right road. The gas station man just told us so. Why should I stop just because you saw a man on the road?"

But Mother would persist. "Why not?" she'd ask. "It can't hurt."

Father, defeated by that logic, would slow the car down and head for the side of the road where the man was standing. But he'd never fully stop the car; he'd just ease over to the shoulder so Mother could stick her head out the window and say, "*Podden* me, gentleman, but do you know if we're on the right road, it should take us to *Lung* Beach, in *LungEyeland*, the *Pockway*?" We would be there just long enough for the "gentleman" to ponder this strange request, nod his head, and open his mouth to respond, when Father would suddenly realize how utterly demeaning the whole situation was. There he was, a grown man, a husband and father, the driver of the car, waiting for some strange man to tell his wife where they should go. It was not to be borne.

Thereupon, Father would hit the gas pedal, turn the wheel away from the curb, and drive off in a blaze of power, leaving the "gentleman" stunned at the curb, Mother speechless in the front seat, me laughing in the back, and Father in control again.

For $4 a year

Some years ago, I learned that the *nadn*—dowry—that almost prevented my parents' marriage amounted to no more than $200. I was appalled. Father always said he married Mother for the dowry, and since they were married over fifty years, he had literally sold himself for $4 a year. How could an astute businessman make such a deal?

Father had a ready answer: "At that time, $200 was a lot of money."

Fishing

My father loved to fish, but he feared that Mother might begrudge him the money he spent on his fishing equipment. Throughout the many years he enjoyed this hobby, he never once admitted to her that he had bought a rod, reel, or other piece of equipment. It was always, "Look what I found on the pier" or "Look what so-and-so gave me. He's going back up North to his children. He won't need it." It was hard for Mother to keep a straight face, particularly when she saw the sales tag still hanging from the item involved, but she never said a word. She simply praised Dad's good fortune in being able to amass such a supply of fishing tools without a cent's outlay.

When not fishing, Dad would lovingly oil and polish his rods and reels. When I came down to Florida for my winter vacation, all was in readiness and the two of us would go fishing. The ritual was always the same. Dad would wake me up around 6 AM, and I'd don one of his old caps and shirts, along with an old pair of my own blue jeans while Mother packed a lunch for us. Then, we'd drive down to the Doughnut Place en route and silently have a cup of coffee and a doughnut with the old duffers at the counter. On the pier, Dad would proudly introduce me to his cronies, though they found it hard to believe that this bedraggled young woman in old clothes was indeed Mr. Pressman's daughter, the lawyer, with the Government in Washington.

I prided myself on baiting my own hook, even when blood-worms were the bait. But Dad was always there to disentangle my line from the rocks below the pier; to tie a new hook on, when needed; and to remove the fish he made sure to help me catch.

Of course, we could never bring the fish home. Father hated eating fish. He just loved to catch them. And I loved to catch them with him.

Not My Daughter

In 1965, when my niece Miriam was twenty years old, she announced her forthcoming nuptials. Naturally, my parents and I were invited to attend the wedding at the Atlantic Hotel in Long Beach. Father was told in advance that as the grandfather of the bride and a member of the wedding party, he was expected to wear a tuxedo. He ignored these instructions and turned up at the synagogue in a nondescript brown business suit. All the other members of the wedding party were aghast. Why wasn't he in a tuxedo? Was it too late to rent or borrow one for him?

"Don't bother to get me a tuxedo," Father said. "I won't wear one. It's not *my* daughter's wedding." I was then thirty-seven years old, had never even been close to getting engaged, much less married—and the prospects for my doing so were dim. Nonetheless, my father, to the consternation of everyone in the family, said he was not wearing a tuxedo to this wedding. He would await the wedding of *his* daughter for such finery.

Miriam got married with her grandfather in attendance in his brown business suit. (It did not appear to affect the marriage. She and her husband Paul have been married over thirty years.) Five years after Miriam's wedding, to everyone's surprise, including mine, I got married. My mother, after practicing for three months, delivered a short speech at the wedding. My father, unfortunately, could not be with us; he had died of a stroke two years earlier. I like to think he was looking down on us from heaven—finally wearing a tuxedo.

A Founder of the Synagogue

In 1968, when he was seventy-four years old, my father had a massive stroke and went into a coma. As soon as I heard, I flew from Washington, DC, to the hospital in North Miami and stood at his bedside. His eyes were closed, so I willed him to open them. I knew he would. His love for me was so great he could not possibly lie there with me standing next to him without opening his eyes. But my will was not strong enough. My father never regained consciousness. He died in that hospital bed.

My parents had not made any funeral or burial arrangements; right after my father died, I made them. They included a service at Beth Torah Synagogue, the Conservative synagogue at Monticello Park in North Miami Beach where my parents lived. I sat in a front pew feeling the eyes of all upon me. "That's the daughter," I could feel them thinking. "The one who's crying quietly in the front."

I heard the rabbi's words in a miasma. What was he saying?

"I didn't know Mr. Pressman," he said. "But he was probably a founder of this synagogue." Broken-hearted as I was, I could not help but smile. A founder of the synagogue? Not my father. My father was not that kind of activist. My father was a founder of our family. May he rest in peace.

Mom

Go a Little Longer

When I completed the third grade, I began to question the wisdom of remaining in elementary school. By that time, I had learned how to read, knew how to write, had mastered Arithmetic, had taken Geography, and done well in History. What more was there to learn? I discussed this with Mother. She, who had only attended school briefly, did not disagree with me. I did indeed have impressive scholastic attainments at the age of nine, but she had the feeling that children in the United States continued to go to school beyond the third grade. "You're right," she said, "but why don't you try it a little longer? And then, if you don't like it, you can quit." I had no problem with that logic. So, I entered the fourth grade—and went to school sixteen more years. At the end of that, on graduation from law school, I realized I knew far less than I thought I'd known at nine. Perhaps I should have quit when I was ahead.

No Birthday Party

I was eight when we moved to Woodridge and every year after that I had a birthday party. Usually, about five to ten of my classmates came: Lotte Proyect, whose father ran the local produce store: Jeanne Becker, whose family ran a gift shop; Shirley Prager, whose father ran a grocery store; Lily Glazer*, whose family was one of the poorest in Woodridge; and the chubby Spingarn* sisters, Masha* and Rhoda*, whose parents were among the wealthiest families in the village—they owned the Savoy Hotel*.

All these children dutifully brought presents each year—except Masha and Rhoda. They came empty-handed, perhaps exercising their own form of droit du seigneur. Masha and Rhoda were always among the first at the birthday cake, ice cream, and other foods served by my mother and always among the last to leave, grasping the party favors in their hands.

One year I could stand it no longer. "I don't want a party this year, Mother," I said, months before the May 30 date. I just can't stand having Masha and Rhoda come again, eat all our food, and not bring me a present."

"Are you sure?" my mother asked. "Won't you miss it?"

"No, I won't. No party this year."

The months passed and I awoke to my birthday. It was a beautiful spring day, but I had nothing to look forward to. There would be no birthday cake, no candles to blow out, no ice cream, no presents, no friends surrounding me and singing "Happy Birthday, Sonia." I would become twelve all by myself. I began to cry.

Mother understood. It was too late to have a party but not too late to do something for me. She and Father took me downtown and bought me the prettiest dress they could find.

I never passed up the chance to have a party again—presents or no presents.

Sex Education

When I was twelve, I awoke one morning to find the pants of my Baby Doll pajamas stained with large, dark red splotches of blood. I was terrified and screamed for Mother. She ran into the room, took one look at the scene before her, hauled off, and struck me sharply in the face. Naturally, I was even more terrified.

That was my introduction to menstruation. I had never heard a word about it before. Now Mother explained to me that henceforth I would bleed for several days each month, that this was a perfectly normal function, and that when a Jewish girl's period began, her mother greeted the occasion by slapping her face. Since the onset of menstruation was a happy event signaling entrance into womanhood, a slap was needed to ward off the evil eye. That's how I was ushered into adolescence.

A year later, Mother decided it was time to explain the facts of life to me. Her explanation consisted of two sentences. The first was, "Don't kiss anyone until you're married." The second, uttered a few minutes later, was "Well, if you're engaged, it may be all right to kiss your fiancé once or twice." These rules had stood her in good stead, and she saw no reason why they wouldn't work equally well for me. Neither did I. I promised to follow them.

But my life did not follow that of my mother, and I broke my promise. We never discussed it, but I think she knew and forgave me.

Three Meals a Day

I go back to the Catskills every chance I get—for a high school reunion, a conference, to see old friends—and I am overwhelmed with nostalgia whenever I return.

But actually while I was growing up, it was not a very happy place for me. I fit in neither with the all-year-round residents in the winter nor with the summer renters. Our bungalow colony was 1¼ miles out of town. While that might not sound like a lot, to a teenager not yet old enough to drive, it might have been 100 miles. Once the school bus brought me home in the afternoon, that was basically the end of any social interaction for me for the day. I didn't have the opportunity to go to a movie with my classmates, get a soda, sleep overnight at a friend's house, or just hang out in town. When I was sixteen, I did get a bicycle, but for someone as unathletic as I was, it was an accomplishment to learn to ride it for even a short distance. Going into town and back was more than I was usually able to manage. Of course, there were school dances when my father drove me into town. But after what seemed like hours of standing around hoping a hole in the floor would open up for me, when someone finally did ask me to dance, there was my father waiting to drive me home.

In the summer, it was no better. I wasn't just another one of the kids. I was the landlord's daughter—someone set apart. Any grievances the renters had toward my father, real or imagined, were picked up by their children and spilled over onto me.

In addition, the Catskills were a cultural desert. In Monticello, there was one movie theater in town, and from time to time there'd be a speaker or some visiting performers at school. No ballets, no concerts, no theater, nothing to stimulate and inspire a young woman's imagination.

Being a good student, my homework didn't absorb a great deal of my time. My disconsolate wandering around the house nonplused Father. "I don't understand what's wrong," he'd say. "You have three good meals a day and a roof over your head. What more do you want?"

By Piltzener standards, of course, I was living a charmed existence. What else could I possibly need?

You Teach Her

To this day, cooking is an art I have not mastered. I blame it all on my mother. *She* was a master of Jewish cooking. She never used a recipe in her life; she just knew how to prepare Jewish dishes. It may have been a genetic trait that I simply did not inherit.

From the time I turned ten, however, she would periodically attempt to teach me to cook. I would be called into the kitchen just as I was reading an interesting novel. "Put away that book," she'd begin. She was never happy to see me immersed in a book. That was not the way to marriage and a family. "Come into the kitchen," she'd say. "I'm going to teach you to cook." Her way of teaching was not to discuss what she was doing and certainly not to let me do anything myself. The way to learn was to watch her.

I'd watch for a while, get bored, begin to daydream, and end by having an accident. I might spill water on the floor, get my hands into her dough, or just disturb her while she was koshering meat so she wouldn't know if she'd salted it on all six sides. As soon as Mother discovered what I had done, she'd order me out of the kitchen. I would gladly leave. And Mother would say to Father, "*You* want her to learn to cook? *You* teach her."

But she was never able to give up her fantasy that her daughter, like all "nice Jewish girls," had the traditional virtues. I walked into the house one afternoon to hear my mother saying on the phone, "She's no beauty, but she's a wonderful cook."

"Who were you talking about, Mom?" I asked.

"You," she said. She looked sheepish.

"Me?" I asked. "Why did you say that about my cooking?"

"I don't know," she said. "It just came to me."

She simply couldn't give up the dream.

Zia complains of having been deprived of a traditional Jewish home where the smell of chicken soup greets you as you enter. I've told her it isn't my fault. My mother never taught me.

The Fontainebleau

In December 1954, during my first year at law school, a spiffy new 550-room hotel opened for business on Miami Beach—the Fontainebleau (now called the Fontainebleau Hilton Resort and

Towers). It was built on Collins Avenue atop the remains of a 1920s
Miami Beach landmark, the Harvey Firestone mansion. We were
astounded when we heard that a room cost as much as $50 a
night! "I could afford to pay $50 a night to sleep," my mother
said, "But, I wouldn't be able to sleep."

No Sports Fans Here

Neither of my parents had any interest in spectator sports. I had
scant interest myself, but the little I had, my mother killed one
Thanksgiving Day. I was home for the holiday while attending
Cornell and was watching the traditional Cornell-Penn football
game on TV. Since my school was involved, and since I knew the
Cornell players—my roommate had even dated one of the stars,
Pete Dorset—I was avidly watching the game. Mother, noticing
my interest, was mystified. "I don't understand," she said. "What
do you get when they win?"

I didn't know the answer then and I haven't been able to come
up with a satisfactory answer ever since. Whenever I'm tempted to
go to a game of any sort, my mother's question comes to mind—
and I stay home.

Hurray for Hollywood!

Mother's overriding concern in life was my welfare. But she was
also an avid movie buff. *Modern Screen*, *Screen*, *Motion Picture*,
Photoplay, and other movie magazines were never far from sight in
our home. Mother scooped them up whenever she passed a newsstand. She devoured them—pictures and text—and prided herself
on being up-to-date on the doings of Humphrey Bogart, Bette
Davis, Jimmy Stewart, and the other famous stars in the Hollywood firmament.

I never thought Mother's concern for me would come into
conflict with her addiction to Hollywood or, if it did, that her

devotion to me would take second place. But I learned differently in the winter of 1959.

On the last day of 1958, Fulgencia Batista, Cuba's longtime dictator, had departed from Cuba, and Fidel Castro officially took office as Prime Minister in February of 1959. Shortly thereafter, my friend, Harriet Dauber, and I headed for Havana for a week's vacation. It was, of course, not the best time to go to Cuba, but we had made our reservations months in advance and were determined to go.

Cuba looked forbidding when we arrived there. Pony-tailed soldiers armed with a variety of fearsome weapons thronged every street. Nonetheless, we witnessed no untoward incidents and were able to go about our holiday undisturbed.

My plane back to Washington, DC, had a brief stopover in Miami and I could not wait to get to a phone and let Mother know I was all right. I rushed to the nearest pay station and dialed my parents' number. "Mom," I began, but I could not continue.

"Did you hear what they did while you were away?" she said. "They've nominated Elizabeth Taylor for an Academy Award. They want to give her an Oscar as best actress for *Cat on a Hot Tin Roof.*"

"Mom," I began again. "I'm back from Castro's Cuba. I'm OK, Mom. Nothing happened."

"That's ridiculous," Mother continued, totally ignoring my announcement. "How can they even say her name in the same breath as Susan Hayward? *That girl* should win. You saw her in *I Want To Live*. How she walked to her death. *That's* acting."

I thought Elizabeth Taylor had done a creditable job in *Cat*, but there was no sense making the case to Mother. She had decided on Susan Hayward.

"You're right, Mom," I said. "But I gotta catch my plane now. Give Dad my love. Glad you're on top of things."

I caught my plane—and some weeks later Susan Hayward won the Oscar. Elizabeth Taylor never had a chance.

A Wonderful Man

Sometimes when I was in a bakery or other store in North Miami Beach shopping with my mother, the clerk would mention having waited on my father recently and comment about what a nice man he was. My mother would heartily agree. "I've been married to him over fifty years," she'd say. "He's a wonderful man."

As soon as we left the store, she'd turn to me and say, "No other woman could live with him." Having thus directly contradicted herself, she was able to comfortably continue her shopping and return home to take care of my father.

Goodbye Columbus

In 1969, on one of her visits to me in Arlington, Mother and I went to see the comedy, *Goodbye Columbus*, starring Richard Benjamin and Ali McGraw. The movie was about a young Jewish librarian who has an affair with a willful daughter of a *nouveau riche* family. When we left the theater, I could see that Mother was disturbed. Finally, she said, "You know, in Warsaw, where I grew up, young men and women didn't go to bed together before they were married."

"Mom," I said. "That was over fifty years ago."

"You know," she said. "You're right."

Jimmy Hoffa

During my years at the NLRB in Washington, DC, from 1959 to 1965, one of my colleagues was a young lawyer of Hungarian descent with the unusual name of Florian Bartosic. Florian, an upstanding young man, left the NLRB and moved to an office a number of blocks away in the Teamsters Building in the Capitol Hill area. He became a top aide to Jimmy Hoffa and later a Teamsters Trustee. Hoffa was the most notorious labor leader in America and the frequent subject of newspaper exposés, detailing charges of fraud, corruption, and mob connections.

On one occasion, when I took Mother to Washington National Airport for her flight back to Miami Beach, we bumped into Florian. "Hi, Florian," I said. "I'd like to introduce you to my mother." "Mom," I said, turning to her, "I'd like you to meet my friend, Florian Bartosic. Florian works for Jimmy Hoffa." Mother was stunned. It was as if I had introduced her to the devil incarnate. But she did not want to insult the well-dressed young man before her who was obviously a friend of mine. Momentarily, she was at a loss for words but not for long. "Some people," she said to Florian, "don't like him."

She Won the Case

After the end of the Second World War, when we were living in Long Beach, Mother asked a local lawyer whether our family had any basis for a claim against Germany. He told her there was no law that would support such a claim. She came home and threw out all the documents attesting to the family's ownership of property that she'd been saving since we left Germany.

Some years later, in the early '50s, while I was in law school, I learned that one of my classmates, Harry Bassett, represented Jews who, like us, had had to flee Germany. Harry, who was of German descent, filed claims against the German government on behalf of his clients. I told him about my mother's experience with the Long Beach lawyer and her subsequent destruction of all her documents. He said that we still had the basis for a claim because new legislation had been enacted in Germany allowing claims for loss of income. I introduced Harry to my parents, who told him the facts of their case, and Harry filed a claim on their behalf.

Some years later, the claim was denied. By that time, I was in Washington, DC, and I learned that one could appeal such denials to the Foreign Claims Settlement Commission in Washington.

I hired an attorney, Samuel Herman, who specialized in such appeals, and he filed an appeal on my parents' behalf.

In 1962, we were notified that a hearing on the appeal was scheduled at the Foreign Claims Settlement Commission. Mother and Dad flew up from North Miami Beach to testify.

I was the first witness called. I had scant knowledge of the facts through personal experience but was able to answer the questions of Sam Herman and the judge based upon what I knew of family history. My answers were direct, to the point, and unemotional, as befitted a government attorney.

Then my mother was called to the stand. She, too, answered the questions of Herman and the judge but in an entirely different manner. She spoke loudly and at great length, gesticulated, cried, took time to compose herself, and, in general, created an emotional scene in the courtroom. I cringed with embarrassment.

"I'm so sorry," I apologized to Herman, after Mother had left the stand. "Perhaps I should have coached Mother in proper courtroom demeanor."

"Don't worry," he said. "Your mother won the case for us."

And she did. The earlier denial of the claim was overturned. For the remainder of their lives, Mother and Dad received a small pension from the German government.

Only When I See It

In 1973, Roberto, Zia, and I were living in Stamford and Mother, at eighty-two, was living alone in her home in North Miami Beach. During her calls to us, she often complained of not feeling well. Her doctor, however, could find nothing wrong. "It's a cry for help," said Roberto. "You've got to bring her up North." Latin that he was, bringing an elderly parent into the home was nothing unusual for him. For me, it meant a complete disruption of my life. My parents had raised me with the maxim, "Two parents can raise ten children, but ten children don't have room for two parents." All their lives, my parents had dreaded ever having to live with their children, and I, much as I loved my mother, did not relish the thought of having her live with me. But Mother's calls became increasingly more frequent. I decided that Roberto was right, and I flew down to Florida. Much against her will, I brought Mother home to live with us.

As soon as she got settled, she resumed her habit of telling me what to do. "Put a sweater on," she'd say before I went out. Or, "Don't forget your rubbers" if it was raining. Or, "Take some more chicken; you hardly ate anything" at dinnertime. One day, when I could take it no longer, I blew up. "Mother," I said, "I'm forty-five years old, and I've been taking care of myself for twenty-seven years." I thought that was a pretty good argument for self-sufficiency, but Mother, as usual, had the last word. "It's one thing when I don't see it," she said, in her most martyred tone.

A Matter of Age

My mother used the ambiguity about her age to her advantage. Towards the latter part of her life, if she was feeling poorly, she'd say, "After all, I'm an old woman—eighty-one already."

On the other hand, a day or two later, when she was full of piss and vinegar, she was apt to say, "After all, I'm not so old. Only seventy-nine."

The Apology

When Mother came to live with us in Stamford, Zia was almost two years old. One day, Mother saw Zia signing her name, something I had taught her. Mother went to a corner of the room, as she did when she was deeply moved by something. "Forgive me," she said, with a pleading, sorrowful look in her eyes. "I didn't do that with you. I didn't know you could teach a child so young." I assured her that it was all right and that I believed I had made up for this terrible educational oversight on her part.

Hermann

Get the Money up Front

When my parents were running their *kokhaleyn* in Woodridge, a Mr. and Mrs. Arnstein came by to rent a room late one afternoon. My mother was out shopping, my father was napping, but Hermann was home. This was his opportunity to show what he could do. The Arnsteins planned to stay all summer and wanted to move in that very night. They had only one small tote bag between them but said their luggage would be coming later. Hermann handled the entire transaction and rented the Arnsteins a room for the season.

When Father awoke, Hermann proudly told him he had rented a room by himself. "Did you get paid?" my father asked him.

"You're supposed to get paid?" asked Hermann.

The next morning Hermann arose at 6 AM, and went down to the Arnsteins' room. He found it empty but spied the couple through the window walking away from the house, with the tote bag in Mr. Arnstein's hand. He ran after them and inquired about their payment for the room.

"We're not going to pay for *that* room," said Mrs. Arnstein. "We won't be staying. The mattress was lumpy; I could hardly sleep. Besides, we don't like Woodridge all that much. Maybe we'll go to Mountaindale."

Hermann, who later became one of Long Beach's most successful realtors, said that's the day he learned that you get the money up front.

The March of Time

Hermann, more than my parents, couldn't accept the fact that I was pursuing a career rather than marriage when I was in my twenties and thirties. Perhaps that was because he had married and left home when I was still a child and hadn't witnessed my developing interests as my parents had.

When I arrived in Washington, DC, in 1957 at the age of twenty-nine, I was away from home for the first time, except for my college years. I was thrilled to finally be on my own and very taken with the glamour of the city. I wrote a six-page, detail-filled letter to my parents extolling the beauty of the city and marveling at all I was doing: the new friends I was making, the interesting cases on my job, the congresspersons I saw around town, the parties I attended. I sent a copy to my brother.

His response, in a letter back to my parents, a copy of which he sent me, and which I never forgot, was, "Sorry there's no news from Sister." I hadn't announced my engagement; therefore, there was "no news from Sister." At that point, I gave up. I realized I'd never make it with my brother. For the next thirteen years, I never communicated with him. And, for some odd reason, he never noticed it.

In 1970, when I announced my engagement to Roberto, I had finally satisfied my brother's dreams for me. The fact that Roberto was Puerto Rican, divorced, had three teen-age children, and no money was unimportant. Hermann was delighted; I had achieved success. I resumed my relationship with him.

When, some years later, Roberto and I divorced, it saddened Hermann but did not remove me from his roster of those who were successful. The important thing was that I had married—to whom and for how long was not material.

Years later, I asked him why he was so proud that his daughter, Miriam, had taken over his real estate business and his granddaughters, Jodi Lee and Linda, were lawyers when he had been so vehemently opposed to my career. "Times change," he said.

Can't Be Buried

On July 8, 1996, Hermann's heart gave out and he died of a heart attack. He was just short of his eighty-second birthday and had been happily remarried to his second wife, Belle, for only nine months. The family gathered at the Riverside Boulevard Chapel in Hewlett, Long Island. During the service, three generations of the family shared their memories of Hermann: his daughter, Miriam; his granddaughter, Debbie; and I. There were stories about how his determination and persistence were responsible for our family's leaving Germany; about the candy store and luncheonette my father bought him in Long Beach, when Hermann married his first wife, Helen; about the first BLT sandwich he made in that store, after which his customer suggested it would improve the sandwich if he fried the bacon; about his diligence in patrolling his neighborhood as an air raid warden in WWII—helmet on his head, armband on his arm—fortunately, it did not occur to the Nazis to bomb Long Beach; about his putting a table in the middle of the candy store, which became the beginning of his real estate business, now the largest real estate office in Long Beach; about his carrying that business on his person—with innumerable keys in his shirt pocket, countless notes affixed to his tie clip, and facts about every house and owner in his head; and about his generosity toward his family and others and his parsimoniousness toward himself. Although he was legally blind, he never traveled by cab. He took a bus or conned potential homebuyers, contractors, and others into driving him around. A building contractor for whom Hermann was a mentor told me he was very flattered when Hermann wanted to ride in his old car when everyone knew he could afford a limousine. The contractor didn't know until I told him that Hermann's preferred mode of transportation was in *yenem's*—someone else's—car. But Hermann gave his children, grandchildren, and great-grandchildren presents on *his* birthday. We laughed and we cried. We remembered Hermann.

Then everyone got into limousines and cars for the ride to

Mount Ararat Cemetery in Farmingdale, Long Island. When we arrived at Mount Ararat, the cortege stopped at the cemetery office. Hermann's daughters, Ruth and Miriam, and his sons-in-law, Mickey and Paul, got out of their limousines and went into the office. I remained in the limousine with Belle, Hermann's bereaved widow. Fifteen minutes passed; the procession did not resume. It was hot, and I wondered what was holding things up. Then Ruth came running to my limousine. "You're an attorney," she shouted to me. "Are you also a notary?"

"No," I said.

She returned to the office. I wondered why she needed a notary.

Five more minutes passed. It was even hotter. Ruth came running back to the limousine. "Sonia," she said. "We need you inside."

Someone came to sit with Belle and I joined Ruth in the cemetery office. The problem was that the Mount Ararat personnel refused to bury Hermann. The name of the deceased on their records was "Herman" Pressman; they were unable to bury a body belonging to "Hermann" Pressman unless one of his daughters signed an affidavit attesting to the fact that "Herman" and "Hermann" referred to the same person. The staff prepared an affidavit for Miriam to sign, but when they asked her for identification, she had none. Miriam, the most successful realtor in Long Beach, didn't have her license or other ID with her. She said she didn't carry her license when she was with her husband and he was driving. I could almost hear Hermann chuckling: "If you carried your office on your person, you wouldn't be in this predicament." I prevailed upon the staff to amend the affidavit so Ruth, who did have ID with her, could sign it. Ruth signed the affidavit, the proceedings continued, and my brother was laid to rest.

I wondered whether he would have been enraged by the contretemps over his burial or have enjoyed the spectacle. I could no longer ask him.

Freddy

In 1990, Hermann, my cousin Fela (the daughter of my father's brother, Iser), and I were together for the first time in our lives. Fela and her husband Toby had survived the war years in Poland, after which they emigrated: first to Israel, then to Germany, finally to the United States, where they settled in Chicago and raised a family. I had been with Fela and her family on numerous occasions, as had Hermann, but all three of us were never together before. We came together to celebrate the bar mitzvah of one of her grandsons.

At the reception after the bar mitzvah, the three of us began to reminisce about my father's side of the family. That gave me the idea for creating a family tree for the Pressman family or as much of it as I could piece together. Fela was not interested in working on it with me; she did not like to look back. But, her daughter-in-law Terrie shared my interest in family genealogy and the two of us put together a family chart.

When I got back home to Potomac, I made copies of the chart and sent one to my cousin, Freddy Fischel. Shortly thereafter, I got an irate call from him. "What's Berta doing on that chart?" he asked. "She's not a Pressman."

"Freddy," I remonstrated. "You've been married to Berta for forty-five years. What does it take to get into this family?" He didn't answer. He just mumbled something and hung up. And so I never found out what it takes to get into the Pressman family but, obviously, forty-five years doesn't do it.

Sarah Bolno

The Silent Partner

One of the success stories in my family involved the sons of my father's cousin, Sarah Bolno. Sarah, whose husband died when their three sons and one daughter were quite young, had raised her children by herself in Philadelphia. Somehow she managed, although there was never much money. In 1935, her sons, David*, Harry*, and Joseph* volunteered their time to a local politician who was running for mayor. He lost the election but was nonetheless grateful for their efforts in his campaign. He told them to come and see him if they ever needed anything in the future.

All three young men served in World War II. When the war ended, they came home. They had no money and no particular skills—in short, no prospects. But they had families to support. They remembered the words of the mayoral candidate for whom they had worked and went to see him. Without a moment's hesitation, he took out his checkbook, wrote a check for $50,000, and handed it to the three young men. He knew of an available store in a good location in downtown Philadelphia and suggested they open a business there; he would be a silent partner. David, Harry, and Joe followed his advice and opened an appliance business, which they called "The Three Brothers." It was a thriving business and they prospered.

In 1956, while I was attending law school, Sarah came to Miami Beach for a visit. The country was all agog at the forthcoming wedding of Grace Kelly and Prince Rainier. Since Grace Kelly came from Philadelphia, I teased Sarah. "Guess you're busy picking out clothes to wear in Monaco," I said.

"No," she answered. "I won't be going. But David, Harry, Joe, and their wives are." The silent partner was John B. Kelly, Grace's father, the well-known sportsman, civic leader, sometime chairman of the Democratic Committee for Philadelphia, and unsuccessful mayoral candidate in 1935.

Roberto

Like Mother, Like Daughter

The first time I told my mother about Roberto was during a routine call to her in Miami Beach from my apartment in Arlington. "Mom," I began. "I'm dating someone. He's not Jewish; he's Puerto Rican; he has no money; and he has three children."

"Is that the best you can do?" she asked.

Several years ago, when Zia came home for the Fourth of July, she was bursting with news when I picked her up at the metro station. But she expressed concern as to whether to tell me; she feared my reaction. Finally, she said. "I'm seeing someone I like a lot."

"So, what's the problem?" I asked.

"Well," she continued. "He's not Jewish, he's not single—only separated, and he's got a baby daughter."

"Is that the best you can do?" I asked.

An Ersatz Puerto Rican

When my sister-in-law, Helen, learned about Roberto, she was not too happy at the prospect of a Puerto Rican in the family. She was a traditional Jewish wife and mother, a Polish immigrant who could barely read and write English; marrying a Puerto Rican was not within her range of acceptable behavior.

She'd heard about Roberto, but she didn't meet him until he and I came to New York City for Thanksgiving in 1969. On that occasion, I threw a cocktail party at the hotel where we were staying so my family and friends could meet Roberto. There, Helen was bowled over by his good looks and charm.

"How'd you like Roberto?" I asked her on the phone the next day.

"He's not a *real* Puerto Rican, is he?" she asked.

A Rabbi from Israel

My mother came to love Roberto and delighted in telling the following story. After my father died, she took to spending Passovers at a hotel in Miami Beach. The meat at this hotel was *glat kosh'r*—scrupulously inspected and prepared according to the dietary laws. On the Sabbath, all the elevator buttons were lit so one did not have to violate the Sabbath by pressing a button.

In 1970, the year that Roberto and I were engaged, we came to Miami Beach to be with her and stayed at a nearby hotel. But we ate with Mother at her hotel and spent a good bit of time there. One or another of the guests coming up to talk to Roberto often interrupted our meals. With his Semitic looks, elegant attire, and presence at a *glat kosh'r* hotel, everyone assumed he must be a rabbi from Israel.

One day, when we were not with Mother, one of the guests came up to her. "Ms. Pressman," she began, "Your daughter's engaged to a Jewish man. My only daughter is about to be married, too—to a *goy*—a gentile."

"What can you do?" said my mother, with a sigh. "That's how it goes."

The Steps

Shortly after our marriage, Roberto and I flew to Puerto Rico. He wanted to introduce me to his family, show me the land where he had grown up, and "the Poly" (the Polytechnic Institute of Puerto Rico), which later became the Inter American University of Puerto Rico. This was his beloved school nestled among the Santa Marta Hills in San Germán, with its revered steps.

An American missionary, Dr. John Will Harris, founded the Poly. The university, which now has nine campuses and 40,000 students, began as a private secondary school, consisting of a single small building with a single classroom. A set of steps led up the hill to that building. At daylight on a morning in March 1912, two individuals walked up those steps to begin a new educational adventure: Dr. Harris, the teacher, and Leopoldo ("Popo") Ortiz Vega, the son of a local carpenter—the only student. Subsequently, other students came and other buildings were erected.

As the Institute grew, the original schoolhouse fell into disuse and disrepair. It was destroyed, but *the Steps* were preserved with the idea of incorporating them into a new building. That new building was never built.

In 1921, the first college-level courses were offered, and, in 1927, the first group of students was due to graduate with bachelor's degrees. Dr. Harris decided to award their diplomas outdoors in the only part of the original schoolhouse that still existed: *the Steps.* Thereafter, graduation ceremonies were always held at *the Steps,* until the classes became too large.

Dr. Harris left $40,000 in his will for the preservation of *the Steps.* When he died in Texas, the board of directors brought his ashes and those of his deceased wife and oldest daughter to Puerto Rico and interred them in the place where his dream and that of his family had been realized: *the Steps.*

The Steps remain on the grounds of the university today as a reminder and symbol of the beginning of the largest private institution of higher education in Puerto Rico and Latin America.

It Depends on Your Point of View

After we were married and living in Arlington, Roberto and I drove over to Gaithersburg, Maryland, one afternoon to visit Bernie and Charlotte Spiegel*. They were the brother and sister-in-law of my friend, Harriet Levine*, who was quite ill in a nursing home in La Mesa, California. Harriet was no longer able to write letters, and we wanted to get word of her. We spent some time chatting with the Spiegels in their garden apartment. Charlotte served us tea and pastries and was most gracious. But as the afternoon progressed, I became increasingly embarrassed. All Bernie and Charlotte could talk about was money—how much he earned as a caterer, how much he planned to earn when he expanded his business, how much they had just spent in redecorating their apartment, and what it was costing them to send their son Steven to college. I looked at Roberto. What was he thinking about all this?

When we left and were on our way to the car, I turned to Roberto. "I'm so embarrassed," I said. "Please don't think all Jews are like that."

"Like what?" he said.

"So materialistic. Always talking about money."

"I didn't notice," he said. "They seemed like very nice people. I'm sorry Harriet's so ill."

Some months later, Roberto and I were in New York City, seeing some shows, dining out, sightseeing, and just walking around. One afternoon, we went to the Bronx, where my family had lived when we first came to the United States. Only now it was a Puerto Rican neighborhood.

Roberto looked around the neighborhood in disgust. "Look how they live," he said. "Like pigs. No wonder they're not treated any better than they are."

"What are you talking about, Roberto?" I asked. "These are poor people doing the best they can in what is, in effect, a new country for them. Have a little compassion."

And then I remembered our visit to the Spiegels and laughed. He was no better than I was. I was overly sensitive to the behavior of Jews and he to Puerto Ricans. We did indeed have a cultural difference.

Abuela

Everything's Relative

When Roberto and I visited Puerto Rico, we drove out to see *Abuela*, Roberto's grandmother. Her name was Carmen, but I never heard Roberto call her anything other than *Abuela*. On the ride over, I asked Roberto how old *Abuela* was. "I don't know," he replied. "I think she's eighty-two."

When we entered her apartment, I was shocked to see a wizened, old woman sitting in a corner, listening to the news on the radio. My mother, who was almost eighty at the time, was tall and robust. This woman was in terrible shape.

We chatted with *Abuela* for a time, with Roberto translating her Spanish for me. Then I asked him to ask her her age. When she answered him, he told me she said she didn't know, but that if he was interested, there was a document at the bottom of her bureau that indicated her age. He got the document, returned with it to me, and said, "My grandmother's ninety-six."

"Oh," I said. "For ninety-six, she looks pretty good. For eighty-two, she looked awful."

Parents and Children

Abuela had raised seven children, all of whom she had survived. "I'm so glad I survived my children," she said to us that day. I was stunned. How could she say that? Wasn't it the natural order of things for parents to die *before* their children? What sort of mother would be glad her children had predeceased her?

Then *Abuela* continued. "I wouldn't want one of my children to need something from me and not be there for them." I'd never thought of that. But she had.

Still a Catholic

While there was a mixture of religions in Roberto's family, *Abuela*, like Roberto, was Protestant. Unlike, Roberto, however, she was fiercely devoted to her religion. During our visit, Roberto asked her how her friend, Maria, was doing. He knew that Maria had been coming to see *Abuela* every Sunday for over thirty years. "Oh," said *Abuela*, "she's still coming—every Sunday." Then, she paused for a few moments, in thought, and added, "But—she's still a Catholic."

Better Than an Atheist

Roberto told *Abuela* that I was Jewish. She was nonplused at first. Then, after giving the matter some thought, she said, "Well, it's better than being an atheist."

Me

Sterotypical/Shmereotypical

The stereotypical Jewish parents are known for their love of learning and their efforts to instill that in their children. Unfortunately, my parents were not stereotypical. They were neither learned themselves nor had they seen any evidence that learning was the road to success for others. They certainly didn't envision having their daughter pursue an education. All they ever wanted for me was that I find a husband and raise a family, the sooner the better. They knew I had to attend school, but it was of no consequence to them.

I, on the other hand, not having any other discernible attractions or skills, applied myself to my studies, with the result that I was frequently the teacher's pet and, therefore, not particularly popular with the majority of my classmates. I generally got straight A's on my report card, a document in which my parents had no interest. As their daughter, I already rated as high as possible with them. Anonymous teachers' evaluations of me were of no moment.

When I was in the third grade in Woodridge, I often heard my classmates talk about the rewards their parents gave them for an A or B on their report cards: a bicycle, a new outfit, or a goodly sum of money. None of them had the kind of grades I had.

When I brought my final report card for the year home, with A's in all subjects, I could bear it no longer. I told my parents that my classmates were receiving money and other rewards for getting good grades. "OK," said Mother, turning to my father. "Give her a quarter." My father dutifully handed me twenty-five cents. I never raised the issue of a reward for grades again. What was the point?

An Apology from Betty Friedan

In the early years of the women's movement, I had occasion to call Betty late one afternoon from my apartment in Arlington. Her husband, Carl, answered, I introduced myself, and then I was amazed to hear him shout, "This fucking—." His last words were unintelligible, after which he hung up. I was totally mystified.

The mystery was cleared up late that evening when Betty called and explained. All that afternoon, her house had been filled with TV camerapersons, equipment, and cables in connection with a television interview of her. Carl became quite annoyed with the disruption. After the TV interview, Betty left for a radio interview in New York City. And then I called. Carl thought I was yet another media person and that accounted for his anger and profanity. That anger, however, later dissipated and was replaced with chagrin. When Betty came home, he told her what he had done. He remembered that it had involved "some woman named Pressman." Gabe Pressman, the New York City radio host, had just interviewed Betty. She shrieked, "Oh my God, you swore at Gabe Pressman's wife." She immediately called the Pressman residence, but Mrs. Pressman had no knowledge of the incident.

Then, Betty thought about me. She called and apologized for Carl's behavior. Some years later, they were divorced.

Repaying a Debt

When my father ran across the border from Poland to Germany as a teenager, he was pursued not only by the border guards but also by the local police. It happened this way.

When Father decided to run away to Germany, he realized he

couldn't do so empty-handed. Establishing himself in a new *medine*—country—would take some money. How to get it?

In the one room, which served as his family's eating, living, and sleeping quarters in Piltz, stood "da Singa." "Da Singa" was an old sewing machine that had long since seen its best days. But it was the only family possession of any value. Undaunted by the fact that the final payment on this relic had yet to be made, Father ventured forth into the marketplace to find a customer. He quickly found his man, who gladly gave him the few rubles he sought and carted away "da Singa."

In the way that news spread in the *shtetl*, the Singer people found out about this transaction and alerted the local police. Thus, when Father raced across the Polish-German border shortly thereafter, the local constabulary as well as the border guards were in hot pursuit. All to no avail. Father made it safely to Germany.

Over fifty years later, one of my colleagues at the NLRB was a handsome young scion of a wealthy Connecticut family, George Horton. George's father was advertising director of the Singer Sewing Machine Company. I shared with George the story of my father's involvement with "da Singa" and the fact that my father later became a tailor. He shared with me the fact that in spite of the importance of the Singer Sewing Machine Company in his family, he'd never learned to sew.

One morning, when a button snapped off George's well-tailored shirt, he asked me if I could sew it back on for him. And so, using a stitch my father had taught me many years before, I partially repaid an old, old debt.

Zia

Another Peaked Child

Mother lived with Roberto, Zia, and me for four months before we lost her to a massive stroke. But during that time she and Zia formed a strong bond. They were separated by over eighty years, but that didn't affect their friendship. They often went for walks, picking up acorns and bringing them home. Mother recalled that she had done the same thing seventy years earlier in Warsaw. Zia was happy on these walks, but if they encountered another child Zia's age, Mother was not. She was troubled because without fail each of these other children was physically superior to Zia in some way. "You know that little girl down the road? With the blonde hair?" Mother would say. "She's the same age as Zia—how come she's taller?" Or heavier? Or has more color in her face? I was hard put to answer. But Mother finally figured it out. I had produced a daughter like the one she had produced—a peaked child.

Gifted Part-Time

During the early '80s, when Zia was attending the sixth grade at the Hilltop Elementary School in Beachwood, I received a notice from the school of the upcoming periodic meeting with her teachers to discuss her progress. When I arrived at the meeting room, only one of her two teachers was there: her regular classroom teacher. She told me Zia was performing well except for one thing: she never participated in classroom discussions. I was surprised and disappointed to hear this; Zia was certainly never shy about expressing her opinions to me. I had just heard this statement when Zia's other teacher walked in, the one who ran the class for gifted children. "Zia's doing just fine," she began, "and she always has something to contribute in class discussions." I was stunned. I turned to the teachers, "Did you two discuss Zia amongst yourselves before calling me in?" I asked.

"No," one of them said. "We don't have time for that." I told them I couldn't understand their two conflicting reports but would go home to see if Zia could explain it.

When I questioned her about it that evening, she said, "No problem, Mommy. In the regular classroom, the kids already snicker and make remarks when we leave for our gifted classes. I don't want to give them something else to talk about, so I never say anything in *that* class. But in the gifted class, they're all like me. So, I can talk there." She had it all figured out.

A Unique View of Williamsburg

A year ago, my California friends, Amalie and Don Meyer, sent me an e-mail telling me that during their one-week visit to the Washington, DC, area over Labor Day, they planned to tour Colonial Williamsburg in Virginia. I immediately invited myself along. The reason was as follows.

When I was living in Stamford in the '70s and the subject of Williamsburg came up, people were always amazed that I had lived in the Washington area for sixteen years and never been to Williamsburg, a three-hour drive away and one of the most visited tourist attractions in the country. But during my years in Washington, I had simply been too involved with my work and career to think about historic sites.

In 1980, however, it looked like I might finally have my chance. The GTE Recreation Association was joining with another recreation association for a bus trip to Luray Caverns and Williamsburg. I immediately signed Zia and me up. When I mentioned the trip to my friend, Ann Kruse, who worked for GTE in Ottawa, Ohio, she said she'd fly in from Ohio and accompany us on the tour.

On the tour, the three of us enjoyed our first stop at Luray Caverns in the Northern Shenandoah Valley of Virginia. When we got to Williamsburg the next day, we checked into our hotel and went immediately to a large Visitor Center for orientation. When we got there, I was dazzled by the array of things for us to see and do. I thought we'd start with the introductory film, *Story of a Patriot*. But, as I was checking the film schedule, Zia looked up at me and said, in a plaintive voice, "Mommy, I don't feel so good."

I asked a member of the Visitor Center's staff what to do, and she suggested I take Zia to the Williamsburg Community Hospital. Ann returned to the hotel to await developments.

At the hospital, a doctor examined Zia, found she had a temperature of 101, diagnosed it as intestinal flu, and advised me to take her back to the hotel and put her to bed.

As the cab was taking us back to the hotel, I noticed a sign on my left that said, "Colonial Williamsburg." "Please," I said to the cab driver, "Can you just drive us through there?"

"Sorry," he said, "cars are not allowed in there."

I could not even drive into the area.

We returned to the hotel, I put Zia to bed, called Ann in her nearby room to tell her what had happened, and suggested she rejoin the tour on her own. She refused to do so and said she would be with us instead.

The following morning, Zia was well enough to join Ann and me on the bus trip back to Stamford.

The trip to Williamsburg was not, however, a total loss. I am one of the few tourists to that historic area with a fairly good knowledge of the Williamsburg Community Hospital.

Role Change

Zia is now twenty-seven. If I have a problem, I talk it over with her. If she has a problem, she works it out herself. "When did it happen," I asked her recently, "that instead of your asking me for advice, I ask you?"

"I think it was when I was twelve," she answered.

The Root of All Evil

In 1997, when Zia came home for Thanksgiving, she was twenty-five years old and had been out of college for four years. She was working as an executive at a corporation in Chicago, earning only a little less than I had been earning when I retired in 1993 after thirty-six years as a government and corporate attorney. She was career oriented and extremely hard-working.

I could not understand this. As a child and teenager, Zia had been dreamy, listless, uninvolved in extracurricular activities at school beyond the marching band, and never displayed any leadership qualities. She told me after graduation from high school that she'd never done any homework in high school. What had given rise to this corporate hotshot?

One evening during her visit, I decided to ask her. "Zia," I said, "I don't understand the success you've been having at work. You never showed me anything while you were growing up. I remember when you were three or four years old and needed to go to nursery school, I couldn't even get you to get dressed in the morning. You'd just sit on the floor staring into space. And now, this. How come *I* could never get you to exert yourself?"

"You never offered me any money," she said.

Fear of Presentations

During Zia's junior year of high school in Potomac, I received a telephone call at work one day from the school nurse.

"Did Zia have a doctor's appointment this afternoon?" she asked.

"Not that I know of," I said. "Why do you ask?"

"She just came to my office," said the nurse, "and said she had a doctor's appointment and had to leave school. It seemed sudden and odd, so I thought I had better check with you."

I told the nurse I was mystified about this, would speak to Zia as soon as she came home from school, and would report back.

When I got home from work, I asked Zia what this was all about. She told me she'd been scheduled to make a presentation in front of her class, was petrified that she'd make a fool of herself, and so came up with this excuse. Instead of making the presentation, she sat in her car and sobbed.

I told her she was not to lie again and tried to comfort her. But I was concerned about her fear of making presentations. Whatever work she chose in the future, she would probably have to make presentations in front of large groups, on occasions considerably more important than a high school presentation. How would she handle that? Was her fear of public speaking related to the fact that *I* was a public speaker? Should I hire a phobia expert to work with her? I consulted a therapist-friend, who didn't feel it was necessary. So, I did nothing and worried about her future.

Early in 1998, Zia told me that I wouldn't be able to reach her by phone during the next few weeks—she would be flying around the country, giving training programs and making presentations about the corporate compensation plan, which she had helped develop.

A week later when she called from the road, I said, "How's it going?" She had just been to Indianapolis and Cleveland.

"Fine," she said. "No problems."

"Aren't you concerned about getting up in front of all those people?"

"No," she said.

"But, Zia," I persisted. "Remember when you told the school nurse you had a doctor's appointment because you were afraid of making a fool of yourself in front of the class. How come you're not afraid now in front of all these corporate executives?"

"I know what I'm talking about now," she said.

PART VIII

38.

HARRY GOLDEN AND
"THE COAT"

My parents were saddened by the fact that as I passed my twenties and then my thirties, there was no prospective husband in sight. But whenever my mother reached her lowest point, my father would hearten her with the story of "the Coat." In Berlin, in the 1920s, in my father's men's clothing store, there hung for many years a long, black overcoat. It had already passed through several cycles of men's fashions and was at a stage beyond fashion and above style. There was nothing really wrong with it, but the years passed and "the Coat" remained. Periodically, Mother and Father would discuss "the Coat." Should they throw it out? Should they give it to someone? It was difficult for them to just give away such a fine-looking coat made of such excellent wool. They always decided to wait just a bit longer. Perhaps they could still sell it to someone someday for 40 marks ($10). And, besides, my father's watchword had always been, "There's a customer for everything."

They were considering what to do with "the Coat" one evening shortly before closing time when a customer walked in. He said he was looking for a coat—but not just any coat. He wanted something special—a coat that would make his friends sit up and take notice. "Lina," said my father, with a gleam in his eye, "Go bring 'the Coat.'" My mother hastened to bring "the Coat" to the customer. My father helped him put it on. It was a perfect fit! The customer admired himself in the mirror. He was plainly delighted. He admitted that this was indeed something different. This was the coat he had been looking for.

"How much for this coat?" he asked.

"Three Hundred Fifteen Marks ($75)?" inquired my father, in a voice that indicated the matter was open for bargaining.

A broad smile flashed across the customer's face. Not only was this coat something special, something none of his friends had, but it was also expensive. "I'll take it," he said. A few minutes later, he was happily walking out of the store with his package under his arm and a satisfied smile on his face.

That was the story I heard my father tell through my adult years to remind my mother that when one had *gute skhoyre*—good merchandise, a customer would always come along. It didn't especially cheer me up to be compared to a coat that had hung unwanted for years in their store, but at least it served to take the pressure off my need to find a husband.

The story of "the Coat" led to my contretemps with Harry Golden. Golden, a short, rotund, Jewish, cigar-smoking colorful writer, was also a bit of a rogue. In 1929, when he was in his late twenties, he pled guilty to mail fraud charges in connection with his activities as a stockbroker in New York City. After serving a four-year prison sentence, he changed his name from Goldhurst to Golden and moved to Charlotte, North Carolina, a most unlikely setting in what became a most unlikely career. As he put it, he was "a Northerner living in the South, a Jew in the most Gentile community on the continent, [and] an integrationist among white supremacists."[10]

In Charlotte, he became the founder, publisher, editor, and writer of the *Carolina Israelite*. In that slight newspaper, with charm and humor, he waxed nostalgic about life on the Lower East Side of New York and railed against racial bigotry in the South. The *Carolina Israelite* became world renowned, and Golden's writings were compiled in over fifteen books. Three of them, *Only in America*, *For 2¢ Plain*, and *Enjoy, Enjoy!* became best sellers.

I enjoyed reading *For 2¢ Plain*, and, in November 1959, I wrote Golden to tell him so. He answered with a postcard and a copy of the *Carolina Israelite*. In that newspaper, I noticed an anecdote sent in by a reader that related to a story called "Buying a Suit for Hymie" that had appeared in one of Golden's books. The anecdote reminded me of "the Coat" story, so I wrote up the story and sent it to Golden with a letter.

The following year, I picked up a paperback copy of *Enjoy, Enjoy!* and what did I find on page 82 but my story under the title, "The overcoat." I was flabbergasted. I immediately wrote to Golden, expressing my outrage, and requesting compensation. Golden responded, saying it was possible that "sometimes an idea remains in your mind that you might have read somewhere and you are not quite sure, and this is particularly true of a man who writes entirely from 'the top of his head' without ever getting out of his chair to look into a dictionary, a reference book, or someone else's work of any nature."

Golden and I then exchanged letters, but he did not agree to compensate me for the unauthorized use of my story. I then consulted several lawyers, but it was not easy finding a lawyer to handle a matter of such small moment. Ultimately, I succeeded in securing the services of Amy Ruth Mahin, who was with the prestigious Washington, DC, firm of Covington & Burling. Miss Mahin agreed to represent me in seeking a settlement of my claim for copyright infringement against Golden. She said that no fee would be due unless money was recovered, and, in that event, she would be entitled to $50 or 25 percent of the gross sum recovered, whichever was larger. In addition, I would be responsible for any out-of-pocket expenses.

In this momentous literary legal battle, the well-known New York City law firm of Greenbaum, Wolff & Ernst represented Golden. In July 1961, a representative of that firm wrote Miss Mahin that after studying "the correspondence closely, . . . the only conclusion to which we can come is that Miss Pressman's claim is without legal merit." Miss Mahin, not to be undone by so cavalier a dismissal, wrote back the following month:

> In your letter of July 28 with regard to Miss Pressman's claim to infringement by Mr. Golden, you do not address yourself either to the controlling facts or to the legal injury actually involved. We trust you will consider the matter further.
>
> Mr. Golden did not take, and Miss Pressman does not ask to be compensated for, merely and [*sic*] idea for a story. As must be apparent to you or anyone comparing the two works, Mr. Golden took substantially both the literary form and content of Miss Pressman's literary piece—to and including her mother's given name, the sequence of narrative and incident, and the actual phrasing.
>
> Moreover, Miss Pressman does not seek compensation for the use of her work on any theory of express promise to pay by Mr. Golden. His use was wholly without notice of any kind to her. And even if inadvertent on his part, it would nonetheless be an appropriation of her rights in the literary piece. You employ the phrase "unsolicited letter" in describing the original manuscript of Miss Pressman's story. If by this you mean to suggest that the law gives an addressee freedom to make an unauthorized publication of any part or version of the contents of such a letter, you are of course in error.

Greenbaum, Wolff & Ernst did not change its opinion, but Golden did. He offered to write a story in the *Carolina Israelite* about me. He also said that when his publishers published a two-volume work entitled *Collected Writings of Harry Golden* scheduled for 1962, he would begin the story of "the Coat" as follows: "Here comes a fine story from a delightful girl in Washington, D.C.,

Miss Sonia Pressman."[11] Finally, he offered to pay me "fifty cents a line, which is what the publishers charged me for using some words of Ernest Hemingway."

I accepted Golden's offer. Greenbaum, Wolff & Ernst sent Miss Mahin a check for $13 made out to me for the twenty-six lines of my story. The next issue of the *Carolina Israelite* carried the following story:

Sonia Pressman Should Write a Book

Sonia Pressman is a lawyer in Washington and has been writing me some nice letters across the years. One of her letters, a true story, eventually found its way into my book ENJOY ENJOY. It was the story of a "schlock" store (a cut-rate clothing store) and how an unmarried daughter figured in a sales secret between the proprietor and his wife.

Sonia should sit down and write herself a book.

Since I was paid only for my story and did not receive any damages, Miss Mahin determined that I did not owe her any fee. She did, however, request $3.20 for Xeroxing, which I forwarded to her.

In 1973, President Richard M. Nixon granted Golden a full presidential pardon for his crime of mail fraud. I could do no less.

39.

VESPERS AT THREE

Nuns and priests have always fascinated me. They give up some of the very things the rest of us are living for: material possessions, sexual fulfillment, and independence. One of my childhood fantasies had been to spend a year in a convent, take notes on my discussions with the nuns, and then write a book based on that material.

The closest I came to satisfying that fantasy was my trip to the Trappist Monastery in the Shenandoah Valley in Berryville, Virginia, in the late '50s. I knew nothing about the Trappists other than that they maintained a vow of silence. That in itself was intriguing to a talker like me.

I drove to Berryville one spring day with Rita LaBrecque, my close friend and neighbor at Arlington Towers. She was single, like me, but, unlike me, she was a Catholic. We had driven about sixty miles when I saw the small sign directing visitors to the monastery to turn onto a small road to the right. We followed the road across a small bridge and over some hills until we saw the dirt road leading to the monastery. On the grounds, we saw a herd of black cattle.

After we parked, we saw the main building, a chapel, a shack, and a small lake, near which sheep were grazing. We went first to the main house, and I rang the bell. Rita blanched at my effrontery. A few minutes later, a portly old monk opened the door. He wore a dark habit that covered him completely, with a belt around his expansive middle. He looked exactly like all the photographs of monks I'd ever seen. I told him that we were visiting the monastery for the day, had heard that they showed visitors around, and asked whether we could have a tour. The monk, taken aback by these two unexpected women visitors, cleared his throat and said, "We only show visitors around—on certain days—and then only men." I told him that even on those certain days, we would still be women. He did not appreciate my attempt at humor, and the conversation came to an abrupt end.

As we left the main house, Rita mentioned that she had heard that the Trappists sold bread on the premises. She suggested that we walk to the little shack since it might be a store. Sure enough, it was a store, a charming one. Its shelves were filled with Trappist bread, honey, and other staples, as well as with a host of religious relics.

When we entered, the monk behind the counter, a young man of about thirty, wearing shell-rimmed glasses, was completing a sale to a young woman. After that, he sold me a loaf of Trappist bread. Rita, who had been browsing, asked him, "Do the monks make this honey, too?"

"No," he answered, with a smile, "We have bees for that." I hadn't expected a sense of humor; it piqued my interest, and we began to chat. The monk handed me an advertisement, which stated that if I liked the Trappist bread, I could make future purchases at my local Giant supermarket. I told him I would buy some lox and cream cheese at the Giant to eat with my Trappist bread; that way I'd be hitting all the religious bases.

Rita purchased one of the religious medals and asked the monk to bless it for her. "Don't be silly," I teased. "He can't do that. Don't you see he's a businessman?" It turned out I was right. "Yes," said the monk. "I have no facility for blessing medals since I'm assigned to selling this year."

I inquired about the Trappists' vow of silence and the reason for it. "We're not supposed to 'chew the fat,'" he said. "Not with visitors and not with each other. We're just supposed to communicate with the Lord."

"Well, you get no back talk that way," I said.

He told us that the rule was relaxed for him and other monks, however, during the time they were assigned to the store. I bought a postcard and asked him where I might mail it. My friends would be surprised to get a card from me with a Trappist Monastery for a return address. The monk took my card and said he'd be happy to mail it for me.

Rita and I said, "Good-bye," and walked outside. We stood for a moment, considering where to take pictures when the door opened, and the monk stepped outside. "It's a beautiful day, isn't it?" he asked. We agreed. "Did you notice the wild onions here?" he asked, pointing to some flowers surrounding the little store. No, we hadn't. "And these, these over here," he continued, pointing to another patch of flowers, "these are crocuses." He then proceeded to tell us whatever he could to hold our attention and keep the conversation going. I don't remember ever meeting a man who was so starved for companionship and conversation. "Did you notice that I'm in brown?" he asked. We hadn't. "You see, Brothers who say Mass and perform devotions wear white; others, such as myself, wear brown." Then he lifted up a piece of his habit and said, "And did you know this material is Dacron? Amazing, isn't it?"

He pointed behind the main house then, and told us the bakery was located there. He told us about the monks working in the bakery and about the two years he had spent herding the sheep we had seen at the little lake. The lake was only for the use of the sheep; it was off limits to the monks.

I asked about the black cattle that we had seen as we drove into the monastery grounds. Those were purebred Black Angus cattle, he told us, which the monks bred. "I wonder, Brother," I asked, "if I could take a picture with you?" Rita began to remonstrate with me that, of course, monks couldn't pose for pictures, but she was interrupted by the monk's immediately adopting a pose. He raised his right hand and pointed his index finger toward the main house. "Go ahead," he said. "I've already broken so many cameras, one more won't make any difference. Why don't you just stand over there and I'll point you the way to the monastery?" A dazed Rita snapped the picture. "How about another one?" the monk asked. "Just in case that one didn't turn out. No sense taking chances." And so Rita snapped another one, and he reluctantly dropped the pose.

Rita and I began to collect our belongings. "Won't you stay for Vespers, the evening service?" the monk said. "We have Vespers at 3. You'll like the singing." And, seeing that we still made ready to leave, he added, "It only lasts half an hour."

"No, thank you," I said. "We'd better be going. We have a long drive back, you know."

"Oh," he said. And stood there forlornly, watching us leave.

I never saw that monk again. When I placed one of the pictures Rita snapped in my album, I didn't know how to caption it because I'd never gotten his name. So, I called it "Brother and Sonia." And so it sits, in my photograph album—a picture of a woman in a gray rayon suit and a bespectacled monk in his brown Dacron habit, pointing to a monastery.

40.

BRUSHES WITH THE LAW

Although I've never run afoul of the criminal justice system myself, a number of people who have gotten legally entangled have crossed my path. They include a call girl, a bank president, a doctor, a bank robber, and a young woman with impeccable political connections in both parties.

Pat Ward

My first such encounter was in 1953 while I was working as a secretary in New York City for *True Confessions* magazine, a romance publication targeted to young women. It involved Pat Ward, who had sold her story to the magazine. Pat had achieved her fifteen minutes of fame as a call girl embroiled in a sex scandal with Minot "Mickey" Jelke III, the heir to a considerable oleomargarine fortune. (His grandfather had invented it.) The papers were filled with the story; it was New York's biggest prostitution scandal—the Heidi Fleiss story of the '50s, except that the accused panderer was a man.

Pat described herself as a "party girl." By the age of seventeen, she'd already had an illegitimate baby, whom she put up for adoption. Then she met Jelke, a pint-sized New York City playboy, at a party. After their second meeting, she began to live with him. In 1953, when she was nineteen, Pat was the star witness in the State's case against the 23-year-old Jelke. She testified that Jelke was the boss of a string of $50-$500 a night call girls, and that after his family cut him off from his trust fund, he pressured her into becoming one of his prostitutes. The case garnered a lot of attention because Jelke's clientele allegedly included café society figures, movie stars, and wealthy businessmen. Jelke was ultimately convicted of compulsory prostitution and sentenced to Sing Sing.

Pat called the office frequently, and we became telephone friends. It turned out she was actually a "nice Jewish girl" named Sandra Wisotsky from the Lower East Side of New York. When she learned I lived in Long Beach, she told me that she'd been at a swim club there that summer when someone recognized her and reported her presence to the manager. Because of her notoriety, he asked her to leave. It was a poignant story and my heart went out to her.

Shortly thereafter, I resigned from *True Confessions* to enter law school. I heard no more about Jelke and Ward—until over forty years later in 1997. That's when I saw *Cafe Society*, a movie based on the Jelke/Ward story at the Key Theater in Washington, DC. I was so intrigued by the new information in this film that I called the movie's writer and director, Raymond De Felitta. He told me that he'd spent five years researching the Jelke/Ward case and concluded that the baby Pat Ward bore before the age of seventeen was the result of her rape by an older man, her father's boss, Lawrence Greenbaum; there was in fact only one prostitute in Jelke's alleged call-girl ring: Pat Ward; and the reason Jelke was targeted for investigation and prosecuted for operating a call-girl ring was because he was a celebrity and his prosecution would garner pre-election publicity to help re-elect Frank Hogan as Manhattan District Attorney.

Jelke spent several years in Sing Sing and then moved to Florida, where he lived reclusively. He married and divorced twice and died of cirrhosis in 1990 at the age of sixty.

Between the first and second Jelke trials, Pat Ward had a brief affair with an Emanuel Trujillo, an unsavory character who was involved with the National Renaissance Party, a neo-Nazi group. When their affair ended, he offered his services to Jelke's lawyers as a witness against Pat Ward. When the lawyers turned him down because of his neo-Nazi affiliation, he wrote a book entitled, *I Love You, I Hate You, My Six Weeks of Free Love With Pat Ward.* Pat later was briefly married to an attorney, Delevan Smith, and she last surfaced in the late '60s when *Esquire* interviewed her in connection with the Jelke case. She is believed to be alive, but her whereabouts are unknown.

Bill Rose

The Catskills have long had a connection with crime and criminals. There were periods in the twenties and early thirties when the Catskills were referred to as "Chicago with pines."[12] Victims of the mob were often found at the bottom of Sullivan County's lakes. Arson was a frequent occurrence, usually after the summer season when buildings were empty and bills were pressing. Due to the fact that many of these resorts were owned and presumably burned by Jews, these fires came to be known as "Jewish lightning."[13] On lazy fall afternoons, my father frequently took the family for a drive to view the remains of the latest conflagration or to Lake Louise Marie in Rock Hill, into which Murder Incorporated deposited its victims.

In the summer of 1955, after my first year of law school, I went to Ellenville, New York, to work as a secretary for Ethel and Joe Kooperman. Ethel and Joe had their offices at 90 North Main Street in a lovely old building, the Wayside Inn (most of which, unfortunately, burned down in the '60s). Ethel and Joe had been a part of my life since 1936 when my family moved to Woodridge. They represented my parents in real estate investments.

Ellenville, a resort village about seventy-five miles northwest of New York City, had a year-round population of 4,200, which swelled in the summer. In 1955, I rented a room in the home of a local family, the Van Gorders, and boarded across the street at the boarding house of Mrs. "Cookie" Peritz. I did routine legal secretarial work, and my duties included frequent visits to the Home

National Bank, a block from the office, to make deposits and with-drawals for the firm.

The bank, located in a modest one-story building at 88 Canal Street, had been founded in 1873, and was the largest of Ellenville's three banks. Being inside the bank was an experience because of the reverential air everyone had toward its president, William Richard Rose. His employees viewed him as akin to a god. Whenever I was in the bank, someone was always running about with a document that had to be signed, calling, "Mr. Rose, Mr. Rose." Eventually, Rose would appear, a portly fifty-year old man, just short of six feet tall, with thinning sandy hair. A hush would fall over the bank as he signed the document. In the bank, Rose was the absolute master.

He was in fact Mr. Ellenville. One writer said that William Rose "may be the most legendary figure to come out of the Catskills since Rip Van Winkle."[14] He was the village's leading citizen, its most influential civic leader, and its most eligible bachelor. He dated occasionally but never married. He lived with his eighty-three year old mother, an independently wealthy widow who was a member of an old Ellenville family. Their home was a seventeen-room mansion of gingerbread, Victorian architecture atop a knoll at 155 South Main Street.

His late grandfather and father, both also named William, were bankers before him. His grandfather had founded the bank, and his father had served as its president.

The William Rose of my day, who was born in 1906, had begun working at the bank summers when he was sixteen. In 1929, at the age of twenty-three, he was a clerk, and in 1940 he became the bank's president.

Ellenville was prospering in the mid-'50s. Part of the community's economy was in the numerous resorts, the best known of which was the Nevele Hotel, but increasingly Ellenville had developed industries. It was home to the Channel Master Corporation, one of the country's largest manufacturers of antennae, employing fifteen hundred people; the Ulster Knife Company, employing about 250; and many smaller enterprises. Rose had fostered all this development. Upon becoming bank president, he had initiated a policy of extraordinarily liberal credit and also encouraged installment loans. The byword in Ellenville was, "If you need money, see Uncle Bill." The bank flourished, too. It was doing 70 percent of the area's commercial business, and employment tripled from ten to thirty during his presidency.

Rose had almost no intimate friends, but almost everybody liked him. He was rumored to be a multimillionaire. He belonged to the Chamber of Commerce, was past president of the six-county District 8 of the New York State Bankers' Association, past president of the Shawangunk Country Club, treasurer and head usher of the local Methodist Church, and a member of the Scoresby Volunteer Hook and Ladder Company. He had gone to Harvard and served as a lieutenant commander in the Navy during World War II. As the most prominent veteran in the village, he was always grand marshal of the military parades.

But he had not lost the common touch. He drove a 1952 two-door Plymouth sedan. He left home at 7 AM every day carrying his lunch—a fried egg sandwich in a little wicker basket—and stopped off en route to his office for a container of milk. He usually remained at the bank until 7 PM or later.

After my summer in Ellenville, I returned to Florida for my second year of law school. A little over a year later, I was studying in my den one evening when my mother called me into the living room to watch TV. She did this frequently as she and my father believed I spent too much time with my books, and they tried to pull me away from my studies. So I did not pay too much attention until she called again, "Hurry," she said. "Ellenville's on the news." I ran right in, wondering what little Ellenville had done to warrant coverage on the Miami news show. But there it was on the screen—not only Ellenville, but the camera was zooming in on the Home National Bank. A minute later, the face of Rose appeared. The FBI had just arrested him!

It had begun on Friday, November 30, 1956, as Ellenville was looking forward to a merry Christmas. National bank examiners, acting on the complaint of a depositor, seized the bank's books. They discovered that Rose had misappropriated half a million dollars of the bank's money. He hadn't done it for financial gain; his stocks, bonds, and cash amounted to no more than $135,000 (all of which he later turned over to the receiver). He was apparently motivated by a desire to create a more prosperous Ellenville and was no doubt also drunk with his power in the bank and the community. And so, like many in positions of power, he seriously overstepped the boundaries. He was profligate with the bank's money and even his own. The most spectacular example involved the Anjopa Board and Paper Manufacturing Company. He lent Anjopa, a financially shaky enterprise, not only the bank's money but also his own, and at one point, he personally took over the financial operation of the company's mill.

Because the bank was so much a part of his life, he forgot the separation between the bank and himself. In his mind, they were one. He made too many loans, and they were often given without collateral and for excessive periods of time. He falsified the bank's records to hide these activities and fooled the bank examiners for years. Two factors led to his undoing. One was a persistent bank examiner named George A. Monahan, who continued to have misgivings about the financial condition of the bank and to conduct examinations of its books. The other was the failure of a depositor's check to clear. The depositor got in touch with the Federal Reserve Bank, and the fateful bank examination took place.

When the examiners confronted Rose with their initial discovery that Black Friday, he resigned as president on the spot. He was arrested that evening at his home by the FBI.

The following morning, the bank's customers swarmed to the bank, not to withdraw funds, but to deposit more as expressions of confidence. One depositor, Ben Slutsky, the owner of the Nevele Hotel, which already had a $100,000 account in the bank, pledged another $100,000 by Monday. And, true to his word, Slutsky withdrew $102,000 from other bank accounts and deposited it in

Rose's bank. Mayor Eugene Glusker told people that "Bill Rose is a great public benefactor. He's done a remarkable job for the small businessman and for private people. We're all united in his behalf."

That Sunday night, two hundred civic and business leaders met to reaffirm their affection and regard for Uncle Bill. On Monday, packing crates were hammered together and a booth erected for the collection of signatures of support. That evening, there was an open air meeting in front of the petition booth with a few short speeches and a great deal of cheering. Eventually, almost three thousand signatures were collected.

One group of four Protestant ministers went against the tide. They issued a statement saying, in part, that they could not condone activities that were unlawful. One of the signers was the pastor of the Ellenville Methodist Church, where two years earlier Rose had had to relinquish his position as treasurer because his financial reports were inadequate.

Then it was learned that the FBI had rearrested Rose, who had been free on $25,000 bail. The check for his bail had been drawn on the now-defunct Home National Bank and, furthermore, the amount he had misappropriated amounted to $1.4 million rather than half a million. The chief recipients of this largesse had been Anjopa and the Hotel Zeiger of Fallsburg, with overdrafts of $926,000 and $235,000, respectively. The Federal Deposit Insurance Corporation (FDIC) ordered the bank closed; it was to go into receivership for liquidation.

The *Ellenville Journal* for December 6, 1956, in reporting these events, had the following box on its front page:

WRITTEN WITH REGRET

The Journal—no different from others in the community—
writes with regret of the events of the past week . . . .

The people of Ellenville began to regret it, too, and to reevaluate their support for Uncle Bill. The petition of support was withdrawn from circulation. Five days after the bank was closed, Ellenville's mayor and leading businesspersons flew to Washington to confer with Treasury officials. As a result of their negotiations, in what was regarded as a miracle of accomplishment in banking circles, eighteen days after the bank was closed, its successor, the Ellenville National Bank, opened for business in the same building as its predecessor. It continues to function to this day, with many branches in the Hudson Valley.

In mid-October 1957, Rose pleaded guilty to seventeen counts of bank fraud, and in December he was given a five-year sentence. During his incarceration at the federal correctional institution in Danbury, Connecticut, he was a model prisoner. As a result, in August of 1959, he was granted parole as of October 1. The warden released him on September 2, however, citing his work in the institution's hospital as the reason for his early release.

After serving twenty-one months of his sentence, on a light drizzly morning, Rose returned to Ellenville to live with his mother. No welcoming committee was on hand to greet him on his return.

Rose resumed the occupation he had taken up while waiting to serve his sentence. Had you lived in Ellenville then, you might have seen him at work. If your toilet was stuck and you called a plumber, the man who would come to your door might very well be a portly, familiar-looking man with thinning sandy hair—Bill Rose.

Dr. Cecil Jacobson

I was more involved personally with Dr. Cecil Jacobson than I had been with Bill Rose. Dr. Jacobson, a professor at the George Washington (GW) University Medical Center, was one of the leading geneticists in Washington, DC. I went to see him in 1971 when I was interested in having a child but was concerned about becoming pregnant over the age of 40. During my two visits to his office, Dr. Jacobson, a heavy-set, jowly man, was most gracious in ex-

plaining amniocentesis, which he had in fact introduced in the
US. On my third visit, he performed the amniocentesis on me,
which revealed no problems with my pregnancy.

In the late '80s, I was watching *60 Minutes*, when, to my
amazement, Dr. Jacobson appeared on the screen. He was in his
mid-fifties, his face was bloated and he was grossly obese, and he
was no longer associated with GW. In 1976, he had opened the
Reproductive Genetic Center, a fertility clinic in Vienna, Virginia,
and ran it for about twelve years. Now he was accused of tricking
women into believing they were pregnant. It was alleged that he
used hormone injections to create symptoms resembling pregnancy;
later he told the women their fetuses had aborted and would be
reabsorbed into their bodies; and then he would begin a new round
of hormone injections and pregnancy tests.

Thereafter, the media was filled with stories about
Dr. Jacobson. It turned out that he had actually had no credentials warranting his setting himself up as a fertility specialist. In
1989, the Federal Trade Commission investigated him and obtained an injunction that led him to close his clinic. He set up a
fund for restitution and refunded $250,000 to more than a hun-
dred former patients. In 1992, to avoid having his medical license
revoked, he signed a consent order, agreeing not to practice medi-
cine in Virginia or anywhere else.

He was criminally indicted by a federal grand jury for fraud
and perjury. In addition to tricking women into believing they
were pregnant, he had also used his own sperm to impregnate
patients by artificial insemination and told them the sperm was
that of an anonymous donor. He had used his own sperm even
where women had brought sperm donated by their husbands to
his office. Prosecutors charged that he might have fathered as many
as seventy-five children in the DC area.

In March 1992, Jacobson was convicted of fifty-two counts of
fraud and perjury. He was subsequently sentenced to five years in
prison and ordered to pay $116,805 in fines and restitution; in
1993, his conviction was upheld. In 1994, CBS aired *Babymaker:*

The Dr. Cecil Jacobson Story, a two-hour made-for-TV film, starring Melissa Gilbert as a patient and George Dzundza as Dr. Jacobson.

To this day, I remind Zia how lucky she is that I was already pregnant when I went to see Dr. Jacobson. Or she might be looking quite different.

Ray Jackson and Christopher Boyce

At the end of 1981, I left GTE to work at the headquarters of TRW in Euclid, Ohio. I was to be director of compliance management with responsibility for the company's EEO and Affirmative Action programs. Prior to my coming aboard, one of the company's executives had served as the interim director of compliance management. He had replaced my predecessor on the job, Jerome Ray Jackson. Jackson, whom I never met, was an African American lawyer, who had been hired at TRW in 1977. He was good looking, well dressed, charming, and made a good impression on everyone he met. After serving as director of EEO for several years, he wanted a change of responsibility and secured a transfer to financial operations. In 1981, he became director of investor relations, but in September of that year, he submitted his resignation. Thereafter, although he was unable to find employment, in the latter part of 1981, *Jet* Magazine and other media reported that he was the front runner for the vacant position of EEOC chairman. Jackson's consideration for the EEOC chairmanship ended on December 30, 1981, however, when he was indicted by a Cuyahoga County grand jury for grand theft and passing a bad check for $2,900. The following day, the IRS filed a tax lien against him for income tax assessments for the tax years 1973-1976 and 1978.

When I began my second week at TRW, on Monday, February 1, 1982, Cleveland newspapers reported a bizarre sequence of events involving Jackson. The preceding Saturday, January 30, Jackson, unarmed, had walked into the Strongsville, Ohio, branch of the National City Bank and handed a teller a note demanding money.

Jackson left the bank, carrying a manila envelope with the money. He hurried to his car in the bank parking lot and got in. A bank employee had, however, tripped a silent alarm and, within minutes, police responded to the alarm and surrounded the bank. Jackson started his car and tried to run down some of them; the police opened fire and struck him in the shoulder and neck. He was hospitalized in critical condition. On February 5, 1982, he was indicted for aggravated robbery, kidnapping, attempted murder, and possession of criminal tools. On March 30, he died of his wounds. He was forty-three years old.

Jackson was not, however, TRW's most notorious ex-employee. That honor goes to Christopher John Boyce, an avid falconer. On July 29, 1974, at the age of twenty-one, Boyce was hired as a general clerk at TRW's Defense and Space Systems Group in Redondo Beach, California, at a salary of $140 a week. Four months later, TRW assigned him to a special project involving the CIA's collection of secret intelligence information from space via satellites. In April 1975, along with his boyhood friend, Andrew Daulton Lee, a convicted drug dealer, Boyce began selling spy-satellite secrets to the Soviet Union. He terminated his employment with TRW in December 1976. In 1977, Boyce and Lee were arrested by the FBI, indicted for espionage, and convicted. Boyce was sentenced to forty years in prison, and Lee was given a life sentence. Their exploits formed the subject of a book, Robert Lindsey's *The Falcon and the Snowman*, which was turned into a 1984 movie of the same name with Sean Penn and Timothy Hutton.

After serving three years, Boyce broke out of California's Lompoc Federal Penitentiary on January 21, 1980. A manhunt followed, and he was arrested on August 21, 1981. The following April, he pleaded guilty to robbing five banks while he was a fugitive, and he was sentenced to another twenty-five years in jail.

With regard to the secrets that Boyce and Lee delivered to the Russians, Senator Daniel Patrick Moynihan said on *60 Minutes* that "nothing quite so awful has happened to our country as the escapade of these two young men."[15]

Deborah Gore Dean

When I joined the General Counsel's office at HUD at the end of 1985, Deborah "Debbie" Gore Dean was the executive assistant to HUD's Secretary, Samuel R. Pierce, Jr. She had come to HUD in November of 1982, as a special assistant to the Secretary and in June of 1984 became his executive assistant—his top aide. She was an attractive, buxom woman of thirty-one with long blonde hair. She was always cordial when we met and easy to work with on the one case in which we were both involved.

Debbie, however, had very little to commend her for a position as prestigious as top assistant to a Cabinet member. In 1980, after eight years, she had graduated from Georgetown University, 507th in a class of 509. Her government experience before coming to HUD consisted of about seventeen months at the Department of Energy. She had secured a job there through the intercession of John Mitchell, President Nixon's former law partner and Attorney General, who had served nineteen months in prison after being convicted of conspiracy, obstruction of justice, and perjury in the Watergate cover-up trial. He was her mother's lover.

On the basis of her family connections, however, her résumé was most impressive. The family patriarch was her grandfather, Henry Grady Gore, who hailed from the politically prominent Democratic Gore family of Tennessee. The Colonel hated Roosevelt's New Deal policies, broke with the party in 1934, and formally changed his party affiliation in 1948. Colonel Gore was a candidate for the US Senate and a close friend of Dwight Eisenhower, Prescott Bush, and other prominent Republicans. The Colonel made a fortune buying and selling Washington real estate. To celebrate his success in the real estate business, in 1932 he bought the Fairfax Hotel (later known as the Ritz-Carlton and now the Westin Fairfax Hotel) at 2100 Massachusetts Avenue, NW. As a child, Debbie lived in the hotel with her family.

The Colonel is probably best remembered, however, as the squire of Marwood, the estate he bought in 1943. Marwood, Potomac's most opulent mansion, was a 33-room house on a 187-acre estate. The building was a copy of Malmaison, the château Napoleon built for Josephine near Paris. Marwood had a driveway that was more than a half-mile long, two 40-foot salons, and a 134-seat screening theater in the basement. The mansion commanded a magnificent view of the Potomac River and the Virginia palisades. Before the Gores, it had housed other prominent people, including the Joe Kennedys and President Roosevelt, who had used it as a summer White House.

Debbie's father, who died in a plane crash on Nantucket when she was three, was Gordon Dean, Harry Truman's first head of the Atomic Energy Commission and a prosecutor at the Nuremburg trials, for which he won the Medal of Freedom. Debbie's widowed mother, Mary Benton Gore Dean, achieved notoriety in the wake of Watergate by succeeding the outspoken Martha Mitchell in John Mitchell's affections. For more than twelve years, Mary Gore Dean lived with John Mitchell, a man Debbie referred to as Dad. After Mitchell collapsed and died of a heart attack on the street outside Mary Gore Dean's Georgetown home, Mary Gore Dean moved back to Marwood.

Debbie's aunt, Louise Gore, was a Maryland state legislator, a two-time unsuccessful candidate for Governor of Maryland, a member of the Republican National Committee, and an intimate of prominent Republicans. Debbie was her protégée.

Debbie's second cousin, Al Gore, Jr., the Vice President, had previously been the Democratic senator from Tennessee, as had his father before him. Gore Vidal, the essayist, novelist, playwright, and memoirist is a distant cousin.

In 1987, when Debbie was thirty-two, Sam Pierce had President Reagan nominate her to be assistant secretary for Community Planning and Development at HUD. In that capacity, she would be responsible for urban programs that cost the taxpayers approximately $4 billion every year. At the hearing before the Senate Committee on Banking, Housing, and Urban Affairs, on August 6, 1987, then-Senator Al Gore and Republican Senators Alfonse d'Amato and Strom Thurmond supported her confirmation. Chairman William Proxmire (Democrat), however, compared her qualifications to those of some prior assistant secretaries at HUD. Before coming to HUD, they had served in positions such as assistant mayor of Indianapolis; director of the Columbus, Ohio, Housing and Redevelopment Authority; and director of the Baltimore Redevelopment Agency. In his questioning of Debbie, Proxmire brought out the fact that Debbie's work experience, other than her six years at HUD and the Department of Energy, was primarily acquired in DC restaurants, where she had worked as a bartender, hostess, disk jockey and manager.

People Weekly, which named her one of "The 25 Most Intriguing People of the Year" for 1989, said, with regard to her qualifications for a position at HUD: "Her only previous experience in housing was that she lived in one."[16]

The nomination languished in the Committee for months. *The New York Times* reported on May 31, 1989, that Bartlett Naylor, former head of investigations for the Senate Banking Committee, stated with regard to the nomination:

> The committee staff was alarmed that someone who was about to be running a $4 billion program had such a poor credit rating and seemed to have money problems, stemming in part from the consistently high bar tabs she charged to her department credit card.

Senator Proxmire said he managed to kill the nomination.

The hearing was the beginning of Debbie's political downfall. She resigned from HUD in January 1988, and, four years later, in April 1992, she was indicted for systemic fraud and influence peddling at HUD. Her indictment was part of an independent counsel investigation into criminal conduct and corruption by HUD officials within the Reagan administration. During her trial at the US District Court for the District of Columbia, she was depicted as funneling millions of dollars in federal housing rehabilitation money from 1984 to 1987 to projects that benefited politically connected Republicans, including John Mitchell. Debbie testified that she was the chief go-between for Secretary Pierce and the hundreds of members of Congress and business executives who wanted favors, but that the Secretary made all the decisions with regard to housing programs. In October 1993, the jury found her guilty of twelve counts of perjury, conspiracy to defraud the federal government, accepting an illegal gratuity of $4,000 from a political consultant, and lying to Congress. On March 15, 1994, Judge Thomas F. Hogan sentenced her to twenty-one months of imprisonment, to be followed by two years of supervised release, $600 in special assessments, and a $5,000 fine. She appealed to the US Court of Appeals for the District of Columbia Circuit, which in May 1995 affirmed most of the lower court's judgment but vacated parts of it, vacated her sentence, and remanded the case to the District Court for resentencing. As of this writing (July 20, 1999), resentencing has not yet taken place, a motion for a new trial is pending, and legal proceedings are continuing.

Samuel Pierce was never charged. In return for his acknowledgement in 1994 that he helped create a climate in which the corruption took place and his acceptance of responsibility for the need to launch the independent counsel investigation, prosecutors agreed not to pursue charges against him.

On October 27, 1998, the two independent counsels who had been involved in the 8½-year HUD investigation submitted their findings to the DC Circuit of the US Court of Appeals— ending the longest investigation in the twenty years of the controversial independent counsel statute. Of the seventeen criminal convictions generated by the investigation, only Debbie Dean's case is still pending. In June 1999, the three-judge panel overseeing the independent counsel statute sent the case to the Justice Department for any future action.

Debbie has, however, managed to survive in Washington despite the scandal. In 1993, she married Richard "Spider" Pawlik, who ran the food service training unit at the Green Door, a mental health social service agency in Washington, DC. She subsequently had a daughter, Jamie Marie Gore Pawlik. In order to pay her massive legal fees, she sold the family pieces in her apartment, which led her to open her own antique business. She owns and operates Gore*Dean, located in two federal-style row houses in Georgetown, and Spider, who left the Green Door, works in the shop with her. In a denouement no one could have predicted, she has become "one of Washington's most respected antiquarians."[17] Her mother, Mary Dean, is ill and lives with her in Washington.

On November 16, 1998, Debbie was quoted as saying: "I am very happy. I don't know, if things had kept going, whether I would be this happy. I would be work-driven." But despite having come from a political family, she will never return to government: "I will always be a felon . . . . the name is tainted," she said.[18]

In another respect, the saga of the Gore family has come to a sad end. In the early '90s, the Gores received approval from Montgomery County to subdivide Marwood into seventy-four building lots. The family owed millions to creditors, including the IRS, however, and went into bankruptcy. The mansion and the estate, worth about $30 million, were the subject of foreclosure proceedings. The Gores received a settlement of about $200,000 to $300,000 and were forced to move out of the mansion. In 1995, the mansion was sold for $2 million to Yonus Zegeye, a neurosurgeon from Ethiopia, who is restoring it for his family. *Sic transit gloria mundi.*

41.

JEWISH GEOGRAPHY

"Jewish geography" is the expression used to explain what happens when two or more Jews meet who share a connection to a particular village, town, city, or locality: they will question each other until they eventually find that they know, or know of, at least one other Jew in common. My most remarkable incident of Jewish geography occurred in the unlikely city of Las Cruces, New Mexico—the City of the Crosses—a place not renowned for its Jewish population.

In the winter of 1996, after Roberto had been dead for over a year, I planned a two-week vacation in New Mexico for the following May with Carmen, his first wife. (I was his second wife; he was married to his third at the time of his death.) Carmen lives in Las Cruces, and we decided to spend a week at an Elderhostel in Santa Fe, followed by a week using Las Cruces as our base while we visited other sites in the area.

When this was arranged, I contacted Nancy Peters Hastings, who lives in Las Cruces, and we agreed to meet while I was there. Nancy was the guest editor of *Café Solo*, the literary journal that was the first publication to accept an excerpt from these memoirs.

When Carmen and I arrived in Las Cruces, I phoned Nancy and she suggested we meet her that afternoon at Nabe's Coffee Bar & Newsstand at 2001 East Lohman. Carmen and I drove there, sat at a table, and awaited Nancy's arrival. Nancy had no sooner come over and introduced herself when she turned her head as she saw a man and a girl leaving the restaurant. "Oh," she said, "there's a man I'd like to introduce to you because he's a writer, too, and also an editor." She waved the man and girl over and, as they approached, she told me that on the preceding Friday, she had attended the bat mitzvah of that girl, who was the daughter of this writer/editor, at Las Cruces' only temple.

Nancy introduced the man as "Ben Nussbaum*" and we said our "hellos." I immediately wondered how someone with a Jewish name had gotten *farblonjet*—hopelessly lost—in the City of the Crosses. To find out, I asked him where he was from.

"Monticello" was the surprising reply.

But there are many Monticellos in this country. I wasn't home free yet. "In what state?" I persisted.

"New York," he said.

"Sit down," I said.

"I'm sorry, I was just on my way out," said Ben, beginning to edge away from the table.

"I said, 'Sit down,'" I told him, in my most imperious tone. He sat down.

"I lived in Monticello," I began. "In fact, I graduated from high school there. But I didn't know anyone named Nussbaum there. But in Woodridge, where I lived from 1936 to 1941, *there* I knew someone named Nussbaum. He was a plasterer."

"That was my grandfather," said Ben. "But we don't refer to him as 'a plasterer.' We refer to him as 'a contractor.'"

"OK," I said, "a contractor. We weren't so fancy in those days. In Woodridge, he was known as a plasterer. He was a friend of my parents."

I was of course amazed that in this medium-sized city in the middle of the New Mexican desert I should meet the grandson of a man I'd known as a child in the Catskills; that he should just have happened to be in Nabe's when we came in (two minutes later, he would have been gone); and that Nancy should take it upon herself to introduce us. Jewish geography.

And then I realized that I could share with Ben a story that I'd been carrying around with me for almost sixty years. "Would you like to hear a scandal about your Aunt Sherrill*?" I asked. He would. And so I told him this story.

I was about ten and attending elementary school in Woodridge when I became aware of a beautiful young woman of about eighteen—Nussbaum, the plasterer's daughter, Sherrill. I'd see her from time to time in the village and was struck by her beauty and look of innocence. She was a sweet, lovely looking young woman, with brunette braids forming a halo around her head.

That summer, a man named Jack Kornblatt*, one of the New Yorkers who frequented Woodridge during the season, met Sherrill, fell in love with her, and asked her to marry him. She accepted, they married that very summer, and shortly thereafter left for his home in Manhattan.

"She always was impulsive," interjected Ben.

There was, in fact, considerable talk in the village about the hastiness of it all, but, beyond that, all agreed that Jack seemed to be a fine man and a wonderful catch for a small-town girl. He was, after all, from the big city.

Several years later, while Sherrill was in their New York apartment one Saturday afternoon, the phone rang and the caller asked for Jack. "He's not here right now," she said. "But I'm expecting him any minute. I'll be happy to tell him you called when he gets home."

"Who is this?" asked the caller.

"It's his wife," said Sherrill.

"That's funny. You don't sound like Betsy*," said the caller. "But have Jack call me anyway when he gets home."

"You don't sound like Betsy"? *Who was Betsy*? When Jack came home, it didn't take Sherrill long to find out who Betsy was. Betsy was Jack's wife, the mother of his three children, the woman he had already been married to when he proposed to, and later married, Sherrill. And the woman he was still married to, and had in fact been seeing, along with his children, that very Saturday afternoon.

After all the reproaches and tears, Sherrill left New York and returned to Woodridge, somewhat in disgrace. Shortly thereafter, however, she married one of the village's most eligible bachelors, a young man from a prominent local family, and I presumed lived happily ever after with him in Woodridge.

"Not exactly," said Ben. "She's now on her fourth—uh, I guess now he's her fifth—actually, I guess he's still her fourth—husband, and last I heard she was in California with him." Apparently, Sherrill had shed her innocence.

Then Ben did get up to leave. And this time I let him go. He said he was running home to call his father—to find out why he'd never before been told about his Aunt Sherrill's first marriage.

I spent a week in Las Cruces and while there visited Mesilla, White Sands, and Ruidoso—beautiful places, all. But nothing matched my meeting with Ben Nussbaum at Nabe's.

PART IX

42.

AN ISRAELI PLUMBER

In 1968, on my first trip to Israel, one of the revelations for me was the variety of occupations engaged in by Jews there. I had previously bought into the stereotypes of traditional Jewish occupations. Jews were doctors, lawyers, professors; they were not taxicab drivers, electricians, and plumbers—except that in Israel, they were. Jews did everything in Israel, everything I'd never seen them do before. But my most memorable encounter was with a Jewish plumber.

I had checked into the famous King David Hotel in Jerusalem and, to my surprise, found that in that elegant hostelry when I flushed the toilet, the water in the toilet bowl rose to a dangerous level. I rushed to the telephone, called the desk, reported the matter, and assumed that a plumber would be up in short order. After a half-hour with no knock on the door, I called the desk again. This went on for two hours until finally, a plumber appeared. I was furious at the delay. "It's taken you two hours to get here," I said. "The entire room could have been flooded in that time." He looked at me calmly and said, "You know how to swim, don't you?"

43.

A POLICEMAN IN MADRID

In 1976, Lucas Isidro invited Roberto and me to join him and his wife Ellen (Ellie) on a trip to Spain. The Isidros, like us, were a couple one of whose members was Hispanic while the other one wasn't. Lucas, a cheerful bear of a man, had come to the States from Havana, Cuba, in 1961 when he was sixteen years old. He was flown over as part of Operation Pedro Pan—Peter Pan, a project that flew over 14,000 children ages 6 to 17 out of Communist Cuba to the US from December 1960 to October 1962 and assumed responsibility for them in the US. Eventually, Lucas made his way to Stamford, where his sister-in-law's aunt worked as a housekeeper for William F. Buckley, Jr., the noted conservative author, editor, columnist, and TV host. After holding a variety of jobs, Lucas met and married Ellie, a nurse at St. Joseph's Hospital, and in 1968 he joined the police force.

He also joined the Spanish International Center, became a Board Member, and became friendly with Roberto, who was also on the Board. In 1976, Lucas learned that Norwalk Community College, of which he was an alumnus, was sponsoring a week's trip to Spain, which would cost $250 per person, including round-trip airfare. He invited Roberto to join him on this tour because he knew that Roberto shared his dream of returning to the land of their ancestors. This trip, with its bargain rate, was a natural for them. Ellie and I were going along for the ride.

The tour included three cities: Madrid, Segovia, and Toledo, and Madrid would be first. After our arrival there at the end of

May, while Roberto and I unpacked and relaxed, Lucas and Ellen went off to explore the city. When they returned, Lucas told us about the interesting buildings and fountains they had seen and showed us a beautiful black leather wallet he had purchased for $90 at *El Corte Inglés*, one of Madrid's leading department stores. It was a bit extravagant perhaps but, after all, it had been made in Spain and was of the softest leather, wonderful to the touch. He had also discovered a charming outdoor restaurant, which would be perfect for our first dinner in Spain.

Lucas was beside himself at the restaurant and kept looking all around. He could not believe he was actually sitting in an outdoor restaurant in Madrid—the culmination of his lifelong dreams. It was fate that had brought him here. Why, the city even had an annual fiesta for its patron saint, San Isidro, who shared Lucas's surname. "I'm only thirty-two," Lucas said, "but if I died this very minute, I would die happy."

During the next few days, we sampled the treasures of Madrid. We visited the Prado, Spain's foremost art museum and one of the biggest art galleries in the world; and we went to the bullfights in Madrid's bullring, *Las Ventas*. Then we heard about *El Rasto*, Madrid's gigantic flea market where everything imaginable was for sale every Sunday morning on the *Ribera de Curtidores* and the surrounding streets. We decided to go there and mingle with the local population.

Next Sunday morning, the four of us set out for *El Rasto*. I wanted to take a cab, but Roberto, as always, wanted to go by subway. He felt you got more of the flavor of a city that way. Lucas and Ellie agreed and, since there was a subway station a block from our hotel, we took the subway. Ellie and I found seats but Roberto and Lucas stood several feet away from us. As the subway doors opened at the first stop, Roberto said, *"Oye"* and gave a sudden jerk. I looked up at him. What had happened? He must have forgotten something at the hotel and now we'd have to go back. But he did not say anything about our returning or motion to me to leave, and we continued our journey.

When we reached our destination, I asked Roberto what had caused him to jump at the first stop. "That *cabron*—son of a bitch—tried to pick my pocket," he said, "and I had to move away quickly." When Lucas heard that, he remembered that he too had been jostled and immediately reached for his new wallet, but it and the $100 in it he'd brought along for shopping were gone. The pickpocket who couldn't steal from Roberto had found his mark in Lucas.

All thoughts of the flea market were abandoned, and instead we went to the nearest police station, where Lucas and Roberto told their stories to the policeman in charge and demanded an investigation and the return of Lucas's wallet. The policeman laughed uproariously. Subway pickpockets were a common occurrence in Madrid, and no one had figured out a way to catch them. He advised Lucas not to ride the Madrid subways in the future with $100 in his wallet.

A considerably chastened Lucas left the police station. He enjoyed the rest of his vacation in Spain with us—but he was no longer ready to die there.

Post Script. On the evening of the following July Fourth, Roberto and I were in downtown Stamford at the block party to celebrate the Nation's Bicentennial when we spied Lucas standing out above the crowd in his policeman's uniform. "*Hola*, Lucas," said Roberto, "What are you doing here? I didn't think you worked at night." With a perfectly straight face, Lucas told us that the promoters of the block party had hired him to look out for pickpockets. He had apparently developed an expertise in that area.

44.

THAI SILK

In 1977, Michael Bennett asked me to go to Southeast Asia for three weeks. Michael was the representative of USIA (the United States Information Agency) with whom I had dealt in the past. On several occasions before a foreign trip, I had called him and asked whether USIA needed a speaker in the country of our destination. USIA had an American Specialist program that sponsored speeches abroad by Americans with expertise in various fields. Under this program, I had given speeches on the women's rights movement in the US and met with leaders of business, the professions, government, labor, academia, and women's groups in Fukuoka and Tokyo, Japan, and Madrid, Spain. On those occasions, I had received an honorarium and travel expenses for the one or two days I devoted to USIA business. This trip, however, was totally for USIA and all my expenses would be underwritten by the agency. Roberto would go with me, and we would be going to Thailand, Singapore, Indonesia, and the Philippines.

Our first stop was Thailand, and our first city there was Bangkok. There were beautiful temples and other sights to see, but it was a crowded, polluted, traffic-choked city. We had been told to look for Thai silk, and there was at least one Thai silk store on just about every block. It seemed as if we went to every one of them, but I could not find anything to my liking.

We were glad when it was time to leave and fly to Chiang-Mai in the northern interior. Chiang-Mai, a city we'd never previously heard of, turned out to be our personal Shangri-la. It was enchanting, with native markets, lovely temples, working elephants, and hill tribes.

On our first afternoon, I addressed the Rotary Club, the first woman ever to do so. That evening, Hugh Ivory, my USIA contact, arranged a small dinner party for us. At the table were Hugh and his Japanese wife, Roberto and I, another USIA representative, and a Thai woman. She appeared to be in her 60's and had the proverbial inscrutable Oriental appearance. She was seated at my immediate right, but I had no idea what to say to her. I finally selected the most innocuous icebreaker I could think of. "I'm staying at a lovely hotel," I said. "The Rincome."

"I'm glad you like it," she answered, handing me her card. "I own it." Her name was Khun (comparable to our Miss, Ms., Mrs. or Mr.) Chamchit Laohavad. Her card stated that she was the owner and managing director of Chiang-Mai's three-level indoor shopping center, owner and director of a finance company, vice president of the Tourist Association of Northern Thailand, honorary secretary of a leprosy foundation, honorary manager of a school for the deaf, and an associate judge of the juvenile court. She later told us that one of her brothers designed the shopping center that she owned and was responsible for the establishment of a ceramics factory; her sister owned the Old Chiang-Mai Cultural Center, which seated two hundred for dinner and had daily performances of traditional Thai dances; and her mother owned a travel agency.

Khun Chamchit told me of the good fortune of Thai women who, she said, had complete equality with men. The next morning, she was at our hotel, with her car and driver, to take us on a tour of the city. As I was about to step into the car, she cautioned me against sitting in the front. Women in Thailand did not sit in front with the driver, she said. Only men did that. When I questioned her about this in view of her claim of total equality the night before, she said women didn't want to sit in front anyway.

At the ceramics factory that had been established through the encouragement of her brother, young women and men did different work for different pay. Only the men, for example, were assigned the more strenuous work at the potter's wheel, for which they received higher pay. When I asked Khun Chamchit about this, she said she didn't want girls doing this kind of heavy work.

I told her of my inability to find Thai silk that appealed to me in Bangkok. "You want Thai silk?" she asked. "Come with me." She took me to a factory owned and managed by a princess, who was the granddaughter of the last ruling prince of Chiang-Mai and the widow of a prince. The princess had six women working for her at individual looms. She supplied this hand-woven Thai silk to the Queen of Thailand and the Queen of England. And that day also to me. Then Khun Chamchit took me to her dressmaker, who created the traditional Thai costume for me from the fabric I had bought: a beautiful, black long skirt, with pink, aqua, and purple embroidery at the hem and a matching pink long-sleeved form-fitting jacket. It hangs in my closet today and reminds me of Chiang-Mai, Khun Chamchit, and the princess who sold silk to a tailor's daughter.

45.

THE ROAD TO BALI

When we were in Jakarta, Indonesia, during our Southeast Asia trip, Roberto and I decided to take a short vacation on the exotic Indonesian island of Bali. We expected to see a land teeming with the bare-breasted nubile women for which Bali was known. But we must have been years too late. During our stay, we saw only one or two bare-breasted women, and they were crones. Instead, we were struck by another phenomenon about which we'd never heard. Every village seemed to be dedicated to a particular art or craft. In one, it might be wood carving; in another, painting; in yet another, fashioning small birds. The mind-blowing thing was that everyone in the village—from a four-year-old child to an elderly grandmother—seemed to be engaged in that village's art or craft. When we entered a village, we'd see what appeared to be all the inhabitants busily working on their art in the village square.

The contrast in expectations between the United States and Bali is what struck us. In the US, we view artistic ability as something limited to a privileged few; in Bali, it was expected of everyone.

But it was dependent on one's place of origin. This was brought home to us one afternoon, as we were about to enter the workshop of a master woodcarver. Sitting on a large stone before the entrance was a middle-aged Balinese man. "Are you also a wood carver?" said Roberto.

"No," said the man, with sadness suffusing his face, "I'm not from this village."

46.

RETURN TO GERMANY

In 1978, Roberto and I began to plan a trip to Greece. Neither of us had ever been there, and we looked forward to exploring its historic ruins and taking a cruise around the Greek Isles.

I called Michael Bennett to see if USIA needed anyone in Greece. "No," he said. "We don't. But we do have a request for someone in France and Germany. One week in France and two in Germany. Would you be willing to go?"

I was taken aback by Michael's request. Germany? The land I'd escaped from over forty years ago? The country of Heil Hitler, marching boots, and swastikas? The country soaked in the blood of my people? Could I go there?

I told Michael I'd need time to think about it.

I consulted Roberto about USIA's request. "Up to you," he said.

For years I'd had a strong desire to return to my birthplace, to see where I would have spent my life if Hitler and his band of murderers hadn't come along. But when I had thought about it, I envisioned a quick trip into Berlin, followed by an immediate departure. USIA, however, was asking me to stay two weeks—something else again.

On past USIA trips, I'd enjoyed sightseeing and local entertainment in my spare time. But how did one enjoy oneself on the site of a charnel house?

I'd always found it challenging, meaningful, and exciting to speak abroad about women's rights. But were women's rights relevant in a country where millions of Jews as well as non-Jews had been slaughtered?

I decided to consult local and national Jewish leaders. The first person I called was Rabbi Stephen Pearce of Temple Sinai, the reform temple to which I belonged. The rabbi, a handsome young man in his early thirties, empathized with my reluctance to go, but he added, "It's not just *their* country. There's Jewish history in Germany, too." I hadn't thought of that. My family alone had lived there for twenty years. "If you do decide to go," Rabbi Pearce continued. "I hope you'll report to the congregation on your return." I agreed to do this if I went but wondered what there'd be to report. After all, the Jewish problem had ended with the war in Germany in 1945, hadn't it? What would there be to report now—over thirty years later?

I spoke with Jewish leaders in organizations such as B'nai B'rith. The consensus was that Germany was a new land with a new people. Israel was trading with Germany, so who was I to resist?

I decided to go. But because of Rabbi Pearce's request, I asked USIA to include in my itinerary meetings with Jewish leaders and a visit to a former concentration camp.

I called Hermann and asked if he remembered any of the addresses of the places where we'd lived, where my parents had operated their stores, and where we owned an apartment building. To my amazement, he reeled off all the addresses, some of which were now in East Berlin. I resolved to try to find them all, if possible.

On November 2, 1978, I flew to Paris, and arrived the next day. Due to some work commitments, Roberto was to join me later. To my surprise, on the night of my arrival, the Jewish question came up. I was having cocktails with a small group of feminists at the home of the woman who was head of the American Cultural Center. A French woman reporter for the newsmagazine *L'Express* mentioned that she had recently interviewed Darquier De Pellepoix, the 80-year-old Frenchman who had been the Vichy government's commissioner for Jewish affairs. De Pellepoix, a major French war criminal who had been convicted in absentia but was never punished, lived in Spain. He told the reporter that the genocide of the Jewish people had never happened; that the 75,000 French and stateless Jews he deported from France to death camps had been resettled in the East; and that only lice were gassed at Auschwitz. The following day, his statements were on the front page of *L'Express*.

The reporter also mentioned that the French had never come to terms with their collaboration with the Nazis. While the NBC-TV film *Holocaust* had been shown all over Western Europe, it had not yet been shown on French TV. A Frenchwoman had, however, started a private fund-raising appeal so the film could be shown there.

Roberto joined me in Paris, and from there we flew to West Berlin, arriving on the night of November 8. The German assistant to the head of Amerika Haus met us at the airport and told us that by an odd coincidence we had arrived on the eve of the fortieth anniversary of *Kristallnacht*. Forty years earlier, Hershl Grynszpan, a 17-year-old Jewish student, had shot and killed Ernst von Rath, an official in the German Embassy in Paris in retaliation for the treatment his family had received at the hands of the Nazis in Germany. Hitler and Propaganda Minister Joseph Goebbels used the incident to incite Germans to wreak vengeance against the Jews. As a result, mob violence began on the night of November 9 and continued into the next day as the regular German police stood by and crowds of spectators watched. Nazi storm troopers, along with members of the SS and Hitler Youth, beat and murdered Jews, broke into and wrecked Jewish homes, and brutalized Jewish women and children. All over Germany, Austria, and other Nazi-controlled areas, Jewish shops and department stores had their plate glass windows smashed, thus giving the terror its name, the Night of Broken Glass. Ninety-one Jews were killed, 267 synagogues were burned (with 177 totally destroyed), 7,500 businesses were destroyed, and 25,000 Jewish men were rounded up and later sent to concentration camps.

We had missed the march commemorating that night but were

in time to see the exhibition at the Jewish Community Center, the *Jüdische Gemeinde Zu Berlin,* on Fasanenstrasse 79/80. The Center was a modern building in the heart of West Berlin. As we approached, we noticed what appeared to be the ruins of another building cemented onto the front of the Center. We wondered about the significance of this.

The Center was thronged with people from the march. The exhibition consisted of pictures of Berlin's magnificent synagogues as they had appeared before the Nazi desecration, the shambles that remained after they had been bombed and ransacked, and how those that had been reconstructed looked today. One of the "before" pictures showed Kaiser Wilhelm visiting one of these synagogues in an earlier period. One of the "after" pictures showed the remains of the synagogue that had stood on the site of the Center. It was two pieces of those remains that were attached to the front of the building.

A poster announced that the following Friday there would be a joint synagogue service in which a rabbi, a priest, and a minister would participate. This would be the first joint Jewish-Christian service in a Berlin synagogue in recent history.

We left the Center and walked around the city. I felt as if I had stepped back in time to the '20s and '30s. It seemed so much like the Berlin of the past about which my parents had spoken.

Both West and East Berlin were a curious commingling of past and present for me. One day in East Berlin, as I was crossing the street, I saw two uniformed Gestapo men coming to get me. I cringed, until I realized they were just two East Berlin policemen crossing the street.

Despite such experiences, I loved being in Berlin—staying at the Hotel Frühling am Zoo on Kurfürstandamm 17, walking on streets on which my parents had walked and seeing street names that had resounded throughout my childhood: Alexanderplatz—Kottbusser Damm—Koepenicker Strasse—Gipsstrasse—and Unter den Linden.

A friend in the States had recommended a West Berlin restaurant named Xantener Eck. We went there one night for dinner. In Germany, if there is no empty table, the maitre d' seats you at one that is partially occupied. On this night, we were seated with two men in their early forties who, we later learned, were printers.

As we poured over the menus, one of them recommended several entrees to us in halting English. With his English and my German, we were able to converse. When he learned I was Jewish, he immediately said, "*I* feel no guilt. I was born in 1937." He then embarked upon a tirade against Jews and Israel and referred to the head of the Jewish Center we had just visited as a Fascist. "Why does he have to be a Jew first and a German second?" he asked. "If I were a member of a proud people like the Jews, I would not take money from Germany, as Israel has done, as individual Jews have done, and as the Center continues to do.

"All people are equal: Jews and Christians, whites and Blacks, Israelis, and Arabs. Why does the Jew think he's better than everyone else?" I shifted uneasily in my seat.

"And look what they've done to the Arabs in Israel," he continued. "Two thousand years ago, Celts lived on the land where my house stands today. Their descendants now live in France. They don't come back here and say they have a right to my house. What gives Jews the right to do this?"

His companion had paradoxical views. On the one hand, he seemed to share his friend's sentiments, if not his vehemence. But he also asked me whether I'd had any special feelings as a Jew returning to Germany. When I told him I had, he said, "You know, my father was involved during the Nazi regime. I have to live with that."

We spent several hours at dinner, during which we shared drinks and reminiscences with these men. When we left, we exchanged business cards, and they promised to visit if they ever came to the States. One of them came close to hugging me when we parted.

I was in a state of utter depression as we walked the foggy streets of West Berlin after this encounter. "Those men really liked me, Roberto," I said. "And yet, it wouldn't take too much for

SONIA PRESSMAN FUENTES

them to come for me again." The discussion in the restaurant brought home to me the fact that what had happened in Germany was still there in some of its people.

A day or two later, I shared the experience with a law professor and his feminist wife while having breakfast in their home. The professor said that he resented the burden of guilt that had been laid on Germans, but his wife did not echo his sentiments. His students did not like being reminded of this guilt, he said. They did not want to be made to feel responsible for events that took place before they were born.

We visited the Center again, this time for a meeting with the assistant to the director. I asked him about the conflict between the Germans' desire to forget and the Center's commitment to remind them. "Do they want to get rid of the past?" he asked. "Or do they want to continue it? It is in the interest of Germany not to forget. It has nothing to do with guilt or responsibility. Germany must cleanse itself of these things. It must be different in the future from what it was in the past. How can this be done without history, without knowing why it happened and how it happened?"

"How long must it take?" I asked. "After all, this happened forty years ago."

"Forty years is not a long time in the history of mankind," he reminded me.

Germany was riven with the tension between the collective obligation to remember and the personal need to forget.

We rented a car and spent days looking for the addresses Hermann had given me, in both East and West Berlin. I knew that Berlin had been reduced to rubble during the war and that I might not be able to locate any of the streets I was looking for, much less the buildings. But that was not the case. We found all the locations for which we were looking. The buildings had, however, all been demolished and rebuilt—except one—the apartment house where I was born at 83-A Linienstrasse in East Berlin. It was still standing, unbombed, intact. There were lights on in some of the apartments. I went inside, knocked on a door at random, and a woman came out.

"Is there anyone here who might remember a family named Pressman that used to live here in 1928?" I asked.

"No," she answered. The oldest resident had moved into the building in 1947. There was no one to remember us.

A friend in the States had given me an introduction to a woman who had lived in Berlin for many years. I visited her, and we had a wonderful time together. We talked, as women do, about our lives, our husbands, our hopes for our children. We hugged, and I turned to leave. She wouldn't have done it to me, would she? I walked out her door. Why not? Why would I have been the exception?

We left Berlin and spent the rest of our trip driving through the German countryside and into the other cities where I lectured: Dusseldorf, Heidelberg, Freiburg, and Munich. I looked at the people; they looked just like anyone else. What had happened to their ancestors? What madness had seized them?

In Freiburg, we stayed at a picturesque hotel high up in the mountains. When I awoke in the morning and drew the curtains aside, an incredibly lovely panorama was spread out before me. As far as the eye could see, there were undulating valleys with picture postcard houses nestled among them. The beauty of it in the midst of the horror that had been struck me.

At the end of my talk in Heidelberg, a woman came up to me and said, "You have made me feel so good personally that you, a Jew, came back to Germany—and that you came back to talk about women's rights. I hope you'll come again."

At Café Kreutzkamm on Maffeistrasse in Munich, I had lunch with two women who were leaders of Jewish women's organizations: one was chairperson of an organization named Ruth and the other was with WIZO (the Women's International Zionist Organization). "How can you live here" I asked, "next to Dachau?" The younger of the two, a woman in her 50's, had, with forged papers, survived the Holocaust by passing as a Christian. "Everyone has his or her own story; we each have a certain degree of schizophrenia," she said. She felt guilty about living in Germany and read every available book on the Holocaust, but she had not encouraged her son to identify with Judaism. He considered himself "European," she said.

The older woman, in her 70's, had, with her husband, spent part of the war years in a Jewish ghetto in Austria. They had returned to Germany because German was the only language he knew. "I don't think about it [the Holocaust]," she said. "I work with German women in organizations. They would be hurt if they felt I was different, and I don't want to be different. When so many people stretch their hands out to you, you forget. Germany's no different from any other country. After all, the Swiss prepared the poison gas for the concentration camps."

She had told her children and grandchildren about the Holocaust. Her son-in-law told his children about the camps once and never mentioned them again. He had enrolled them in an exclusive private school, where they were the only Jews. There, they were being educated as "cosmopolitans." She was nonetheless pleased when her young grandson came to visit, donned his *yarmulke*—skullcap, and accompanied her to the synagogue. She was optimistic about the future of Jews in Germany.

In Munich, I was interviewed and taped by Dr. Michaela Ulich, a feminist who was preparing an American Studies program for German high school students. And so, I, who had to flee Germany for my life in 1933, would, through the medium of tape, have a chance to talk to the young people of Germany.

We left Munich and talk of the future and drove on Dachaustrasse into the past—to Dachau, the first of Hitler's camps. Dachau was full of tourists, most of whom were young Germans. In the midst of the crowd, one couple stood out—a man and woman in their late 50's, walking arm in arm. Wherever I looked—at the gate with its ironic *Arbeit Macht Frei*—Work Makes You Free—sign, at the museum, on the grounds where the barracks had stood, at the gas chamber (which had never been used), and at the crematoria (which had)—they were everywhere. Finally, I could stand it no longer. I walked over to them and said, "What is it with you people? Wherever I look, there you are." The man responded in Yiddish. He was a German Jew who had been imprisoned in Auschwitz at the age of fourteen for five years. He now lived in Israel with his Israeli wife and children. He had come to Germany to testify at the war crimes trial of a former official at Auschwitz and had done so the day before. Now, he was showing his wife a camp such as the one in which he had been interned. Tears welled up in her eyes as he told us that on one occasion he had been beaten six times with a whip such as was exhibited at Dachau; he had thereafter been unable to sit for two weeks.

He pointed to the chimney of the crematorium and told us that on his first day at Auschwitz, one of the officials had directed his attention to the smoke coming out of the chimney there and said, "Tomorrow that smoke will be coming out of you."

Roberto asked to see the number on his arm. "Do you still think about it?" I asked.

"Think about it?" he said. "I wake up in the middle of the night saying this number." Like Primo Levi, he "felt the tattooed number on . . . [his] arm burning like a sore."[19]

I asked him how he could identify the camp official at whose trial he had testified when he hadn't seen him in forty years. The passage of time was not an obstacle for him. "That is a face I will never forget," he said.

We left Germany and returned to the States. Shortly thereafter, I received a postcard from one of the women I had met. She wrote:

> Those last moments in Freiburg when I walked down the steps and you stood there at the top have impressed themselves hard-edge in my mind. It occurred to me that my life could have been yours, and yours mine.

Perhaps.

ENDNOTES

1 Elie Wiesel, *Memoirs, All Rivers Run to the Sea* (New York: Alfred A. Knopf, 1995), 150.

2 Stefan Kanfer, *A Summer World* (New York: Farrar Straus Giroux, 1989), 71.

3 Caroline Bird with Sara Welles Briller, *Born Female: The High Cost of Keeping Women Down*, rev. ed. (New York: David McKay, 1970), 14.

4 Remarks, NYU Annual Conference on Labor, 61 LRR 253-5 (Apr. 25, 1966); Bird with Briller, 15.

5 Dick Berg, "Equal Employment Opportunity Under the Civil Rights Act of 1964," *Brooklyn Law Review* 31 (1964): 62, 79.

6 Research has since revealed other dangers in pregnancies of women over thirty-five.

7 Decades later, it was discovered that some children of mothers who took DES during pregnancy had severely deformed sexual organs, cancer of the vagina or cervix, could not have children, or had impaired immune systems.

8 Currently, however, testing is recommended by the National Tay-Sachs & Allied Diseases Association even if only one prospective parent is of Ashkenazic Jewish ancestry or is a member of another high-risk group, such as individuals of French-Canadian, Cajun, and Irish ancestry.

9   Deborah Tannen, *You Just Don't Understand* (New York: William Morrow, 1990), 61.

10   Harry Golden, *Enjoy, Enjoy!* (New York: World Publishing, 1961), Frontispiece.

11   This work was never published.

12   Kanfer, 121.

13   Kanfer, 148.

14   J. Richard Elliott, Jr., "The Ellenville Story," *Barron's* 28 Oct. 1957, 3.

15   Robert Lindsey, *The Flight of the Falcon* (New York: Simon and Schuster, 1983), 317.

16   "The 25 Most Intriguing People of the Year," *PEOPLE WEEKLY*, Dec. 25, 1989-Jan. 1, 1990: 85.

17   Susan Watters, "The Unsinkable Deborah Dean," *W* 27, no. 12 (1998): 90.

18   Ann Gerhart and Annie Groer, "The Reliable Source," *Washington Post*, 16 Nov. 1998: B3.

19   Primo Levi, *Survival in Auschwitz, The Reawakening (Two Memoirs)*, trans. Stuart Woolf (New York: Summit, 1985), 370.

90000>

9 780738 806358